THE AMERICAN PAINT HORSE

by Glynn W. Haynes

UNIVERSITY OF OKLAHOMA PRESS

NORMAN AND LONDON

The paper in this book meets the guidelines for permanence and durability of the Committee on Production Guidelines for Book Longevity of the Council on Library Resources, Inc.

Library of Congress Cataloging in Publication Data

Haynes, Glynn W.   1936–
  The American paint horse.

Bibliography: p. 340
  Includes index.
  1. Pinto horse. I. Title.
SF293.P5H39   636.1'3   75-9645
ISBN: 0–8061–2144–0

Copyright © 1976 by the University of Oklahoma Press, Norman, Publishing Division of the University. All rights reserved. Manufactured in the U.S.A.   First edition, 1976; second printing, 1983. First paperback printing, 1988.

To my wife, Dolores, whose inspiration and assistance made possible this work, I affectionately dedicate this book.

PREFACE

I am particularly glad to take this opportunity of introducing the American Paint Horse to the horse lovers of America. Over the past decade a few articles have appeared on this breed in various equine magazines, but this is the first volume to be compiled about these colorful horses, which contributed their part to our American heritage.

Many people do not realize where these horses actually came from or understand the true identity of the Paint Horse. It is this background of history and breed development, as well as the story of individual horses, both past and present, that I have attempted to tell in this book. Additionally, I have tried to provide a certain amount of information on breed characteristics, color patterns, bloodlines, and breeding principles with the special view in mind that it should be useful to the many breeders and owners of Paint Horses. It is my hope that this book will create a better understanding of this admirable horse and familiarize more individuals with the breed.

I would like to acknowledge here my debt to many owners,

breeders, trainers, and exhibitors with whom I have corresponded and discussed Paint Horses in compiling this book. Their wholehearted cooperation and assistance in answering questions, supplying material, and finding pictures is deeply appreciated.

A particular debt of gratitude is owed to Robert M. Denhardt and Joe M. Huffington for their contribution of historical information, which was most helpful in the preparation of the text.

Also I would like to thank Marge Spence for the loan of many outstanding photographs taken by herself of Paint Horses, included in the book.

Most of all I want to thank Sam Ed Spence, first Executive Secretary of the American Paint Horse Association and Managing Editor of the *Paint Horse Journal*, for the many kindnesses shown along the way. He and his staff patiently and understandingly allowed me access to the association files for information concerning rules, regulations, activities, statistics, and show records.

My sincere thanks to you all.

G. W. HAYNES

Shongaloo, Louisiana

CONTENTS

ILLUSTRATIONS

PART I **HISTORY**

1 THE EARLIEST PAINT HORSES

The horse is known to be one of the earliest surviving animals. Throughout Europe and Asia geologists have discovered fossil remains of horses in almost every country dating back many, many centuries ago. The Paint Horse probably had his beginning with the appearance of these first horses, for his ancestors can be traced in Spain, southern France, Arabia, and North Africa from as early as 20,000 B.C.

The coat colors of the earliest horses did not differ greatly from the colors that are known today. Generally, the black, brown, and white shades were predominant, but frequently the two-toned coloring appears in drawings and artifacts depicting the horses and horsemen of ancient civilizations. Early equestrian art shows plainly that the colors and patterns of today's horses were present in the past—possibly throughout the existence of the horse.

There are two schools of thought about the evolution of this two-toned coloring. Some authorities believe that the spots may have been the original marking of horses and were present in nature's beginning. These horses were given a two-colored coat, while others received a solid coat of the colors common to horses. Another belief is that this mixed coloring appeared through the centuries for the purpose of camouflage in areas where there were sharply contrasting light-and-dark shadows. Such color contrast is apparent in the zebra and the giraffe.

From prehistoric times nature has protected many of her animals by camouflage. The polar bear of the Arctic is as white as the snow that surrounds him. The camel is a drab, yellowish color that blends into the vast desert through which he roams. The horse, not on his own a courageous animal, depended on speed for his survival. His only other advantage was a coat color to blend into the background against which he moved.

In countries of conflicting colors with dense shrubbery and flowering bushes and trees, light filtering through the close-growing vegetation casts strange light-and-dark shadows. A horse of varied coloring, one containing light-and-dark shades, would find this location a natural habitat. In these surroundings the two-toned horse could move more freely, particularly at night, against the arabesque patterns formed by moonlight shining through trees and shrubbery.

From what source has the modern Paint Horse descended? The origin of all breeds of horses is of historical interest to most horsemen. There are many diverse and conflicting conclusions, and when trying to trace origins of the various breeds and their migrations over Europe, North Africa and Asia, one finds oneself going through page after page of contradictory material.

One common belief is that all breeds are descended from one original ancestry, a small, four-toed animal. The extreme differences among today's breeds are attributed to the many changes in climate and ecology resulting from geologic up-heavals over millions of years. The environmental changes produced corresponding anatomical changes in the horses of each era.

Some authorities think that all breeds developed from two distinct stocks—the light, or hot-blooded, stock of the North

African desert and the heavy, or cold-blooded, stock that ranged over northern Europe and Asia. Others believe that all modern breeds trace their origin to three ancestral groups: the Libyan horse of northern Africa, the Mongolian pony of upper Asia and southern Europe, and the Celtic horse of northwestern Europe. Still others advocate that the domestic breeds can be divided into six types, each type tracing back to a specific group of wild horses.

These varied beliefs are confusing, to be sure. There is agreement, though, that the modern light-horse breeds have roots in common and can be traced to a limited group of ancestors. To meet his varying standards of performance in different locales, man began to crossbreed the various types of horses at an early date. From this voluntary crossbreeding, and from environmental pressures, the specific breeds emerged.

There is a scarcity of facts concerning the origin of the odd colors and variations of color found in today's horses. Because the Arab is the original source of the hot blood and has contributed to the development of many modern-day breeds, any unusual markings are attributed to Arab blood. While Paint Horse markings are not usually found among the purebred desert Arabian horses, the paint coloring has existed for centuries in many breeds and was characteristic among the offspring of mixed blood. It might be pointed out that very few "purebreds" are in existence today, which could be one reason why the paint coloring is found in almost every breed of horse.

Horses of the Arabian type[1] have existed in Persia, North Africa, and Arabia for thousands of years. The Arab horse, of course, derived its name from the breed's development and growth in the Arabian Peninsula. Arabia was not always a dry, desert area. From prehistoric eras to as recently as 600 B.C.,

---

[1] The "Arabian type" is a group of animals with similar characteristics in one certain category. Breed characteristics are not considered at this point. The Barb and the Turk horses were closely associated with the Arabian, and some authorities maintain that all three shared a common ancestor, making them of the same type, to fall in the Arabian category.

Arabia was a fertile land with a mild climate and many rivers surrounded by dense forests. The Bible abounds with allusions to the "forests of Arabia," and in the intervening years fossils of these forests have been uncovered.

The passing years brought extreme changes and, some writers believe, the extinction of horses in this region for a few thousand years. As is the usual case when the historical background is obscure and often legendary, there is a completely opposite theory. The Paint Horse with his more remote antecedents is known to have existed in this area during the earlier years, giving some credibility to the theory that environmental conditions do affect the coloring of animals, and the paint coloring could have developed over a span of years in an atmosphere such as this.

Whether the paint markings evolved here and in other similar regions or was already present in prehistoric horses may never be known for certain. Nevertheless, the early existence of the Paint Horse is uncontestable. Primitive cave paintings, some of which survive today, are proof of this. The earliest cave paintings to be found showing painted horses are dated to a period between 20,000 and 15,000 B.C. The caves are in a remote area of south-central Europe, where the terrain consists of numerous mountainous ridges and open, grassy slopes. The horses of that region were depicted in carvings and colored cave paintings to be of medium build and suitable for riding. Some of the paintings are of horses of a solid color; others are of horses with varying color patterns of light and dark spots. The point is that the artists of ancient cultures sketched events and figures of animals familiar to them, and these pictures, some in vivid color, reveal that Paint Horses have been around for a very long time.

As horses were domesticated and their use increased throughout the Near East, men began to crossbreed different types. Breeders in countries bordering Arabia (now known as Turkey, Iraq, and Iran) improved their stock with Arab stallions.

Many beautiful horses, half Arab in blood and often splashed with color, were bred with utmost care. These early breeding practices opened the door to the wide spread of hot-blooded Paint Horses across the land.

Of crossbreeding horses it has been said that a union of hot- and cold-blooded horses will often produce a horse with paint markings. This seemed to hold true when the hot-blooded Arab horses were crossed on the heavy, cold-blooded stock of northern Europe. Yet despite the insistence by many writers that Paint Horse spotting is a result of mixing hot and cold blood, it seems likely that if the paint-spotting gene was present in particular horses then the paint gene could be transmitted no matter what the cross. This is not to say that a Paint Horse would always result; modern breeders know that this does not always happen. In the past decade most thinking horsemen have agreed to this logic, since Paint Horse spotting is so apparent in many hot-blooded breeds that may or may not be influenced by cold-blooded stock.

The first horses known to the Egyptians were introduced by the Hyksos, who ruled Egypt around 1600 or 1700 B.C. After conquering Palestine, Babylon, and Assyria, the Hyksos with their mobile force of charioteers brought their sturdy Mongolian horses into the Nile Valley. They were spirited horses, moderately well bred, and in color usually bay or black, with some showing Paint Horse spotting.

For about one hundred years the Hyksos ruled supreme. As the Egyptians discovered the art of horsemanship in warfare, they imported horses of their own and finally were equipped with a deadly chariot division that subdued the Hyksos. The remains of Egyptian horses and the many paintings

Following page: From the painting on the tomb of Menna, dated 1400 B.C., a Paint Horse pulls the chariot of a wealthy land steward of the Pharaoh. Courtesy American Paint Horse Association.

from this period indicate that the horses imported by the Egyptians were of Oriental[2] ancestry, stood about fifteen hands, and weighed around one thousand pounds.

In all probability the Paint Horse was highly esteemed by the Egyptians, since several articles have been found displaying the role he played in their lives. On the wall of the tomb of Menna, a wealthy Egyptian land steward of about 1400 B.C., is painted a scene depicting a Paint Horse pulling Menna's chariot. The horse appears to be of the Oriental type, reddish-brown (sorrel) in color, with overo markings. The painting, executed in honor of a very significant event, is supported by biblical statements that Egyptians were using horses at that time: "And the Egyptians pursued and went in after them to the midst of the sea, even all Pharaoh's horses, his chariots, and his horsemen" (Exodus 14:23).

Ever since man invented sharp, pointed tools, he has had a strong urge to decorate the objects around him. The many hand-carved decorations tell a visual story of personalities, developments, and events in great eras of the past. A noteworthy discovery from early Egyptian times is a mummy case with a Paint Horse carved and painted on the cover. The case ranks as one of the finest in the field of art. Moreover, it is a unique record of a period of time in Paint Horse history.

Other civilizations in existence before Christ that have recorded the presence of the Paint Horse are those of China, Tibet, and India. The painters and sculptors of China left behind some magnificent equestrian art. One treasured piece is a statuette from the Hun Dynasty, dating from 206 B.C. to approximately A.D. 220, of a horsewoman mounted on a horse with definite paint markings.

In Tibet one of the prehistoric breeds was a small, sturdy horse that stood about 52 inches high, or, in horse terms, 13 hands. Many of these horses had a two-color coat, overo in

---

[2]The term "Oriental horse" is a catch-all phrase for any horse from eastern Europe or northern Africa. The three breeds most commonly referred to as Oriental are the Barb, the Arabian, and the Turk.

pattern, and resembled the early American mustangs in some respects. They were famed for their great speed and fortitude. These horses were captured and tamed by later inhabitants, but some bands remain wild today.

In many countries there is no evidence to indicate either the presence or the absence of Paint Horses. If there is mention of horses in the written chronicles, all too often descriptions of color and markings are sparse. To make matters worse, some early writers did not clearly describe the "spotted" horses they wrote about. Appaloosas and Paint Horses were included in one general grouping, making it difficult to distinguish between the two and impossible to trace the movements of each breed. To cite one instance, both Appaloosas and Paint Horses lived in China in the early centuries before and after Christ. The reference to their existence is constant, but only "spotted" horses are mentioned. Statuettes and paintings reveal that horses of both color types were present and were apparently rated as very special animals.

Not long after the Greek Olympic games were inaugurated, large breeding establishments appeared in the nations east of Athens. There the best Arab mares and sires were bred for the specific purpose of providing horses for the many equine events that became popular during the period. The caliph of Motassen, a wealthy monarch of a later century, operated one of the largest breeding farms, with some 130,000 head. His horses were described as spotted, speckled, and splotched circus-type Arabians. No doubt the stable was made up of Appaloosa and Paint Horses, which were raised to be colorful performers in the circuses and equestrian performances that flourished first in Greece and then in Rome and other centers of the civilized world.

When Rome was at the height of power in the first centuries of the Christian era, her boundaries extended to nearly every great horse-raising country around the Mediterranean. All the good breeding stock of the ancient nations was in her hands. Although the Romans did not use horses extensively as war horses in their military campaigns, they did put them to the

Statuettes of glazed earthenware from Chinese Hun Dynasty (206 B.C.–A.D. 220). Courtesy Pinto Horse Association of America, Inc.

test in their barbaric sports events. Among the favorite activities were horse racing and chariot racing. Two-horse and four-horse teams provided fiery action with no regard for careful driving. Amid the clouds of dust collisions of horses and drivers were common. The Oriental horses from Arabia, North Africa and Egypt, noted for their stamina, endurance, and speed, were well suited for these contests.

The Romans were also famed for their pomp and pageantry, as demonstrated by their long costumed parades and festive tournaments. For these affairs horses were adorned with elaborate trappings of gold and silver, bright colored plumes, and fancy harness. Throughout equine history man has shown a fondness of and desire for color. Rome is only one of the wealthy nations of historical consequence whose lust after the flamboyant was vividly displayed by its showy animals. In the absence of colorful horses decoration was added sometimes by a paintbrush and other times in the form of tassels, rosettes, and ornate harness. In this respect the Paint Horse was (and is) well suited to serve man's pleasures.

After the fall of Rome, for almost a thousand years progress paused, and there is little record of the Paint Horse. Throughout the Middle Ages he was found at fairs, joustings, and other public gatherings. During this period the wandering minstrels with performing horses were putting together shows and exhibitions, and the phenomenon of the circus was born.

The Germans experimented with the breeding of horses during the Middle Ages to produce a spotted or paint coloring in their animals.[3] Their only purpose in breeding was to produce horses with amazing spots and patches of color; their

[3]Charles Phillip Fox, *A Pictorial History of Performing Horses,* 14.

Facing page; A tobiano horse of India—the pulwhari, *or "flower-horse." Courtesy Pinto Horse Association of America, Inc.*

ideal was not a fine pleasure horse or a sleek racing animal. The German horses were a coarse, cold-blooded stock with very little refinement or beauty and were primarily work horses used for farming and as a means of transportation.

Horse breeding was carried on at this time more as a necessity than as a desire to improve a breed. In Britain and western Europe horses were bred to huge size and were used in the feudal wars and in riding to the hounds. Another popular kind of hunting demanded a lighter, faster horse, which was obtained by crossing the light, hot-blooded horses on the large northern varieties. Much of this earlier breeding, before arrival of the Byerly Turk, laid the foundation for the Thoroughbred that emerged in eighteenth-century England.

There is no record that the English ever bred for color in their horses. In fact, the gray Thoroughbreds, which appeared quite early from the Barb importations, fell into disfavor in England, and a breeding campaign was begun as early as 1700 to eradicate the color.[4]

The big grays were bred in the heart of France, where color seemed to be very popular with Thoroughbred and Arabian breeders. Later the strain was re-established in England through Roi Herode and his famous son, The Tetrarch. The Tetrarch, nicknamed the "Spotted Wonder," was a big steel gray covered with large white spots. His name is prominent in the ancestry of many Thoroughbred horses that were well splashed with white stockings, heads, and body markings. The French Arabian breeders bred many colorful Arab horses, and

[4]Letter from Lowell H. Rott, Morocco Spotted Horse Co-operative Association of America, Ridott, Ill., November 14, 1971.

Facing page: An overo Paint Horse of the sixteenth-century Spanish Riding School in Vienna, Austria. The horse is of Andalusian stock from Lipizza. Courtesy Pinto Horse Association of America, Inc.

A Spanish tobiano horse, about 1650. Courtesy Pinto Horse Association of America, Inc.

the French Arabians are particularly noted for their spotted coats.

Horses had existed on the southern peninsula of Spain, known as Iberia, many centuries before recorded history, as evidenced by the cave paintings found at Santander. The prehistoric paintings and engravings of animals in the Altamira Cave show unusual skill. During the third century B.C. the Carthaginians were driven from Sicily by the Romans and sought refuge in Spain. The many fine stallions they took with them were bred to the native horses, producing a stock superior in speed and strength. Some Iberian vases dating from the third century B.C. verify that the Paint Horse was already in residence in Spain before the arrival of the Arabian and Barb horses some one thousand years later. The pottery was decorated with floral motifs and elaborate pictures of hunting scenes, ritual dances, and battles on land and sea. One striking piece shows the Iberian soldiers fighting another tribe whom they had caught hunting wild boars. One of the soldiers is mounted on a Paint Horse. The horses depicted could be either the fine stock brought in by the Carthaginians or descendants of those horses that resulted from crossbreeding with the Spanish horses. In either case, they appear to be well bred, with smooth, trim body lines and clean, slender legs.

There were two breeds of horses in Spain in 1492, when interest was sparked for exploration to the west. The older of the two was the Andalusian. It has been said that every breed has a story, and yet the origin of these ancient horses is vague. The Andalusians were a substantial breed, showing characteristics of a cross between the northern Gothic type and the hot-blooded Orientals. The Spaniards found the Andalusian very durable and dependable in their long war of liberation against the Moors, and extremely valuable in their conquests of the New World territories. As was apparent in most crossbreeds, among the Andalusian strain were many varicolored animals of the Paint Horse color patterns.

The second Spanish breed developed as a result of the Moslem invasion of Spain in A.D. 710. Before their entry into Spain, the Moslems had conquered much of North Africa, including the Barbary States—Algeria, Tunisia, and Morocco. In the years of their expansion into these lands, the small, light, fast horses of the Barbary States were improved principally by the animals from Arabia, and the blood of the desert-bred Arabians was so thinned by crossbreeding with the native Barb horses that they were no longer purebred Arab horses. It was the Spaniards, in the end, who benefited the most from the best equine blood to be found and the new tradition of horsemanship that the Moslems had brought into Spain in their 710–1492 domination.

The Barb and the Arab are generally considered to have their origin in the same ancestors. During the early history of the two breeds the Arab was probably indistinguishable from the Barb. Contemporary illustrations, however, show different characteristics. The Barb does not have the arched, rounded neck of the Arab; the Arab does not have the low tail set and the sloping rump that is characteristic of the Barb horses. Today the home of the Barb is Algeria, where a relatively pure strain still exists.

With Spain so near the Barbary Coast there is every reason to believe that Barb horses were imported from North Africa, possibly in great numbers, between the ninth and fifteenth centuries A.D. During the eight hundred years that Spain was under Moorish rule, the newly imported Arabian-Barbs were crossed on the fine horses already in the country, producing a breed that gave Spain an unequaled reputation for horse breeding.

In the centuries that elapsed before the colonization of America, Spain was a country as unforgettable for its bull fights as for its fine working and using horses. Bullfighting, at that time called *rejoneo*, was conducted from horseback. The horses bred for this rugged sport were trained to watch the bull, move when it moved, and stand obedient and quiet when it was motionless. These are the basic skills inbred in any good cutting horse today. The Spanish horses had been crossed as desired by breeders for centuries with apparent improvement in their horses' stock sense and fighting bull sense. From these early breeding practices a new generation of horses ensued, the ancestors of the cow-country horse for which the American West later became famed.

The Spanish Barbs of the fifteenth century were developed to perfection. Their superiority was due primarily to the logical outcross that had been employed through the years by adding to the original blood the strength and stamina of the Carthaginian horses and the speed and refinement of the Barbary horses of North Africa. The plains of Córdoba in the southern region were recognized in every part of Europe as the greatest horse-breeding center, where some of the best Spanish stock was available. After the Moors were successfully defeated and driven out of Spain, an age of discovery and exploration followed. Looking toward the west, the conquistadors and their horses embarked from the ports of Cádiz, Seville, and San Lucas, all near the Córdoba plains. From these ports the Paint Horse, whose ancestry could be traced through many centuries and many generations to the horses of North Africa and Asia Minor, made his first voyage to America.

2 ARRIVAL IN NORTH AMERICA

When Columbus discovered the New World, there were no horses here. This is strange, for horses were abundant in North and South America over ten thousand years ago. Why these animals became extinct is still a puzzling question: conditions were excellent for their development with the open grassy plains and the high plateaus of the interior. Some unknown factors were involved in their extinction, since other prehistoric animals disappeared at the same time. Because horses were at one time hunted for food, it is possible that migrant hunters from Asia, by constantly hunting and chasing them from their grazing lands, were responsible for their extinction. It is also possible that a plague or drought exterminated the original horses. Yet none of these theories seems adequate to explain the extinction of selected animals, while others thrived and multiplied. Whatever the cause, in the fifteenth century horses were absent from the Americas.

Like all other horses, Paint Horses arrived in America in two general ways. The first, and most significant, was by way of the Spanish conquistadors. The second was through importations from England.

Most of the horses of the first Spanish expeditions were of the Barbary, Arabian, and Andalusian strains from the plains of Córdoba in southern Spain. The conquistadors in their narratives wrote of their own experiences in the new country and of the horses that played a part in their quests. From all accounts the mounts of the nobly born adventurers were the finest to be found, and even the breeding stock that followed was as good as Spain could send. For one thing, the Spanish adventurers were rich and could afford the top-blooded horses. Too, the long ocean voyages to the New World took their toll of the weak and unsubstantial horses; only the strong and stalwart survived. In that time and place the horses of those first American "cavalrymen" had to have a certain rugged power that could be depended on, possibly for life itself.

As for the Paint Horse, the first record of his arrival was made in 1519. Hernando Cortes, the Spanish explorer who conquered Mexico, brought the first horses. The records of his voyage list sixteen horses, one in foal, of the Spanish Barb type aboard ship as it sailed from port. Bernal Díaz del Castillo listed in his diary a complete roster of the horses, giving their characteristics, coloring, and abilities. He listed among the horses that arrived at Veracruz: "Moron, a settler of Bayamo, had a pinto with white stockings on his forefeet and he was well reined. Baena, a settler of Trinidad, had a dark roan horse with white patches."[1]

Díaz del Castillo's account of the landing and conquest is accepted as authentic. From his descriptions there is no doubt that these two horses were Paint Horses, and their markings, although not fully detailed, would suggest that one was of the tobiano pattern and the other of overo design.

In the years intervening between 1492 and settlement of

[1]Robert M. Denhardt, *The Horse of the Americas*, 50–51.

the mainland, it must have become apparent that there were no horses in New Spain. Letters to the homeland continually stressed the need for additional mounts, and those that arrived were more precious than the soldiers who accompanied them. It is reasonable to assume that the horses that arrived in the Southwest during the sixteenth century were of the same type as those ridden by Cortes and his men and that their coloring and characteristics were much the same.

The mounted Spaniards held the upper hand over the Indians. To prevent the natives from obtaining their horses, they issued decrees forbidding Indians to own or ride horses. Despite these ordinances many tribes built up horse herds by stealing, bartering, and attacking the Spanish ranches and missions.

There was a time when the tribes in the interior along the eastern fringe of the grasslands lived as farmers and practiced agriculture. They had permanent villages and raised large fields of corn and other crops. Short hunting trips out on the plains provided their supply of meat. With the introduction of the horse and the techniques of riding and use, they adopted a new culture. Horses extended their range and allowed them to follow the buffalo herds. Some of these people, who became fierce horsemen in the nineteenth century, made the transition from grassland farmers to nomad hunters.

Indians living farther out on the plains were more nomadic, making periodic migrations with the buffalo herds. They adapted themselves easily to the horse. They could now race along the flanks of the buffalo herds more closely and be assured of bringing home abundant supplies of meat.

Because they had an eye for anything bright or colorful, the Indians sought out the painted horse. They seemed to prefer the gray, white, and Paint Horses above all others. The grays and whites could easily be colored Paint-style by the imaginative Indians if there were not enough spotted horses to go around. Besides their love of color, the Indians had a practical reason for owning Paint Horses. The colors were the easiest to alter to coincide with the changing seasons. The American Indians were experts in the ancient art of camouflage. They devised protective tactics of camouflaging their horses and themselves in enemy territory and ably outmaneuvered seasoned soldiers and unfriendly tribes. So that both horse and rider could pass unobserved across open plains, the Indians chose horses of a coloring to blend with the natural and seasonal background of the country. The warriors, skillful riders that they were, dropped to one side of the horse and passed undetected by the human eye. Horses of the color of the prairies—dun, roan, or light sorrel—were ridden in summer and fall. In winter white or Palomino horses were indistinguishable traveling across the snow. In sagebrush country the gray and blue roan colors were ideal. The techniques employed by the Indians were in no way unusual. They utilized nature's own mode of concealment to aid animals in protecting themselves from predatory animals.

The Paint Horse was the Indian's favorite horse. He was variable and could be transformed to suit any surroundings or any season of the year. Simply by shading or rubbing out one color, his owner could easily alter the body colors. If the Indian wanted a dun or gray horse, he had only to darken the white areas of the body. For a light-colored coat the dark areas could be rubbed with sand or ashes and faded out.

Many western tribes decorated their horses for battle with paint, feathers, and beads. As the warriors painted themselves with war paint, they also decorated their horses for the battlefield. The Paint Horse, already decorated by nature, added color to the visual spectacle, and in the heat of battle his colors would not run and blur as would those with paint added for the occasion.

Other tribes considered the colorfully marked horses magical and effective in conflict. The Comanches and Cheyennes, for instance, desired a type of Paint Horse which they called a Medicine Hat. This type of mustang, loudly splashed with color, was to them a prince of a horse. Only the braves who had

San Domingo, stallion of Robert Brislawn, regarded to be of Spanish Barb ancestry and registered in the Spanish Mustang Registry. He is a type of mustang known as a medicine hat by the Plains Indians and often called a war bonnet by some because a bonnetlike marking covers its head and ears and a dark shield "protects" its chest. Courtesy Hope Ryan, New York City.

proved themselves were allowed to ride them, and a Comanche warrior who rode a Medicine Hat into battle considered himself invincible.[2]

To the Indian the horse was more than a war horse or a means of travel. He was a medium of exchange and a status symbol. An Indian's wealth was determined by the number of horses he owned, and any wealthy hunter owned at least a half-dozen horses. Paint Horses were especially treasured and prized. Even though they never bred their horses carefully, the Indians took pride in their animals and made some attempt to breed for the paint coloring they admired so much.

The Paint Horse has always been associated with the Indian in legends, stories, songs, and even in today's television programs. At the siege of the Alamo, at the Fetterman massacre, at the Battle of the Little Big Horn, the Paint Horse was there.

An interesting story has been told of an Indian and his Paint Horse who played a part in the massacre at the Little Big Horn in 1876. The army under Custer went down in defeat before the nearly three thousand Sioux warriors who had gathered to protest the invasion of their buffalo lands. After the victorious warriors rode back to their camp, the only survivor on the battlefield was a horse called Comanche, whose rider had been Captain Myles W. Keogh of the Seventh Cavalry. Unknown to anyone at the time, one other horse survived, a tough, range-raised Indian pony belonging to one of the army scouts. The Pawnee and Arikara tribes have honored in a war-dance song a spotted horse who walked into the Arikara village alone some time after the battle, still wearing an army saddle with the reins up as if he had been ridden.[3]

The Pawnee and Arikara tribes have similar languages and

---

[2]Hope Ryden, *America's Last Wild Horses*, 56–58.

[3]Brummett Echohawk, "The Spotted Horse Alone," *Western Horseman*, October, 1964.

customs. Annually they held ceremonies together, with singing, dancing, and exchanges of gifts. They were at peace with the whites, and some of the younger would-be warriors served as scouts for the army.

As Custer's Seventh Cavalry marched from Fort Lincoln, members of each company rode different-colored horses: A Company rode black horses, B Company rode bays, and C Company rode sorrels. The Arikara scouts rode army horses and their own ponies, which were mostly Paint.

After the Sioux had their revenge at the Little Big Horn, there was mourning in the Arikara village for the three Arikara scouts slain with Custer. The song originated at that time and handed down from generation to generation refers to a young warrior and his spotted horse. The words of this song, translated into English mean: "Little Soldier's [the Arikara scout killed with Custer at the Little Big Horn] spotted horse has returned [home] alone."

The horse they were singing about was the Paint Horse who walked all the way from the hard-fought battle and arrived early in the morning at his village, scarred, injured, and showing signs of a hard journey. The Arikaras knew the horse and knew how far he must have traveled. They also knew the young scout who did not return as Little Soldier, and today on a granite marker at the Custer National Monument in Montana listed under Scouts is the name Little Soldier.

In the nineteenth and early twentieth centuries vast herds of wild horses roamed the western deserts and plains. Although the wild horses of America were not of the unrestrainable character as the truly wild horses of Europe and Asia, they ranged freely in great numbers and could be claimed by anyone willing to attempt their capture. These horses, known as mustangs and broomtails, had their foundation in Spanish Barb stock. They were descendants of the domestic horses imported from Spain and the islands off the Florida coast that had been driven off or stolen by the Indians.

Today mustangs are known as small horses, standing less than fourteen hands and weighing from seven hundred to nine hundred pounds. This was not always so. Many western writers of the nineteenth century left records that the average mustangs of that century and earlier were horses of greater height with a good, hardy build. The best specimens were refined, handsome horses. Their colors ran largely to bay, black, brown, and chestnut, with some grays, whites, and Paints scattered among them. Judging from the fairly large number of Paint Horses in the herds of the early twentieth century, the paint coloring must have reproduced steadily and consistently over the years.

Centuries of survival in a harsh existence on semibarren ranges after the advancing ranchers and settlers drove them off the best ranges, as well as generations of inbreeding, resulted in deterioration of the mustangs. The same decline would have occurred in any other kinds of horses under the same circumstances. But helped by a combination of speed, self-reliance and defensive perception, they continued to survive and multiply. Later, however, mustangs were crossed with every type of horse and lost their identity.

Old-timers like Frank T. Hopkins, probably the greatest long-distance endurance rider who ever saddled a horse, proved the virtues of the American mustang many times. A former dispatch rider in the United States Army, Hopkins developed his endurance-riding ability carrying dispatches for frontier generals and his horse-handling skill as a specialty rider in the Buffalo Bill wild-West shows. All in all, Hopkins won more than four hundred races in the late 1800's, when endurance riding was the rage, and for most of those rides he was mounted on a mustang.

One of his lengthy rides started at Galveston, Texas, and ended at Rutland, Vermont. He covered the eighteen hundred miles in thirty-one days and finished two full weeks ahead of the rider who came in second. Another of his best performances was made in October, 1893, when he covered approximately one thousand miles from Kansas City, Missouri, to Chicago, Illinois. Hopkins was the only man to complete the grueling ride, which he did in twelve days six hours.

One of the first proponents of the mustang and the Paint Horse, Hopkins became internationally known not only for setting unbeatable records in endurance racing but also for the excellent quality of the horses he rode. His ranch in Wyoming Territory was the home of a number of good western-type stock horses and one outstanding Paint Horse, Hidalgo.

Described as a cream-and-white Paint Horse, Hidalgo was bred on a Sioux Indian reservation in South Dakota. Since he came into the world before the days of pedigrees and family lines, it can only be assumed that he was of "western stock-horse blood," and was descended from horses brought to this continent by the Spanish conquistadors. He was known as an American mustang and possessed the indefatigable endurance typical of the breed. Hopkins obtained the young Paint from the Sioux about 1882 and owned him until 1890.

At the World's Fair in Paris in 1889, Hopkins was approached by Rau Rasmussen, a freighter who dominated most of the trade from Aden to Gaza, to enter his Paint Mustang in a three-thousand-mile endurance race across the Arabian desert. Rasmussen had heard of the American mustangs' hardiness and asked Hopkins if he would be willing to pit one of his best against prized Arabian horses. Hopkins accepted the challenge.

The desert endurance race was a true test of a horse's strength and stamina. To be able to complete the course, a horse must have a healthy constitution, incredible power, a staunch spirit, strong legs, and sure steps. Beginning in Aden, in southern Arabia, the course followed the Persian Gulf and then turned inland over the barren sandy land along the borders of Arabia, Iraq, and Syria.

The contest had been held annually for a thousand years, and in the past had always been won by an Arab horse. In the words of Anthony A. Amaral, writing of this famous race:

Slightly over one hundred horses started on the ride from Aden. The great caravan of skilled Arabian riders rode their most prized mounts. They were spirited, accustomed to the difficulty of the sands, accustomed to the sun that sprayed exhausting heat upon them. Even among the mass of mounted horsemen, Hopkins stood out with parti-colored, 950 pound Hidalgo from the American plains.

Hopkins held Hidalgo at a steady pace as they made their way through the dry heat and over sandy soil. The march progressed to the Persian Gulf and up toward Syria and then along the border of Iraq and Arabia. Each day the riders started with the sun, following it until they were marching into it. Horses dropped by the way, some exhausted, some lame. At the end of the first week, the scarcity of water and the meager diet the horses were forced to exist upon in the barren country, had culled the inadequate horses. The strung line of riders dwindled daily.

Entering the second week of the grueling trek, Hopkins made his move and started to pass the other desert riders. In the wake of the sand kicked up by Hidalgo, treasured Arabian horses of the Bedouins fell farther and farther behind, while Hidalgo kept to a steady pace.

On the sixty-eighth day of the ride Hopkins rode Hidalgo to the finish stone, leaving behind him three thousand scorching miles.[4]

The tough Paint Mustang was the winner by thirty-three hours over his nearest competitor. The only American Paint Horse in the history of Arabian endurance racing ever to win the historic race, Hidalgo did it, and did it on merit.[5]

In the eastern United States horses transplanted to the

[4]Pers Crowell, *Cavalcade of American Horses*, 294–95.

[5]Anthony A. Amaral, "Hidalgo and Frank Hopkins," *Horse Lovers*, July, 1962, pp. 28–29.

mainland from the islands off the Florida coast were called Chickasaws by the early English settlers. There was little difference in this breed of horse and the Spanish horses in the southwestern United States and Mexico. Both were descendants of sixteenth-century Spanish stock and were endowed with the same fine Oriental blood. The Chickasaw was of a more even temperament, but that can be attributed to his close association with man, while the Spanish cow horses and mustangs roamed freely in the rough, unsettled West. The early colonists acquired several Chickasaw mares and mated them with their own well-bred stallions imported from England and France in an effort to improve their using stock and to produce a running horse for short distances up to a quarter of a mile. This successful blending of blood formed the foundation of today's American Quarter Horse.

Early Americans closely associated themselves with the horse. Horse racing was their sport, horse trading their delight, and horse breeding, but a slight necessity, was in some respects their challenge. Consequently, the appearance of light, trim "blooded" horses in England had tremendous effect on American horsemen and horse breeding. Following the pattern set by the English for improvement of their racing stock by infusing a generous amount of Oriental blood, settlers in the eastern colonies brought in horses of Barb, Arabian, and Turk breeding.

Importations of Paint Horses were relatively few and were for the most part of the Hackney and French Coach lines, which were by and large indirectly descended from the early English Thoroughbred foundation sires, the Godolphin Barb, the Darley Arabian, and the Byerly Turk. The painted horses of this blood were showy animals with a natural gait, making them excellent harness horses.

By 1700 the sport of horse racing was well established and had spread throughout Maryland, Virginia, and the Carolinas. In the beginning "short" races for distances up to a quarter-mile were popular among the plantation owners and backwoods settlers. As Thoroughbred horses entered the American scene, longer courses were laid out in major racing centers for racing "pedigreed" horses. The Thoroughbred became the gentleman's flat-racing breed, and the little Quarter Horse followed the western migration. In the cattle country of the American West the Quarter Horse met with the mustangs and Spanish cow horses. Their blood and qualities naturally blended well.

By the time the Quarter Horse reached Texas in the middle 1800's, the Spanish horses had been working cattle for over three hundred years. The mingling of the blood of the eastern Quarter Horse and the Spanish cow horse created a western stock horse with the physical stamina of the mustang, the flesh and muscle of the Quarter Horse, and the cow sense and fighting bull sense of the Spanish cow horse. The racing blood from the Quarter Horse proved to be just what was needed to produce the dependable cow horse that virtually "won" the west.

In the nineteenth and early twentieth centuries the western stock horse was an "all-purpose horse" who could do his work handling vast herds of cattle and in his spare time run a matched race at one of the local brush tracks. And where was the Paint Horse when the western stock horse was born? He was hazing cattle out of the mesquite thickets, bringing up strays during the roundups, and taking part in the bulldoggings and calf ropings alongside his solid-colored brothers and sisters.

Stock horses were of many bloodlines and of every color. The cowboy had his own curious names and preferences for certain horses. The dun horse that was a favorite among many was a buckskin with a dark dorsal stripe of brown or black. Horses of this color were called bayo coyotes, and some hands claimed them to be the toughest cow ponies. Another shade of dun was often referred to as a claybank, and another, a light-dun color, was a bayo blanco. A gray, freckled with black hair, was flea-bitten, a blue roan was a moro, and a mouse-colored, bluish-gray horse was a grullo. Bay horses were supposed to be the most dependable, while dun horses were supposed to be the best rope horses. Appaloosa horses that were white or light gray with dark spots over the entire body were called leopard horses or polka-dots, and all white horses were said to be albinos.

Because of his many varied coat colors and patterns, the Paint Horse probably has been called by more names than any other horse. Dating back to the earliest Paint Horses in Arabia, the Moslem called him a kanhwa, which meant blotched with white and chestnut or black. In India a Paint Horse was a pul-wahri, meaning a white horse that "flowers" with black spots, and in Spanish his name was derived from the word pintado, meaning painted or mottled.

The cowboys applied such names as piebald, skewbald, calico, overo, spotted, pinto and old paint. Generally, piebald horses were black and white, calico horses were roan and white, and skewbald horses were bay, sorrel, or dun with white. Among the ranch hands there were mixed views on the ability of a Paint Horse. As in every breed there were superb performers and mediocre ones. Those who rode one, owned one, or worked one knew that most Paint Horses possessed action as quick as any horse of their time. They were willing to give credit where credit was due.

The Paint Horse could have suffered a serious decline in western America similar to that of the mustang, had it not been for a new form of entertainment involving horses that began in 1883—the wild-West shows. For the next four decades enthusiastic crowds applauded the rip-roaring performances that toured the country bringing to easterners a new look at the West. The first exhibition of its kind was put together by the master showman William F. Cody, known worldwide as Buffalo Bill, for a Fourth of July celebration in his home town, North Platte, Nebraska. By the turn of the century there was an abundance of shows performing nationwide. Next to Buffalo Bill's shows, the most successful in attracting customers in large numbers was probably the 101 Ranch Wild West Show.

Facing page: A colorful poster of Buffalo Bill's Wild West Show. Courtesy Circus World Museum, Baraboo, Wisconsin.

Indians mounted on tobiano Paint Horses awaiting their performance in the Miller Brothers 101 Ranch Wild West Show. Courtesy Circus World Museum, Baraboo, Wisconsin.

These shows were designed to present to the American people the highlights and excitement of western life. Flashy horses, Indian races, trick riding and roping, sharpshooting, and dramatic events were magnificently displayed. Hundreds of horses, Quarter Horses, Paint Horses, Thoroughbreds, and Arabians, billed as bucking broncos, wild mustangs, Indian ponies, and military drill horses were utilized in the spectaculars. Indians demonstrating sports of the plains rode Paint Horses. The trick riders, standing on their heads or somersaulting, looked even more daring on a vivid Paint Horse. The Paint Horse added a touch of brilliance to these colorful affairs.

For the thousands of annual performances western-reared horses were in great demand. Since they were put to specialized use, the stock horses were well selected for their intelligence, spirit, and color. Ranchers near the market cities, striving for improved Paint Horses, bred from good cow-country stock colorful animals that were valued as much for their intelligence and energy as for their color. Most blood of all kinds and description was tried out on the Paint Horse at one time or another. None, though, nicked as well as that of the Quarter Horse, and none used then, or since, has proved to be any more beneficial.

Each of the forty-odd wild-West shows added its own special features, sometimes bulldogging, calf roping, wild-cow milking, or steer wrestling. When the shows faded in the 1920's, one of the most spirited of American sports, the rodeo, came into national prominence. Rodeoing had begun years earlier among the cowboys after roundup. Annually in cow towns throughout the West at these roundups, stampedes, or rodeos the Paint Horse gained a new recognition for his terrific action, strength, and athletic ability. Paint Horses, whose ancestors a few generations back were applauded for their good performing ability in conveying the message of the wild-West Shows, were now cheered for bucking or cutting skills that brought to the arena a true frontier background. There is no denying the fact that the Paint Horse contributed his part to historic Americana extremely well.

3 PAINT HORSES IN SOUTH AMERICA

The first South American horses disappeared at the same time that horses vanished from the North American continent. In all probability they met the same mysterious fate as that of the horses on the north. The first "native" horses were introduced to South America with the expansion of territories from the islands off the Florida coast. They were Spanish horses, predominantly Andalusian and Barb, and of the same blood and physical appearance as the mounts of the aristocratic adventurers that made possible Spain's conquests and victories in the New World. They had the same characteristics that distinguished the Spanish cow horses of the southwestern United States: they were strong and had endurance. Seeing the excellent qualities of this stock of horses, the early ranchers put them to the task they had been bred for, that of working cattle.

In the Spanish-speaking countries the word for "native" is *criollo*; and in Portugese it is *crioulo*. Hundreds of years before the criollo breed was established, horses of like characteristics native to the country were designated criollos. Today the breed is found mainly in Argentina, Brazil, Paraguay, Peru, and Chile. The horses resemble the western stock horses of the American plains in shape, size, color, and action. They are a uniform type, and traces of Spanish blood remain in most of them. The average criollo stands about 14.3 hands. He has a short, well-set head, a body that is fairly heavily muscled, and stout, sturdy legs. There is little difference in the breed standards throughout the South American countries, and any variation in size or build can be attributed to differences in environment rather than to differences in breeding.

The criollos, like the western stock horses, come in all colors. The Paint Horse pattern appears frequently and seems to reproduce easily. The early South American Criollo Paint Horses had a characteristic dark coat with roan patches of white, and were called overos by the gauchos of Argentina and Brazil. The South Americans employed a number of color terms for overos, such as negra overo for a black horse with white patches and bayo overo for a dun or yellow horse with white markings. The use of the word overo has continued to the present and is now the term for Paint Horses that are basically dark in color with the white extending upward from the underside, usually in patches or in an irregular, scattered design.

From all available records it appears that the overo color pattern was more common in South American Paint Horses and the color design termed tobiano was found more often in North American Horses. This is not to say that the overo pattern was not present in North American horses; there is evidence of the presence of both color patterns in horses. On the other hand, the tobiano coloring did not appear in early Argentine criollo horses, and the inhabitants have a story that has been repeated from generation to generation about the arrival of the tobiano horse.

In the middle of the nineteenth century a new type of horse was introduced into Argentina by an individual named Tobias. He was reported to be a São Paulo revolutionary who departed his country in 1842 after being defeated in the revolution in southeastern Brazil. He and his men arrived in Argentina seeking safety and asylum. Several of the men were mounted on Paint Horses that were unlike the native horses. Instead of the usual dark horse with irregular white areas on the underside, some horses were more white than dark, and the white appeared to cover the back and "slide" down the sides. To distinguish these Paint Horses from the overo horses already in the country, they were called tobianos.[1]

It is possible that Tobias and his men had acquired horses that were of the type found in northern and northeastern Brazil. The northern districts were settled by emigrants from Friesland, a province of the Netherlands that had been inhabited by Germanic peoples. The horses of that region were of a different stock from the *criollo* breed developed from the Spanish horses left by early conquistadors. Their origin is not known, but they appeared to be of the European type with a touch of Arab blood. Since the Brazilian settlers were from the region in Europe where experimental breeding for color was carried on during the Middle Ages, perhaps the horses traced back to the Paint Horses of that period.

The account of the arrival of the tobiano horse in Argentina, as told by many of the old inhabitants, cannot be proved, but since there is no reference in Argentine history to the tobiano horse before the end of the nineteenth century, there is a basis for giving some credit to the story.

In 1925 a young schoolteacher from Argentina, Aimé Tschiffely, brought fame to the Paint Horse by making one of the most remarkable rides ever attempted on horseback. Having a great desire to see North America, he planned a trip that would take him from Buenos Aires to Washington, D.C. To be assured of a successful trip, Tschiffely needed dependable, intelligent horses, reinforced by good, sound breeding. With

[1]Denhardt, *The Horse of the Americas*, 171–72.

A champion crioula *at Bagé, Brazil, 1941. Courtesy University of Oklahoma Press, Norman, Oklahoma.*

the help of a friend, Emilio Solanet, he selected two *criollo* horses, Mancha and Gato, for the long ride. Solanet, a professor in the Agricultural and Veterinary College in Buenos Aires, was most responsible for starting the *criollo* movement to preserve the breed.

Mancha, probably so named because *mancha* in Spanish-speaking countries is a term generally used for spotted horses, was a Paint Horse. Today neither Mancha nor Gato would be considered exceptional in conformation, but the prime con-

Mancha and Gato with Robert Denhardt and Aime Tschiffely, photographed in Argentina. Courtesy University of Oklahoma Press, Norman, Oklahoma.

sideration was performance under the most extreme conditions, and in this they were not lacking.

Tschiffely, riding alternately the two *criollo* horses, traveled a distance of approximately ten thousand miles over mountains, across arid regions, and through dense jungles and swamps. Mancha and Gato served him well, and he never had reason to regret his choice of horses. After months of hardship, all three arrived in Washington, D.C., in good condition. The two horses were later shipped back to Argentina and lived for many years in the best of health.

Tschiffely's ten-thousand-mile ride was in itself a worthy accomplishment. Of greater import is the fact that he depended on Paint Horses for a safe and successful journey—proving once again the outstanding ability of this breed.

4 FORMATION OF AN ASSOCIATION

For centuries horses have played a role in the sports, recreation, and general enjoyment of mankind. Although the Paint Horse has been around for thousands of years and present on American soil since 1519, he has only recently received appreciation for his contribution to the American scene. His past experiences in cattle roundups, rodeos, race meets, trail rides, and parades attracted horsemen to his versatility, and by 1960 the magic spell of the Paint Horse had begun to weave its way across the country. With this stimulus a few Oklahoma and Texas breeders got together in a serious effort to establish a Registry for Paint Horses to perpetuate for future generations the ancestry and descent of this "new breed" of horse.

Two associations, forerunners of the present American Paint Horse Association, were formed in the early 1960's—the American Paint Stock Horse Association and the American Paint Quarter Horse Association. For the first time the "sport model of the horse world" had a destiny. Because of the well-laid foundation of these two organizations the American Paint Horse Association has become one of the most successful breed associations in the United States.

The American Paint Stock Horse Association

The key figure in the organization of the American Paint Stock Horse Association (APSHA) was a unique horsewoman, Mrs. Rebecca Tyler. She conceived the idea of a registry for preservation of the lineage of Paint Stock Horses and laid the groundwork for such an association with informal get-togethers in the kitchen of her ranch home. This outstanding lady was a prominent breeder of both Paint Horses and Quarter Horses and one of the most knowledgeable authorities on bloodlines and pedigrees. The great-granddaughter of a Cherokee judge, Mrs. Tyler inherited her love of breeding and raising fine horses from her pioneering forefathers.

With the help of a few dedicated—and sentimental—Paint Horse breeders, who had as their purpose recognition of this breed of horse, the APSHA became reality in February, 1962. The association was incorporated as a nonprofit organization managed by an executive committee and a board of directors. It stated as its purpose: "To promote and develop a long neglected type of Paint Horse into a breed that will take its rightful place beside other American breeds in livestock history."

The organizational meeting was held in Gainesville, Texas, by Paint Horse breeders from northern Texas and Oklahoma. C. C. Teague, Sherman, Texas, was elected president; Dick Barrett, Ryan, Oklahoma, was elected vice-president; and Mrs. Tyler, who had done so much toward formation of the association, was the first secretary-treasurer. Directors were Junior Robertson, Waurika, Oklahoma; Ralph Russell, McKinney, Texas; and L. N. Sikes, Sherman, Texas. Russell and Sikes were also named as the association inspectors.

Three departments were set up for registry: the appendix

for all colts, the regular registry for Paint stallions and mares, and the breeding-stock registry for Paint-bred colts of a solid color, which could be valuable for breeding purposes. Among other rules and regulations of the association, it was stated that single-foot or pacing horses were not eligible for registration, a dark horse must have at least three white spots three inches in diameter on the body to be registered, and a white horse must have a minimum of one spot at least six inches in diameter to be registered. No discrimination was made against blue, glass, or dark eyes. Requirements for registration were kept lenient for the first few years, with plans formulated to tighten up in the future for the betterment of the breed. A stallion-inspection program was instituted to inspect all stallions at two years of age or older before the horse was accepted for registration and given a number.

By the time the organization was two years old, it had members and horses registered in forty states, including Hawaii, and in Canada. Affiliate organizations were formed to create interest in the Paint Horse and to sponsor shows in local areas. Interest grew in this new breed through association-sponsored shows, races, and awards.

The association had something to offer every member of the family, such as halter classes, performance events, racing, and youth activities. To promote the breed and create additional interest in the APSHA, a substantial purse was offered to the first Paint Stock Horse to be listed in the top ten of the official standings of the National Cutting Horse Association and another purse for the first Paint Horse to be listed among the top ten in the Girls' Barrel Racing Association standings.

The American Paint Quarter Horse Association

Formation of the American Paint Quarter Horse Association (APQHA) brought together two registries of horses—the Paint Horse and the Quarter Horse. Many of the founders of the association were owners of Quarter Horses and members of the American Quarter Horse Association (AQHA). These founders, who had a number of Paint Horses produced by Quarter Horse parents on both sides, felt that the animals deserved recognition and that they were, in fact, Quarter Horses with color. Since the AQHA registry would not allow registration of the horses, this group of individuals organized their own association for registering these outstanding animals and recording their bloodlines.

The charter for the new association was obtained in Abilene, Texas, in 1961, under the laws of the state of Texas. A trademark featuring a Quarter-type horse with paint markings standing on a map of the United States was registered with the United States Government. (The trademark was adopted by the American Paint Horse Association in 1965.)

The first president of the APQHA was W. L. "Bill" Jones, Abilene, Texas. The APQHA was organized along the lines of the AQHA. Registration in the association was not limited to horses with two Quarter Horse parents, since there were not enough Paint Horses with full Quarter Horse breeding on both sides to carry out the program that had been established. Selected animals either with known Quarter Horse bloodlines or with a definite Quarter Horse conformation were accepted for registration. Since it was inevitable that some solid-color foals would result, the *Appendix Breeding Stock Registry* was established for the solid-colored horses with one or both Paint Horse parents.

The association gained momentum in its early years and celebrated its second anniversary with publication of the first issue of the *Paint Quarter Horse Journal*. By the time the third year had passed, headquarters had to be moved to larger offices, at the Starlite Inn Motor Hotel in Abilene.

In 1964 the APQHA held fifteen approved shows across Texas. An active campaign for membership in all states was under way when, halfway through 1965, a merger with the

APSHA was concluded, resulting in the present American Paint Horse Association.

The American Paint Horse Association

The APSHA and APQHA were in existence for three to four years before work toward a merger of the two associations was begun. Since the purpose and objectives were the same and registration and show rules almost identical, consolidation would be a further advancement to the Paint Horse. In May, 1965, officers and directors of both associations met and made preliminary arrangements for a merger. On June 3, 1965, it was ratified by the memberships of both organizations. The new organization was called the American Paint Quarter Horse Association (APHA).

Through the efforts and leadership of Paint Horse breeders such as J. D. Hooter, Mrs. Tyler, A. J. Campbell, E. J. Hudspeth, and the late Art Beall, the merger was a major milestone in Paint Horse history. Guiding the young association during the early years was not easy, and all breeders and owners of Paint Horses are fortunate to have had these individuals at the helm.

A great deal of credit for much of the success of the APHA— and the Paint Horse— is due another individual, whose skill and management cannot be overlooked. With a deep affection for Paint Horses and a concern for their future, Sam Ed Spence, as executive secretary of the American Paint Horse Association, has given his time and talent in an effort to promote and establish the American Paint Horse as a permanent breed. Spence, a graduate of Texas A&M University, earned degrees in journalism and business administration and served as assistant editor of the *Quarter Horse Journal* in Amarillo, Texas, before joining the APHA in 1964. Except for a brief period in 1968–69, he subsequently served the association in the dual capacity of executive secretary and editor of the *Paint Horse Journal* with wholehearted devotion.

The early breeders, the founders of the APHA, and Sam Spence did much to sustain the breed and lay the foundation of

Sam Ed Spence, first Executive Secretary, American Paint Horse Association.

the modern Paint Horse. Too often the names of distinguished horses are of more importance than the individuals who are responsible for their success. The Paint Horse owes much to the founders of his association. Their efforts and diligent work is reflected in the tremendous interest that has developed in the

Officers and members of the APHA Executive Committee, 1973.
Left to right: Colin Beals, president; Stanley Williamson, immediate
past president; James V. Apple; Mott Headley; Paul Harber; I. M.
"Chuck" Dearing, Jr.; Junior Robertson; Sam Ed Spence.

American Paint Horse, and he is a better horse because of their
endeavors.

J. D. Hooter, Alexandria, Louisiana, was elected the first
president of the combined associations; Horace L. King, Cross
Plains, Texas, first vice-president; and A. J. Jack Campbell,
Douglas, Wyoming, second vice-president. Sam Ed Spence was
retained as the full-time executive secretary, and the head-
quarters were established in Fort Worth. The executive com-
mittee included Mrs. Tyler, Gainesville, Texas; Art Beall,
Broken Arrow, Oklahoma; William L. Jones, Abilene; Jewell
McClinton, Fort Worth; Joe S. Boone, Springdale, Arkansas;
Eddie Courtney, Levelland, Texas; and the three officers.

All horses that had been registered in either of the two
associations before the merger kept their respective numbers
and papers. The young association closed out the year 1965

with a total paid membership of 1,546, total registrations numbering over 3,900, ten regional clubs representing twelve states and horses registered in forty-three states, Canada, Mexico, and Guatemala.

In 1966 the APHA noted a 30 per cent growth in registrations, memberships, and transfers over the previous year. During the first six months 1,097 horses were registered, and by the end of the year there were over 5,600 in the registry.

The first *Stud Book and Registry of the American Paint Horse Association* was compiled and printed to provide a reference source and guide for breeders. The first volume contained all the old APSHA and APQHA numbers. In addition to registration data on some three thousand horses, the registry provided historical articles and full-color pictures of some of the leading Paint Horses in the country, a membership list, the board of directors and officers for 1965, and a history of the APHA.

Another accomplishment of 1966 was the appearance of the first issue of the *Paint Horse Journal*. The journal, published bimonthly, includes articles on breeding, care, and showing of Paint Horses; show results; coming events; and sales. Before its appearance the APHA issued the *Paint Horse Newsletter*, mailed monthly to all members. Between issues of the *Journal* the *Newsletter* is still mailed to subscribers to keep them current on activities and events.

In 1967, Volume II of the *Stud Book and Registry* was published, which included all numbers from 2,600 through 6,000. The volume contained a listing of the 1966 and 1967 officers and directors, a membership list, APHA champions, and a pictorial section of Paint Horses.

For the next six or seven years the association's growth was tremendous. By the end of 1969 the APHA had outgrown its office space in the Western Building in Fort Worth. Headquarters were moved immediately after Christmas that year to new, modern offices in the Calmont Oaks Building, 6801 Calmont, just off Interstate 20 West, Fort Worth. Five years later, with a new computer system and a half-dozen or so more employees, the APHA office was once again filled to capacity. Three acres of land were purchased on Interstate 35 West, about twelve minutes north of downtown Fort Worth, and in early 1974 a new APHA office building was completed and ready for occupancy.

Volume III of the *Stud Book and Registry*, containing numbers 6,001 through 12,000, was published in 1970; and in 1974, Volume IV was off the press, together with the first *APHA Racing Chart Book*. The *Racing Chart Book* gives the chart on every official race run from 1966 through 1973, as well as a listing and record of every official race starter in those years and tables on leading money and point earners.

The changing shape of the Paint Horse is a result of the regulating factors of the association. Although the books are still open for registering all Paint mares and geldings foaled before January 1, 1964, provided they meet certain conformation standards, it appears likely that they will close within a few years. The open registration was set up to allow entrance into the registry to all quarter-type Paint Horses whose ancestry had never been recorded. To meet the goals and purposes of the association of bloodlines, conformation, and color, revised rules adopted in 1970 provide that all horses foaled after December 31, 1963, must have a sire and dam registered in the APHA, the AQHA, or the Jockey Club. More recently the requirement was added that stallions registered with the AQHA and Jockey Club that are used for breeding to Paint mares must be identified and listed with the association before registration of their foals.

Intelligent planning to standardize the Paint Horse breed has paid rich dividends. The founders of the APHA recorded what the Paint Horse must look like, and they have not allowed horses that do not meet these standards to be registered. The association's rigid stallion-inspection program is one of the many "police actions" that has helped ensure uniformity in the breed.

An inspection of all stallions at two years of age has guaranteed a minimum of undesirable, inferior stallions in the

APHA headquarters and office building.

registry. The program is selective in the stallions that are passed, or approved, and given a number, since approximately 40 per cent of the horses inspected do not measure up to the APHA standards. The inspectors are men of experience and ability. It is their job to see that only stallions are passed who will serve as progenitors of the qualities desired in today's Paint Horses.

Most breeders find it difficult to judge objectively their own horses, keeping in mind over-all breed improvement. It is not an easy task to cull out those horses that do not come up to standard, and yet one should bear in mind that not all stallions can pass inspection and that those with less desirable qualities are better off gelded and given some kind of training. In some associations without an inspection program inferior stallions allowed to stand at stud could have serious effects on the breeds.

The complete registration rules pertaining to the Paint Horse are found in the *American Paint Horse Association Official Handbook*. Listed below are a few selected rules from Volume I of the *APHA Stud Book* that apply to all horses:

(1) *A horse must be at least 14 hands (56 inches) tall at the withers as a two-year-old, and it must not be gaited. These rules were set up expressly to adhere to the desired stock and quarter-type Paint as opposed to the pony and gaited or parade-type individual.*

(2) *Each stallion must pass a personal conformation inspection before he can be advanced to the Regular Registry and receive a number for breeding purposes. Perhaps no rule in the APHA is more universally praised by horsemen than this stallion inspection rule, which prevents any stallion from being "born with a number." Every stallion must pass inspection as a two-year-old to earn his place in the Regular Registry.*

(3) *All horses foaled on or after January 1, 1964, must be sired by a horse with a registration number in the APHA, the American Quarter Horse Association, or the Jockey Club. This bloodline requirement rings true to the Association's never-ending endeavor to up-breed its stock.*

The Paint Horse registry is faced with one problem that most other breeds are not concerned with, the question of color. How much color is a Paint Horse? The original rule stated that a horse had to be recognizable as a Paint Horse from two sides. A new and simpler rule has been adopted, stating that a horse must be recognizable as a Paint Horse. Since color is one basis for registration, a horse must show Paint Horse characteristics and must be immediately identified as a Paint Horse when in the show ring or on the race track. Each case is passed on individually, questionable cases being referred to the registration committee and then to the executive committee of the association for the final decision.

Breeding-stock numbers are given to horses lacking enough color to qualify for the regular registry. The letter *B* precedes such registration numbers. By this number the APHA is not passing on the quality of the animal but merely indicating that the horse does not possess enough color to be recognizable as a Paint Horse and cannot be shown in APHA shows. Beginning in 1969 all solid-color grade mares that were bred to Paint Horses had to be registered in the breeding stock so that their 1970 foals would be eligible for registration.

To increase interest in raising and showing Paint Horses, points are awarded to registered horses entered and exhibited in approved APHA shows. Points won in performance contests qualify a horse for the "Register of Merit," the "Superior Event" title, the "APHA Champion" title, and the "Supreme Champion" titles. The point system used by the APHA is similar to that used by the AQHA. In shows endorsed by the association the same rules must be used in all classes, only approved judges must be employed, and results must be furnished to the APHA secretary. The judges must be listed either on the recommended list of the APHA or on the approved list of the AQHA. Moreover, the judge must be a member in good standing in the American Paint Horse Association. The scale of points is given below:

Scale of Points

Number of Horses in Class	Placings					
	1st	*2d*	*3d*	*4th*	*5th*	*6th*
3–5	1					
6–8	2	1				
9–11	3	2	1			
12–14	4	3	2	1		
15–17	5	4	3	2	1	
18 and over	6	5	4	3	2	1

Paint Horse shows are classified according to the number of entries in all halter and performance classes. This classification is set up as follows:

Class A Show   126 or more entries (minimum of 40 horses)
Class B Show   76 through 125 entries
Class C Show   51 through 75 entries
Class D Show   0 through 50 entries

The "Register of Merit" award is a recognition of performance ability. Horses are advanced to the "Register of Merit" when they have won at least ten points in any one performance event, as outlined in the "Scale of Points" above. The title APHA Champion may be awarded to any stallion, mare, or gelding registered in the Regular Registry of the association. To qualify, a horse must win a total of forty or more points in competition in official shows and contests recognized by the APHA. The points for this title must be won in five or more shows and under five or more judges. Sixteen of these forty points must be won in halter classes, with a minimum of ten points won in A- or B-class shows. Sixteen points are required in performance events, and at least five points must be earned in each of at least two categories of performance events.

A Paint Horse may become the Superior (Event) Horse upon earning fifty or more points in one recognized event. For example, a horse earning a minimum of fifty points in halter is designated an APHA Superior Halter Horse; a horse with fifty points in Western Pleasure becomes an APHA Superior Western Pleasure Horse.

The title American Paint Horse Association Supreme Champion is presented to a Paint Horse elevated to noble eminence by outstanding ability. To receive the award, the horse must meet these requirements:

(a) Has been named Grand Champion in at least five approved APHA shows under five different judges. These shows

must also have been classed as A shows.

(b) Has won a total of at least 80 points in recognized halter and performance shows approved and classified as A shows by APHA.

(c) And that at least 30 of those points have been won in approved halter classes.

(d) And at least 50 of those points have been won in performance events approved by the Association.

(1) And no more than ten (10) points may be won in any one performance event.

(2) And must have earned at least one Register of Merit in four of the five categories of performance events as set forth in Rule 230.

(3) And must have earned at least four (4) racing points as indicated under Category V in Rule 230 (Racing) and have run at least one race in an official Speed Index of no less than 70.[1]

From 1970 through 1974 twenty-two horses qualified for the title American Paint Horse Supreme Champion. They are shown in the accompanying list.

Supreme Champion No.	Name	Supreme Champion No.	Name
1	Snip Bar	12	Red Mount
2	Yellow Mount	13	Lady Bar Flit
3	Joechief Bar	14	J Bar's Lady Bug
4	Lady Rimbo	15	Rapid Ranger
5	Bar Mount	16	Our Sir Prize
6	Nightwatcher	17	Cowboy Ranger
7	Ceasar Bar's Dinero	18	Rio Retta Bar
8	Cherokee War Chief	19	Bar Patches Reb
9	Yellow Mount's Pride	20	Silly Filly
10	Skippetta	21	Spunky's Blaise
11	Gill's Q Ton	22	Awhe Honera

[1]American Paint Horse Association, *Official Rule Book*, 9th ed.

PART II **BREEDING AND COLOR**

5 BREED CHARACTERISTICS

A "breed" is defined as a variety or stock of animals related by descent with certain inherited characteristics and capable of reproducing those characteristics. Furthermore, the word breed has come to mean a specialized group of animals or pedigreed animals registered in some association or club. In these respects the American Paint Horse, now related by descent, possessing the same qualities of body and limb, and capable of reproducing the precise conformation, character, and coloring in the progeny, became a breed in 1961 with the formation of the first Paint Horse Association.

As discussed in Chapter 1, it is extremely difficult to trace the origin of all the modern breeds of horses. An assumption may be made that through migrations and importations a considerable exchange of blood occurred over the years, leaving most horses of mixed ancestry. A descendant in a very long line of hot-blooded horses, the Paint Horse received a liberal admixture of Oriental and Spanish blood in the early centuries and, beginning in the 1950's good foundation Quarter Horse and Thoroughbred blood.

The Paint Horse is a "hot blood" and possesses the characteristics common to all hot-blooded breeds: smooth body lines, trim legs and feet, quick movement, and maneuverable speed. The Orientals were the original hot bloods and were set apart from the cold-blooded stock by their ancestry and performance ability. Their blood formed the basis of all modern light-horse breeds, and through the years environmental conditions, crossbreeding, feeding, and use have molded each distinct type.

Development of the Paint Horse breed is along similar lines to that of the foundation of all other modern-day breeds. The colorful "horse of the plains" was crossed with stock that was more stylish and popular, and over the years the Paint Horse type developed. Of course, the Paint Horses of today do not look like the Paint Horses that Cortes first landed in the New World. The changes that have been made were intended changes. Like the Quarter Horse, the Paint Horse can claim to be "made" in America.

In the Thoroughbred and Quarter Horse breeds it is fashionable to have families that can be traced for many generations past. Most individuals interested in bloodlines and the breeding of horses feel that it takes several generations of recorded and scientific breeding to establish a family or strain. It could very likely be many years before Paint Horse families are important in the same sense as are Quarter Horse and Thoroughbred families. Although the recorded history of the Paint Horse dates from 1961, when the first horse was registered, a few Paint Horse families were in existence before that time. Actually it would be difficult to make a distinction between Paint Horse families and Quarter Horse families, since most Paint Horses trace directly or indirectly to the known Quarter Horse families or strains.

When the American Paint Horse Association was formed, it was felt that horses carrying Quarter Horse and Thoroughbred blood should and must be used in the foundation stock. Although Quarter Horse bloodlines will show up most often in the Paint Horse pedigree, many Paint Horses carry a good deal of Thoroughbred breeding. Crossbreeding with the Quarter Horse has had the greatest influence on breed improvement, quite similar to the influence of the Arabian in the improvement of English racing stock three hundred years ago.

Except for his color the appearance of the Paint Horse closely resembles that of the Quarter Horse. His heritage is the same, his environment is the same, and he is being used in the same capacity as the Quarter Horse. Until a few years ago "Paint" was a color classification rather than a type or breed. It is not the intent of this chapter to prove that the Paint Horse is just another Quarter Horse with color or a different type of Quarter Horse or Thoroughbred. Having a background tracing back through many generations to some of the best Spanish stock available, and having served well the early ranchers in herding cattle and the Indians in running buffalo, he has earned a respectful place in the equine world. There is no other horse of like character more brilliantly colored that is any better suited to the western way of life. The American Paint Horse typifies all that is distinctive in the twentieth-century-model horse.

While individuals may have differences of opinion about the standards required for the ideal Paint Horse, certain basic physical characteristics are desirable in the Paint Horse as a breed. The more closely breeders bring together the important combinations of traits, the more firmly the breed is established and the more alike future generations of Paint Horses become.

The general characteristics of appearance, structure, and shape of the Paint Horse have been outlined by the American Paint Horse Association. They are as follows:

Head

The head should be well proportioned to the rest of the body, refined, clean-cut, with good width between large clear eyes.

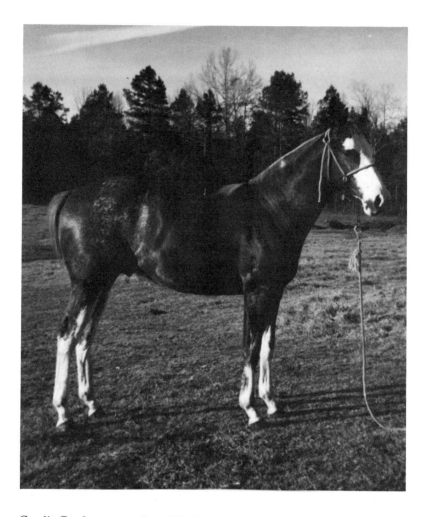

Credit Card as a yearling. His dam was an AQHA registered mare, and his sire was a Paint Horse whose pedigree is solid Quarter Horse and Thoroughbred breeding.

The face should be straight, the muzzle relatively small, the mouth shallow and the jaw broad and strongly muscled. Ears should be short to medium size, well carried and active.

Neck

The neck should be fairly long, and neatly join long, smooth sloping shoulders. Short, thick necks are most undesirable. The neck should emulate keenness, and the throatlatch should be ample, but clean-cut. The head and neck of the Paint Horse should show boldness and masculinity in the stallion, refinement and femininity in the mare.

Chest

The chest should be deep, fairly wide, but well forked. It should denote good power, but ample mobility.

Back

The back (topline) should be short, with a strong loin that fits into a heavily muscled croup. The Paint Horse should also sport a good set of withers— "a place to put a saddle and have it stay there."

Rear

The rear quarter of the Paint should feature a long croup, heavily defined stifle, and a hip that runs well down into the leg. The gaskin should be powerful proportionally both inside and outside.

Legs

The legs should be straight, true and squarely set. Hocks should be clean-cut, correctly set and not too high. The knees should be straight and taper gradually into the leg. The fetlocks should be naturally clean with no excess hair.

Balance

The Paint Horse should show balance, a harmonious development of all parts. His disposition should be highly manageable, but still imply alertness and animation. He should show style and beauty, balance and symmetry—overall quality.

Action

Basically the Paint Horse should be short–coupled for a high degree of action, and have the ability to move quickly for any stock horse event he is called upon to perform. His motion should be straight and true, with fluidity and good stride.

The American Paint Horse is at a point in his history comparable to that once occupied by the American Quarter Horse, the American Thoroughbred, and, in fact, most breeds at one time or another. The breeders of the 1960's and 1970's control the future of the breed. What principles they employ today will determine what tomorrow's Paint Horse will be.

When setting up a breeding program and selecting suitable foundation stock that will produce the desired conformation, performance, and color, breeders would do well to follow the advice of a most knowledgeable breeder of Quarter Horses, Ott Adams, who said that "performance and conformation both are secondary considerations, you need not worry about them, both will come with the right kind of blood in your horses."[1]

The Paint Horse breeder should, then, begin with blood. It is through blood that type is preserved, and, to infuse the right kind of blood that will ensure uniformity of breeding beyond the first generation, an outcross to the Quarter Horse has been necessary.

[1]Ott Adams to J. M. Huffington, "Letters," *Quarter Horse*, Vol. 1, No. 5 (August, 1946).

Since the Paint Horse breeder is striving to preserve the paint coloring, one goal in his breeding program is color. As other desirable traits are added to the list—conformation points, specific utility, and temperament, to name a few—discriminate crossbreeding becomes necessary. Still in an early stage of development, the Paint Horse can be bred into superior lines through selective outcrossing, but the type selected should be one that will ensure the fundamentals of Paint Horse breeding stock.

Any constructive breeder aims to maintain the uniformity of quality already attained in a breed and improve those characteristics that are not up to standard. An important force involved in maintaining the excellence of quality is heredity, the genetic channel through which qualities are transmitted from one generation to another. For the laws of heredity to apply, horsemen must breed for one type. Emphasis should be placed on the intelligent mating of breeding stock that possess the distinct characteristics that have been cultivated in the breed. Certain basic qualities are desirable in the Paint Horse breed, and they have been listed and identified in the registration rules of the association. One phrase sums up in very simple language the force of heredity: "Like begets like."

Heredity includes not only the individual horses mated but the ancestry of the horses. Breeding a particular sire to a particular dam is in reality breeding from the ancestry of that sire and dam. Some breeders feel that ancestors beyond the fourth or fifth generation have little influence. For one thing, it is not possible to determine a horse's performing ability from fifth-generation ancestors. Yet it should be pointed out that the better a horse is bred the more surely are his characteristics likely to be fixed and the greater assurance of obtaining such characteristics in the offspring. The genetic influence does reach back beyond the parents, to the grandparents, to the great-grandparents, and to the great-great-grandparents. The strength of the hereditary force of every characteristic is decided by the extent to which the characters are represented in the ancestry, and unknown individuals in the ancestry can introduce unknown traits into the offspring.

Another important aspect of breeding that should not be overlooked is upgrading, a system of introducing new characteristics into a group of animals. The Paint Horse has come up through the years to his present breed type by the substitution of characters through an outcross to the Quarter Horse. Upgrading is the mating of common mares of unknown breeding to purebred stallions, thus increasing the amount of pure blood in the progeny. When these "half-breds" are later mated to purebreds, the percentage of increase of pure blood will follow the proportions of three-fourths, seven-eighths, and fifteen-sixteenths for each successive generation. The greater the number of generations through which this up-grading process is carried the higher will be the percentage of pure blood. Continuing the upgrading process for six generations will result in over 98 per cent pure blood in the sixth-generation offspring.

To follow an upgrading process in a breed such as the Paint Horse, the most logical beginning is to take a Paint mare, who may be of unknown breeding but whose general appearance resembles that of the stock horse, and add the characteristics and refinements of a Quarter Horse sire. The offspring will have at least 50 per cent pure blood. This process should be continued with each generation until a complete substitution of characteristics has been made. The other alternative is to cross a quarter-type Paint Horse with Quarter mares. The resulting foals will inherit most of the traits and general qualities that constitute the ideal for the Paint Horse breed. There will always be some variation from the accepted standard, but years of selective breeding with a concentration on quality horses of excellent bloodlines will produce results. When attempting breed improvement, the influence of a well-bred stallion, and his ancestry, may be enormous, and in that respect the American Quarter Horse has been used with much success.

It is obvious that any marked improvement of a breed involves a long period of time and a great number of animals.

Squaw Cat and C-Note, Jr., a Paint mare and foal by a Paint Horse sire. Photograph by Margie Spence.

Good horses are not produced overnight or in a matter of a few years. It takes time, research, and insight to produce top-notch horses. Pedigrees are traced, performance records are studied, and compatible characteristics are sought. Years of planning and developing a sound breeding program are necessary. "Like father, like son," and "Every good horse, like every good man, has a good mother," is still good advice, even in today's sophisticated, mechanized world.

6 COLOR PATTERNS

Paint Horses come in a wide variety of colors and designs. Their coat is always a combination of white with any of the basic colors common to horses: black, bay, brown, chestnut, dun, grulla, sorrel, palomino, gray, and roan. Each Paint Horse has his own markings, and no two horses are exactly alike in color and design.

There are two distinct patterns of coloring designated overo and tobiano. These two patterns do not refer to color—that is, black and white or brown and white—for there are overos and tobianos of all colors. The color patterns are decided by the type and location of marking, or, in other words, body contrast.

The amount of white predominant on the horse does not affect the pattern. Some horses are almost completely white; others are dark with a few white spots on the body. There is no limitation on the amount of white or the darker color that is predominant. What makes the two patterns distinct is the location of the white on the body, not the amount.

Annie Rose, an overo with four white legs. Photograph by Margie Spence.

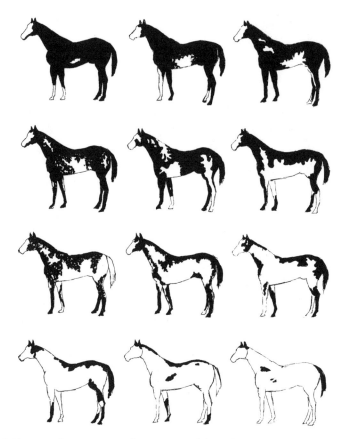

Variations and extremes of overo markings from very little white to almost all white.

Genetically, the two patterns are different. Only tobiano-spotting genes cause tobiano coloring, and only the overo genes are responsible for overo coloring.

Overo

An overo may be either predominantly white or dark, although the darker coloring is more common. The white areas originate on the underside of the horse and extend upward in an irregular design, giving the impression of a dark horse splashed from underneath with white coloring.

One way to determine whether a horse is truly an overo is by taking a look at the back. If there is a line of solid dark color from the withers to the tail set, in most cases the horse is an overo. Very rarely does an overo have white crossing the back, withers, or tail set. There are exceptions to every rule, and a few horses do not have this solid dark line of coloring.

In most cases the mane and tail are a solid color and not mingled. They are either solid white or solid dark, and usually the tail is the latter.

The head is almost always white, or bald. A bonnet face is common, as well as an apron face. The bonnet face is identified by the dark color that frames a white face from the forehead, over the ears, and under the jaws, giving the appearance that a white head is fully covered with a dark, close-fitting bonnet. Characteristics of the apron face are the dark forehead and dark ears, as in the bonnet face, but in contrast the area around one or both eyes is dark, and the dark color is "splashed" on the sides of the face and under the jaw. It is very unusual to find an overo without some white on its face or head. The neck is basically dark with splotches of white color. Most overos have dark legs. Sometimes one or two show some white, but, in contrast to the tobiano, the overo almost never has four white legs from the knees down.

An additional trait of the overo pattern is the irregular, rather scattered or splashy white markings on the body, which is one reason why these horses have been called calicos. A roan coat is also very common in the overo, with the white coloring appearing in many small ragged patches.

Tobiano

On the tobiano horse the white area starts on the back and spreads downward, usually in a regular or clearly marked pattern. The most noticeable feature is the white area extending

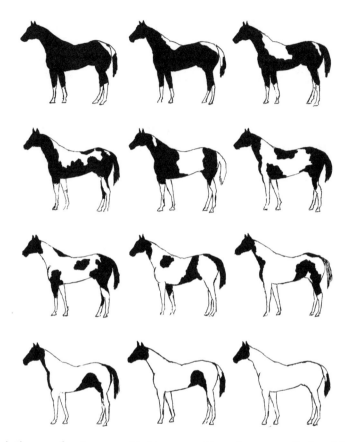

Variations and extremes of tobiano markings from very little white to almost all white.

up and over the withers. Often the tobiano has a dark neck and chest with white front legs, and when viewed from the front he gives the appearance that he is wearing a shield.

The head is usually dark with markings similar to horses of solid colors, such as a snip, star, strip, or blaze. There are only a few exceptions to this rule, where the head is completely white or bald; this is often the sign of a tobiano-overo cross.

One typical characteristic of the tobiano that seems always to hold true is that the legs are white, at least below the knees

Sky Bar, a predominantly white tobiano. Photograph by Margie Spence.

and hocks. It may be accepted as a general rule that a tobiano never has more than one or two solid-color legs.

The mane and tail are the color of the region from which they extend, and the tail is sometimes two-toned or mingled in color. The tobiano usually has a dark spot in each flank, and the spots are normally regular in shape, often in oval or round patterns. Presently the tobianos outnumber the overos about four to one.

In a tobiano-overo cross, a colt with a predominantly white coat seems to be the most common result, often with overo traits showing up on the head (bonnet or bald) and dark ears. Since these crosses have produced perfectly marked overos and perfectly marked tobianos, there is no way to predetermine what color pattern will result. Crossing the two color patterns can produce an indistinct color pattern that is difficult to identify, and the offspring becomes one of the "exceptions to the rule."

Glass Eyes

Both the overo and tobiano may have "glass eyes" (often called "blue eyes" or "white eyes"), although this trait seems to be more common in the overo. This is not a good rule to follow in determining whether a horse is overo, since there are many tobiano horses with one or both blue eyes.

The glass-eyed horse has eyes that are any color other than "normal," usually a shade of blue. Horses with glass eyes have perfect vision and can see as well as horses with dark eyes. Because blue eyes have been referred to as "glass eyes" does not mean that they are inferior. Blue eyes are just as serviceable as brown eyes.

Glass eyes are hereditary and have come down to the

Facing page: J Bar's Trooper as a yearling, an overo-tobiano cross. Photograph by Margie Spence.

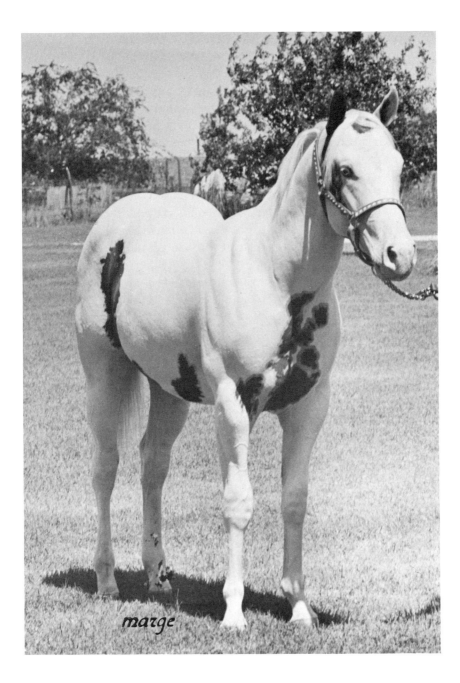

Quarter Horses, Paint Horses, and even the Thoroughbred horses of today. This trait was of some concern to Quarter Horse breeders as long as one hundred years ago. Though glass eyes were once thought to be the result of mixed blood, geneticists have recently concluded that they are probably related to color inheritance. Now and then glass eyes appear in a horse whose parents have normal dark eyes. Cotton Eyed Joe by Little Joe by Traveler is a good example of a glass-eyed horse in the Quarter Horse breed. He was out of Little Sister by Little Joe, and was bred by Ott Adams, of Alice, Texas. Cotton Eyed Joe was a bald-faced sorrel horse with one glass eye and two white feet.[1] He showed a lot of roan color in his flanks and at the root of his tail. Owned by Tom East of the King Ranch for a short time, he was sold because many of his get inherited the extra white coloring and glass eyes from their sire.

The question of glass eyes, their source, and the reason for their occurrence has never been fully answered. J. M. Huffington, secretary-treasurer of the old National Quarter Horse Breeders Association, was deeply interested in this outcropping and researched the subject some twenty-five years ago. He learned from an old horse trainer in Illinois, who was about seventy-five years old at the time, that Barney Owens,[2] a Quarter Horse by Old Cold Deck, had white under his stomach, glass eyes, and a skunk mane and tail (a description often applied to horses showing white in the mane and tail and at the tail set). Barney Owens sired a number of celebrated horses, and yet from this description of him it seems likely that he was actually a Paint Horse.

Robert Moorman Denhardt, one of the best-informed writers on Quarter Horse history and bloodlines, discussed family strengths, weaknesses, and traits in his book *The Quarter Horse*. In Volume III he wrote: "The Joe Reeds, Old Freds,

[1]Robert Moorman Denhardt, *The King Ranch Quarter Horses,* 124.
[2]Barney Owens was by Cold Deck by Old Billy by Shiloh and out of a steel-dust mare. He made a strong impression on Quarter Horse breeding through his son, Dan Tucker, the sire of Peter McCue.

and the Travelers often have too much white on the face and the legs. A few spots appear on some of these horses, as does an occasional white eye."[3]

In the Traveler line one of Traveler's sons, Blue Eyes, had glass eyes, and a great-grandson, Hobo, by Joe Moore also had blue eyes, as well as Cotton Eyed Joe.

What is interesting about Old Fred and Barney Owens is that Old Fred is a great-grandson of Old Billy, and Barney Owens is a grandson. Some might be inclined to say that Old Billy by Shiloh is responsible for glass eyes. This could be true, since glass eyes appear to be a trait of this strain. But their appearance in Traveler horses and Joe Reed horses is not satisfied by this one and only source. There is no known link between these two Quarter Horse sires and Old Billy; however it may be possible that far enough back there were some ancestral ties.

Old Billy's influence extends to the Old Freds, Peter McCues, Cold Decks, Sykes Rondos, Blakes, and Lock's Rondos—just about every foundation family of Quarter Horses. With so wide a spread and the mixing of blood with the Printers and Steel Dusts, glass eyes and other Paint Horse characteristics could easily appear in any of the modern-day horses.

Huffington, as well as Adams, who owned Blue Eyes and Cotton Eyed Joe at one time, discussed on many occasions the cause of blue eyes and why they appeared in some horses. Adams believed that "it was from stock away back that was strong in hot blood." This opinion led Huffington on a search into past generations of Quarter Horses, where he found that blue eyes appeared early in American horses in a Spanish mare, described as black and white in color, who was bred to Janus.[4]

[3]Robert Moorman Denhardt, *The Quarter Horse*, III, 160.

[4]Janus, the greatest of early Quarter Horse progenitors, was foaled in England in 1749 and was imported to the United States about 1752. His sire is recorded as the Godolphin Barb and his dam as a mare by Fox. Janus is the stallion most responsible for the early development of the Quarter Horse. At least eight of the founding families in early Quarter Horse history are related to him. The story of Janus is best told by Barbara Muse in *The Grand Twenty*.

He could not learn the identity of this mare with the blue eyes and Paint Horse markings, but he did establish the fact that blue eyes were present in horses before Old Billy's time by almost one hundred years.

An example of a Thoroughbred with blue eyes was an imported English blood horse, *Silver Eye, who had stocking legs, a bald face, and glass eyes. He is described in *Edgar's Stud Book*, published in 1833, as "a pale sorrel horse with a white face, raw nose, and glass eyes. Very well formed, but light; with all four legs white above the knees before, and hocks behind."[5]

Whether or not glass eyes are a color inheritance, there does appear to be a close association between blue-eyed horses and the paint coloring. Most of the horses with glass eyes, and those previously described, had in common large amounts of white on the face, the legs, the feet, and occasionally the body.

The appearance of the occasional blue eyes is still one of the most puzzling riddles of horse breeding. While it is not expected to get a blue-eyed foal from parents with normal dark eyes, it has happened and happens in some strains much more frequently than in others. It is also worth noting that, when there has been some inbreeding, recessive characteristics—and blue eyes are generally considered a recessive inheritance—are brought out that otherwise might remain hidden under dominant traits. Inbred lines of families of horses where these genes are present become more homozygous as they continue to develop, increasing the chance for blue eyes to appear. Such mating develops more pairs of genes in which the members are alike and the animals more uniform in type and more prepotent than the average horse.

[5]Franklin Reynolds, "They Called Him Traveler," *Quarter Horse Journal*, May, 1957, p. 35.

7 COLOR GENETICS

For many years color in horses has been a topic of interest to breeders and geneticists. In the study of hereditary factors some progress has been made in the selection of and breeding for a particular coat color, but color inheritance in horses is complicated. Several genes and their alleles affect color. An animal can receive either one or two variations of a gene, but no more than two. The various combinations of these genes make it difficult to predict the color of an offspring and even more difficult to predict the two-toned coat of the Paint Horse.

(Before proceeding, I should explain that genetics is the branch of biology that deals with heredity in similar or related animals. It is the study of the transmission of characters by parents to the offspring—more specifically here, the transmission of the paint color.)

Very little information is available about the genetics involved in breeding for the paint color. During the past several years during which studies have been made, some important facts have been learned. With the increasing interest in the breed and more individuals recording data about their breeding programs, it is expected that in the coming years more reliable knowledge may be gained.

In their breeding of Paint Horses, most breeders take advantage of the many generations of breeding available in the Quarter Horse for the type, conformation, and ability. In addition to these traits Paint Horse breeders want color, but for most of them color inheritance remains a jigsaw puzzle. While progress may seem slow to the breeder who is trying to produce Paint Horses that breed true, it is encouraging to know that progress is being made.

For each and every color characteristic a gene is involved. A gene is that part of a chromosome that transmits hereditary characteristics. The horse's color, sorrel, dun, black, or any of the colors with the white Paint coloring is determined by his color genes.

The inheritance of the genes that control color and color pattern in horses is autogenetically the same as for other traits. Genes control everything about the horse: size, conformation, speed, intelligence, and color. Every foal receives at least two genes associated with every trait, one from the stallion and one from the mare. One way, and no doubt the easiest way, to determine the genes a horse may have is to study his ancestors and his offspring. It is possible to determine whether the genes received from each parent are the same or dissimilar. As the number of offspring studied increases, the progeny color becomes more meaningful.

Genes exist in groups and are located at a particular spot on the chromosomes. Chromosomes occur in pairs, as do the genes within them. A gene for a certain characteristic will be in a specific place on the chromosome, and the gene for its complement will be in the same place on the other chromosome of the pair. A normal horse has sixty-four chromosomes, and these chromosomes form thirty-two pairs. When fertilized, the thirty-two chromosomes from the male (the sperm) pair with the thirty-two from the female egg. Thus the new foal has sixty-four chromosomes, or thirty-two pairs. Since the chromosomes from the stallion contain genes that control the same traits as the chromosomes from the dam, the young foal now has two genes for every trait.

The problems of inheritance depend upon the ways in which genes are passed on from the older generation to the younger and upon how genes act and interact. The paired genes, one from each parent, always deal with the same hereditary characteristic, such as hair color, but their effect may differ. It is purely chance which gene of a pair may be passed on to any particular offspring.

The most widely accepted view regarding the genes that influence coat color divides the genes into two or perhaps three groups. One group of genes acts directly on the color; the second group influences the pattern, or the way in which a given color is distributed over the horse's body; and the third group affects both color and pattern. To put it another way, the genes in one group are associated with the color of the horse—bay, brown, sorrel, chestnut, black, dun, palomino, and grulla—and determine his color. The genes in the other group control the presence or absence of color and are evident by patches of hair that are not colored. The genes from one group give a Paint Horse his black, brown, or sorrel coat, and the genes from the second group determine which hair is colored and which is not. The same is true of the roan horse. The genes from the first group give him color, and the genes from the second group control the nearly 50 per cent of hair that is not colored.[1]

The color pattern of many animals is known to change from season to season or with advanced age. Some color patterns in the Appaloosa do not appear at birth but are apparent at two to three years of age. On the other hand, the Paint Horse

---

[1]The information on the group division of color genes was taken from Jim Brown, "Color Inheritance in Horses," *Paint Horse Journal*, March–April, May–June, 1970. Brown is animal geneticist and research assistant at Texas A&M University, College Station.

is born with a coat pattern, and the extent and location of the spotting does not change with maturity. The paint-color patterns resulting from the combination of genes in the second group with those in the first group occur long before birth, during development of the embryo.

Color genes are either dominant or recessive. It is not necessary here to discuss in detail the various theories regarding recessive and dominant genes.

In general, a dominant gene is a ruling, or controlling gene; superior to all others; a recessive gene is a receding, or subordinate one. If one gene masks the other of the pair, that gene is dominant. The gene that is covered is said to be recessive. When the effect of only one gene can be seen in the individual, this gene is dominant to the other of the pair. For some traits other than color it is possible to see the effects of both genes: therefore, neither gene is dominant over the other.

The tobiano gene is dominant because it is stronger and obscures the action of the solid-color gene when both occur in the offspring. In the mating of a tobiano horse with a solid-color horse, when the offspring receives a paint gene from the tobiano parent, the tobiano spots will be visible, even though the offspring has received a solid-color gene from the other parent. The tobiano gene, then, is a dominant spotting gene, and the tobiano coloring is an "all-or-none" inheritance.[2]

If a solid-color foal results from the mating of two tobiano horses, it is believed that this offspring has no paint gene, having received only solid-color genes from his parents. The all-or-none theory, therefore, means that the paint gene, if received, is evident in the foal; if it has not been received, the foal has no tobiano markings.

The American Paint Horse Association has officially recognized the theory of the dominant tobiano gene and requires

[2]For further information on the tobiano spotting gene and "all-or-none" inheritance, see William E. Jones and Ralph Bogart, *Genetics of the Horse*, 299, 319–20.

that at least one parent be tobiano in order for a tobiano foal to result. For registration of a tobiano Paint Horse out of two registered Quarter Horses or any two solid-colored horses, the APHA requires in all instances notarized affidavits and inspections of both sire and dam and in most cases blood tests of sire, dam, and foal.

The recessive color gene is the weak gene; its action recedes from view when combined with the solid-color gene. This does not mean that recessive genes are undesirable because they are subordinate or weak. These terms are used only to contrast dominant and recessive relating to color inheritance. One point to remember is that a recessive gene can be exhibited only when both genes in the pair are recessive. Both parents must contribute a recessive gene for a certain characteristic to appear.[3] With this oversimplified explanation, it may be easier to understand how a solid-color horse can have the color gene and yet not show the characteristics of color.

Most authorities hold the opinion that the recessive gene is responsible when overo coloring crops out in a foal whose parents do not show Paint Horse markings. If the overo spotting gene is assumed to be recessive, then it can be present but not in evidence in solid-color horses. In other words, a solid-color horse could carry the overo spotting gene and transmit the gene to an offspring. A paint offspring will result only when the recessive gene is transmitted by both parents.

Today there is a theory concerning a dominant overo gene that appears to be present in some overo horses. By this theory the overo spotting gene would completely dominate any color gene and would exhibit its action in the offspring, as in tobiano coloring.

Whether or not overo and tobiano color genes are genetically present in all horses is a matter of individual opinion.

[3]Robert S. Temple, "Inherited Characteristics in Horses," paper presented at the Louisiana Quarter Horse Association Field Day, Cankton, La., July 9, 1960.

Some experts point out that the presence of the color gene in solid horses is visible in blaze faces and stocking feet. Others support the idea that these isolated white areas are not evidence of the spotting genes producing tobiano or overo color patterns but are distinct and separate genes that restrict white spotting to faces and feet.

An overo foal or solid-color foal will always result when two overos are bred. The same is generally true when two tobianos are bred: either a tobiano or a solid-color offspring is foaled. In very rare cases an overo foal is produced by mating two tobiano horses if there is overo breeding in the parents. This could happen only when an animal's ancestors are the product of a tobiano-overo cross, both tobiano genes being transmitted and the overo genes lying dormant. The overo offspring that may result would be a crop-out, like the offspring that would be produced by two solid-color horses.

Dr. W. M. Irving, Jr., Irving, Texas, made a survey of American Paint Horse Association records of 1969 foals to determine the percentage of total Paint foal production. Of the 2,096 solid mares bred in 1968 to Paint stallions and Paint mares bred to solid color stallions, 937 Paint colts were registered. This represents nearly 45 per cent Paint-colt production. At the time of the survey some of the foals from these breedings may not have been registered, and so this percentage could be a little higher. The survey was run on an over-all average and included both overo and tobiano horses. Many Paint stallions and Paint mares produce near 100 per cent Paint foals each year, and so the average includes both high and low production. It is believed that 45 per cent Paint-foal production is good and will improve through the years with more selective breeding.

Of particular significance from the survey was the fact that the largest number of Paint foals resulted from breeding solid-color stallions to tobiano mares. This was not as apparent when breeding solid-color stallions to overo mares.[4]

[4] W. M. Irving, Jr., "Genetics at Work," *Paint Horse Journal*, January, 1971, pp. 10, 11.

More tobiano foals are registered each year than overo foals. An examination of APHA records indicates that tobiano horses now outnumber overo horses by more than a four-to-one margin. From their registration data, the conclusion may be drawn that the overo color pattern is more difficult to reproduce than the tobiano color.

Tobiano horses are not necessarily more popular because there are more of them, nor are the overo horses valued any higher because they are harder to breed. There are APHA champions of both color patterns, and the demand is great for *good* Paint Horses, whether they are overo or tobiano.

8 WHAT IS A PAINT HORSE CROPOUT?

Most horses have color genes that affect the stocking legs, sock feet, and face markings. This form of white spotting is very common and often admired, but in some families of horses the spotting has been controlled by selective breeding and is almost never apparent in the animals. The King Ranch has for years followed a scientific breeding program that has produced sorrel horses with no visible white markings.

In other horses the white-spotting characteristic is more apparent and has been transmitted from generation to generation. Parents are responsible for the color of a horse's coat—a statement that is much oversimplified. It is surprising how much influence comes not from the parents themselves but from the parents' ancestors. With all the color genes involved, some dominant and some recessive, and with both parents transmitting the genes they have inherited, occasionally an offspring with an additional amount of white coloring is produced.

Cropout coloring is nothing new to the horse industry. For many years horse breeders have been confounded by the unexpected appearance of color markings on the bodies of some colts from two solid parents. The appearance of the occasional cropout remains one of the riddles of horse breeding. While one does not expect to get a loudly marked colt from parents with a solid coat color, it has happened, and it occurs in some strains with much higher frequency than in others.

It bears repeating that a recessive gene is responsible for overo color cropping out in a foal whose parents do not show Paint Horse markings. Some characteristics, including recessive coloring, are transmitted through a number of generations and are present, although not visible, in certain horses. There are exceptional instances in which this transmission occurs and the offspring receives the recessive color genes that both parents originally had. This happens rarely, but when it occurs in exact combination, cropout color results. No comprehensive explanation of the cropout color can be given. The genetic phenomenon takes place in the same manner that two brown-eyed parents have blue-eyed children. When the color gene is recessive in the solid-color horses and is transmitted to the offspring to pair with the same color gene from the other parent, then paint coloring appears in the foal, just as blue eyes occur in the human child.

It is believed that cropout horses result from earlier inbreeding in family lines. Inbreeding is the mating of animals more closely related than the average of the breed, such as brother to sister, sire to daughter, son to dam, and cousin to cousin. Inbred lines, as they are extended, become more homozygous—that is, when close inbreeding is practiced, large numbers of gene pairs have identical members. Horses that are closely related would be more likely to have the same genetic formula than those that are not closely related. Of course, brothers and sisters will not have exactly the exact genetic content, but they will have more genetic cells alike because they would have received an aggregate of like genes from their parents.

The practice of inbreeding is employed to keep quality

high in a superior line of animals, to obtain more uniformity in the offspring, and to improve a horse's capacity for speed or his adaptability for performance. Another advantage of inbreeding is that it strengthens recessive characteristics. Inbreeding enables one to identify recessive genes and bring out the recessive inheritance that otherwise might remain hidden under dominant traits. Since cropout color is a recessive inheritance and inbreeding increases the likelihood that recessive genes will be paired, the frequency of cropout color from inbred lines also increases. However, the appearance of undesirable recessive traits in the offspring of inbred sires and dams has caused some breeders to criticize this breeding method.

One can quickly look at a pedigree of a particular horse and note the influence of certain ancestors. If a name appears on several lines in close proximity, indicating inbreeding, relationship to this ancestor is high, increasing his or her importance in a pedigree. While certain bloodlines tend to predominate in cropout horses, it may be the way in which these family lines are brought together that gives a cropout his color. Close inbreeding of horses in a family line for several generations may lead to a fixation of recessive genes, after which selected outbreeding is ineffective. Therefore, a horse considered suspect as a producer of cropout color may actually be the victim of breeding methods employed years before.

There is as yet no precise system of breeding to obtain a cropout colt. When one is seeking the ideal cross, it is important to keep in mind that, if paint color has cropped out, both the sire and the dam of the offspring possess and have transmitted the recessive paint gene. Since they carry the gene, some of their solid-colored offspring could also have received this recessive gene from one of the parents. Every animal has its own genetic composition and can transmit only hereditary characteristics received from the ancestors—it will breed only those characteristics it possesses. If the records show that a number of ancestors of a certain horse were producers of cropout color, there is some assurance that other offspring without any color markings will have inherited a recessive color gene and may later transmit it in turn to their offspring.

A stallion that has sired a cropout colt has proved that he can transmit the recessive color gene. Mating this stallion to a mare that has also produced a cropout will not always result in a second Paint offspring. By following this procedure, the breeder could eventually produce a cropout. Should this occur one out of four times bred, the record would be considered extremely good.

A number of families in the Quarter Horse breed have at various times produced Paint foals, and particular crosses have produced several painted horses. The colored foals in every case possessed the conformation and characteristics of their Quarter Horse parents and solid-color brothers and sisters. Although the bloodlines of parents producing a cropout vary considerably and all old foundation Quarter Horse families are represented, indications are, after investigation, that certain family lines transmit the cropout-color genes more regularly than do others, as demonstrated by the constant appearance of cropouts produced from these family lines. To judge from the pedigrees of cropout horses, the predominant family lines are those of Joe Reed (usually when Leo appears in a sire line); Little Joe, by Traveler (usually in King [AQHA P-234] and Joe Moore [AQHA 1856] horses); Peter McCue (found in almost all Quarter Horse pedigrees); and Skipper W and Nick Shoemaker (both linebred Old Fred horses).

The cropout Paint foal is not limited to Quarter Horse breeding. The mating of two Thoroughbreds or a Thoroughbred with a Quarter Horse has also resulted in the cropout colt. In the American Paint Horse Association significant numbers of overo foals have been registered out of solid-color horses in every year since 1961, but, if one keeps in mind the large number of solid-color horses bred each year, this percentage is very small.

Cropout colts have no similarity in the extent of their markings. Some horses, such as Painted Robin, Sallisaw Rose,

Painted Breeze Bar, and Mr. Pale Face, are loudly marked with white. Others, such as High Bars, Honey Bee, Jacket Bars, and Mr. Pokey Bars, have white areas that are limited to the stomach areas, faces, legs, and feet, with occasional splashes of white extending up from the shoulders. The dark overo cropouts often have wide blazes on the face and do not have the bald or apron faces that are associated with the overo color pattern.

Several years ago a Paint Horse that resulted from the mating of two registered Quarter Horses was an outcast because he could not be registered in their association. The authenticity of the breeding was also questioned by some horsemen who did not understand that a few of their finest horses carried recessive paint genes, and sporadically the action of these genes was exhibited in one of the foals. The Paint cropouts were usually gelded, sold, or disposed of to avoid embarrassment to the owner and futile explanations. It made no difference what names could be found in their pedigrees; they were of little value to their owner, and their selling prices were no more than those of good-grade stock horses.

Today these horses with the Quarter Horse breeding, conformation, refinement, and ability have been elevated to their rightful place and have become a cornerstone of the Paint Horse breed.

Facing page: Our Sir Prize, a cropout Paint Horse by Smuggler Clegg (AQHA) out of Pretty Jackie (AQHA). Photograph by Johnny Johnston.

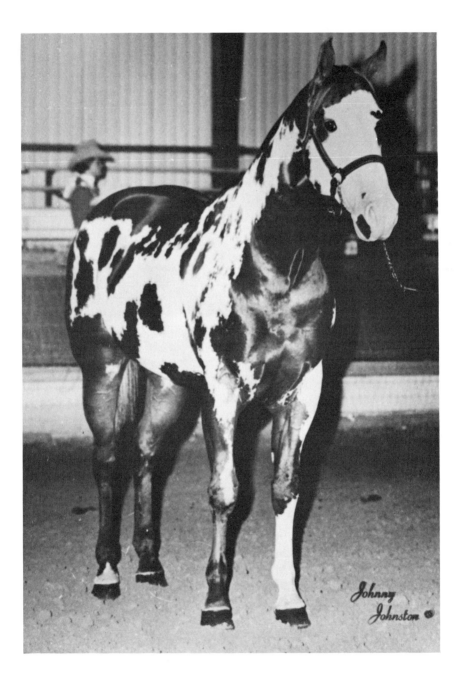

Johnny
Johnston

9 CROPOUT PAINT HORSES

In southern Texas is a region known for its fine breeders and fast short horses. One of the most renowned breeders was Ott Adams, Alice, Texas, who bred a number of great horses, such as Monita, Pancho Villa, Grano de Oro, Cotton Eyed Joe, Stella Moore, and Joe Moore.

Ferminio

Uncle Ott, as he was affectionately called by those who knew him, was a believer in the value of blood. He felt that all fast horses were the product of two outstanding bloodlines. The crossing of his sire, Joe Moore (AQHA 1,856), and mares of Chicaro Bill breeding was a step in the right direction. From this crossing of families came many excellent horses, among them a cropout foaled in 1949 who was later registered in the American Paint Horse Association as Ferminio (see Appendix 1).

From his sire, Joe Moore, Ferminio traces through Little Joe to Traveler. His dam, Blaze A (AQHA 40,851), was a

Ferminio, a cropout Paint Horse by Joe Moore out of Blaze A by Chicaro.

daughter of Chicaro Bill and was out of Dolly by Black Joe. Chicaro Bill was by Chicaro (TB) and out of Verna Grace or Fair Chance (AQHA 1,439) by Little Joe, thereby giving Ferminio two crosses to Little Joe.

The Joe Moore horses were bred to a uniform type. The

grand old Quarter Horse stamped his get with the same quality, head, and muscle, making them easily identifiable as his sons and daughters. Ferminio was no exception—he inherited his sire's conformation, characteristics, and action. He was not a loud-colored Paint Horse. In fact, he was almost completely dark, the largest area of white appearing on the front legs and left forearm and a white spot in his right side.

After living most of his life unknown, in May, 1965, Ferminio was purchased by Edgar Robinson, Happy R Ranch, Abilene, Texas, from Ray Claver, Fort Stockton, Texas. Robinson, another breeder who relied on the pedigree to produce outstanding individuals, purchased Ferminio primarily to establish a breeding program to preserve the Joe Moore bloodlines in the American Paint Horse. His concentration of good blood and his dedication to breed improvement are apparent in the progeny produced by Ferminio. Although he was never bred to more than five mares each year while Robinson owned him, Ferminio sired a number of fine Paint Horses: Dodgerette, Copperella, Happy Joe, Karen Moore, Mr. Abilene, Jo's Ditto, Ferminiette, Copper Joe, Happy Traveler, and Ferminio, Jr. Robinson kept nine daughters of Ferminio in his band of broodmares at the Happy R Ranch, revealing to the world the true breeding worth of their sire.

Ferminiette was without exaggeration a beautiful filly. Her dam was Miss Dodger, an APHA champion retired to a life of leisure in the Happy R broodmare band. Foaled in April, 1966, Ferminiette was shown for the first time at Wichita Falls, Texas, on July 22, 1967, and stood first in a class of twelve 1966 mares. She was regularly a winner at halter that year and was named Reserve National Champion of the 1966 mare class at the 1967 national show.

In the same year that Ferminiette won her national title,

Facing page: Ferminiette. Courtesy American Paint Horse Association.

Copper Joe, by Ferminio.

Copper Joe, one of Ferminio's outstanding sons, was named Reserve National Champion Two-Year-Old Stallion and the Texas High Point Two-Year-Old Stallion. As might be expected, Copper Joe's dam was a good one—Copper by Painted Joe.

Happy Traveler, a 1969 sorrel overo colt out of Miss Hackberry, reached back into his great family background for the speed bequeathed to so many of Joe Moore's get and grandget. He got not only the speed but everything else that combines in the making of an outstanding running horse.

Ferminio has had other colts to run, and among them it would be hard to find anyone better than Happy Traveler. At three years old he won the 1972 Texas Paint Horse Maturity at Ross Downs, Colleyville, Texas, in 20.69, for a very good 88 speed index on the 400-yard event. His greatest race that year was run at the Centennial Track, Littleton, Colorado, against nine of the top Paint Horses in the National Champion Maturity. Happy Traveler finished two lengths ahead of the betting favorite, Spoiler, who had won most of the stakes races available to Paint Horses over the past three years, and took home over $4,300. He retired from the track in 1974 with a Superior Race Horse Award and AAA ratings at 350 and 400 yards.

During his lifetime Ferminio was not raced and was never shown in Paint Horse shows. His get, however, earned him the title of Reserve National Champion Get of Sire at the 1968 National Show. Because of old age and poor health, this gallant Paint Horse, one of the last living sons of Joe Moore, was put to sleep on June 6, 1970.

Wildfire

In the spring of 1961 the blood of Flit Bar (AQHA 74,572) and Bar V Fanny (AQHA 12,323) nicked well, and a brilliantly colored little colt opened his eyes for the first time on the Earl Foreman ranch at Denton, Texas. When he stood on his wobbly legs, his short, sensitive ears picked up as he surveyed the crowd gathered around. What they were looking at was not an ordinary colt out of two ordinary Quarter Horse parents. He was Wildfire, a bright sorrel crop-out splashed with plenty of white under his stomach and up his sides.

An examination of Wildfire's pedigree (see Appendix 1) reveals that Flit Bar was by Sugar Bars and out of Flit by Leo. So, Flit Bar, Wildfire's sire, was a desirable product of the best of two bloodlines. Sugar Bars is respected as a sire of Quarter Horses of great speed and working ability. Through 1971 he had sired twelve Top AAA, 45 AAA, and 59 AA colts. Flit Bar's record at the stud is a good one: his get include five AQHA Champions, five Register of Merit (ROM) running Quarter colts, and many ROM arena horses.

The mare who foaled Wildfire, Bar V Fanny, carries the blood of Ben Hur on the top and Peter McCue through her dam.

Wildfire had plenty of zip as a yearling colt. By the time he was a two-year-old, he looked and ran as if he had a good quarter-mile in him, and during the next couple of years he was sent out to spend part of his life on the brush tracks. He turned out to be an excellent match-race horse, and that is not surprising since his veins were filled with some of the same blood that had produced many of the leading money earners in quarter racing.

While he was on the tracks, Wildfire was owned by Bob and Jean Buck, Rockin "B" Ranch, Bolton, Mississippi. In 1965 they sold him to Martha West, Hollandale, Mississippi, and she began grooming him for halter. Martha had a special talent for putting the "Sunday britches" on a horse. She did an exceptional job with Wildfire, partly because, in her words, "he was so easy to work with." Shown six times the following year, he easily won his class and stood Grand Champion once and Reserve Champion twice. Still having the heart to run, he made a good showing running the barrels and picked up several barrel-racing points.

When he was about seven years old, Wildfire was put in

Facing page: Miss Lena Bar, by Wildfire. Photograph by Margie Spence.

Margie Spence ©

cutting training with Ralph Russell, McKinney, Texas. Shortly thereafter, in the first months of 1969, Martha West sold him to LaVell "Bud" Hall, Readland, Arkansas. Already owning one of his daughters, Miss Lena Bar, Hall was pleased with the progeny of this well-bred stallion and took him across the Mississippi River to stand as sire over the broodmare band he was putting together at that time. He kept Wildfire in cutting and won a few open cuttings on him in Arkansas. Although Bud did not get the chance to work him in any APHA shows, he said: "Wildfire had the heart and motivation of a true cutting horse. He could turn on a dime and would get down and work right with the calf."

In April, 1970, Wildfire suffered a pinched nerve in his back. He was treated at the University of Auburn veterinary clinic for over a month and was unable to breed the 1970 season. Bud relates that while Wildfire was at the university clinic one of the veterinarians told him that Wildfire was the easiest stud to handle that he had ever worked with. He added matter-of-factly, "Those spots just might make a difference." Bud planned a full breeding season for Wildfire in 1971 but lost him early in the year when the horse developed acute colic and died.

Of his few descendants Miss Lena Bar is in all probability the one who stands out for her high-level performance. She carries full Quarter Horse blood herself, having as her dam Miss Grande (AQHA 136,476) by Tejano Grande (AQHA 30,904) by Tejano, a King Ranch horse. Miss Lena Bar is an APHA Champion, a Superior Halter Horse, and a National Champion Western Pleasure Horse.

Another daughter, Lady Wildfire, has done extremely well in Mississippi Four-H and Paint Horse shows. She is owned by Kit Gorman, Redwood, Mississippi. Lady Wildfire has a Register of Merit in Trail and has acquired seventy trophies and ribbons in open and Four-H shows. She was bred to Joechief Bar in 1969, and their colt was as good as a young foal could be. He was shown five times as a yearling and won his first Reserve Championship shortly after his first birthday.

It is unfortunate that Wildfire's stud career was so severely hampered. There is no doubt that he would have left many descendants worthy of his great name.

Flying Fawago

Some of the finest Paint Horse stallions received little or no recognition in their early years. Before the American Paint Horse Association moved forward and gained prestige, only a handful of these horses were seriously appreciated. Flying Fawago was not one of the lucky ones. He spent his first four years running wild, unbroken and untrained. Until his purchase by Donna Loomis, Elkhorn, Nebraska, in April, 1967, nothing is known for certain of his young life.

Flying Fawago, a beautiful bay overo bred by W. E. "Bill" Evans, Scottsdale, Arizona, was foaled on March 3, 1963 (see Appendix 1). He stands 16 hands and weighs around 1,300 pounds. Well proportioned and well balanced, Fawago is a true representation of the middle-of-the-road horse that the modern breeder of today is producing from his breeding program. He is descended from some of the best bloodlines and has good body length and depth and genuine show-ring refinement.

Yendis (AQHA 114,109), the sire of Flying Fawago, is by Top Deck and out of Sue Bob by Flying Bob. Top Deck stood fifth on the all-time Leading Sires of Money Earners List for 1949–71. He has sired such well-known Quarter Horses as Go Man Go, Moon Deck, Glory Be Good, and Rebel Cause. The earnings of his get through 1971 totaled $1,641,884. Yendis was another good horse, but he was overshadowed by the more notable accomplishments of his brothers. He was AAA-rated and holder of the track record for 350 yards at the Pinal County, Arizona, Fair Track. He too has sired many ROM running colts and ROM arena colts in the AQHA.

The dam of Yendis, Sue Bob, was by the famous Flying Bob, a sire of short-horses that were virtually unequaled in the early days of quarter racing in the 1940's. Sue Bob was officially rated A, but has produced three AAA winners: Bobbie Bruce, Ridgetta, and Yendis.

Flying Fawago's dam, Tango Scooter, was a registered Quarter mare by Brown Chips and out of Scooter's Tango, who traces back to Cowboy (AQHA P-12) and Oklahoma Star (AQHA P-6).

In 1968, Flying Fawago made his first appearance at halter and in western pleasure events at the Paint Horse shows. In January he won the Senior Paint Horse Western Pleasure class at the Denver Livestock Show over a class of twelve and then the Marysville, Missouri, show over a class of thirteen top horses. He was shown throughout the spring of 1968 in Iowa, Missouri, Illinois, and Oklahoma and accumulated four Grand Championships, one Reserve Championship at halter, and many firsts in western pleasure and trail. At the 1968 APHA National Show he was named Co-Reserve National Champion Aged Stallion and became an APHA Champion on November 1, 1968.

Not shown in 1969, Flying Fawago was used in the stud and trained in reining and English pleasure. In 1970 he earned thirty halter points and won the title National Champion Aged Stallion over seventeen other entries at the Amarillo, Texas, National Show. He now had a Register of Merit in Western Pleasure and added in 1971 a ROM in English pleasure and reining.

Donna Loomis, an excellent horsewoman, has ridden several Paint Horses to their APHA champion titles. She handles Fawago with ease and finesse. She says of Fawago, "He is the best-dispositioned stallion I have ever been around and all his colts seem to have his gentle manners and affectionate personality."

Because he was bred only in recent years, Flying Fawago's

Facing page: Fawago Star, by Flying Fawago.

get have not yet had an opportunity to become show colts or establish outstanding performance records. The Fawago Kid is a 1969 gelding by Fawago that developed into a good pleasure horse. He has several halter and western pleasure points on his record and has been named an APHA Champion.

One of Flying Fawago's daughters is Fawago Star, a 1969 foal bred by Dean Miller, Hornick, Iowa. A glossy black overo standing just over 15 hands and weighing around 1,150 pounds, she is the epitome of grace and balance. As a two-year-old, Fawago Star was named Grand Champion Mare at the National Western Stock Show in Denver, Colorado, in January, 1971. At the National Show in October of the same year she was named Reserve Champion Junior Western Pleasure Horse. One of the highlights of her career came in winning an APHA championship in the fall of 1971 after compiling 28 halter points, 5 western pleasure points, 13 English pleasure points and a Register of Merit in English pleasure. In 1972 she was named the National Champion Three-Year-Old Mare.

These and other good performers are surely making an unforgettable name for their sire, Flying Fawago.

Dial-A-Go-Go

Dial-A-Go-Go, a dun overo mare, was foaled on April 23, 1964 (see Appendix 1). She was bred by Ray Claver, Fort Stockton, Texas, a long-time Quarter Horse breeder who has bred, raised, and owned some of the fastest running horses and best working horses to come out of southwestern Texas.

From the blood of two distinctive families of running horses Dial-A-Go-Go inherited the speed to become a AAA running horse and the conformation to become an APHA Champion. She is the daughter of Go Johnny (AQHA 185,226), whose sire, Breezing Johnny (AQHA 51,597), was by Johnny Dial, a prime figure in quarter racing.

Breezing Johnny earned a AAA rating in a very limited racing career from 1955 to 1957 and has sired two AAA sons and one AAA daughter. Johnny Dial was the 1952 World Champion Quarter Running Horse and the sire of thirteen Top AAA and forty-eight AAA qualifiers.

Flaxy West (AQHA 80,027), Dial-A-Go-Go's dam, is of the Little Joe–Della Moore blood that is so prominent in crop-out Paint Horses. Flaxy West by Sandy West (AQHA 46,510) goes back to Joe Moore, a product of the Little Joe–Della Moore cross.

Dial-A-Go-Go's racing career was not as spectacular as were those of some of her solid-colored brothers and sisters. In 1966, Paint Horse racing was just beginning to take hold, and the Racing Division of the association had not yet been set up to record races, winners, and results. In her first futurity as a two-year-old, she ran a third in the first half of the Texas Paint Horse Futurity trials at Lubbock Downs, Texas, defeated by Painted Jewel and Christi Leo in the 250-yard race. Although the outcome was disappointing to her owners, it indicated she had some speed.

The next year Dial had the opportunity to show her true ability. The Texas Paint Horse Derby was run on July 30 at Manor Downs, Texas, and to some it was the outstanding event of 1967. Three Paint Horses, all in great running shape, earned their Registers of Merit in one of the fastest races run up to that time. Dial-A-Go-Go and Sentimiento ran a very close race, both in AAA time, with Sentimiento nosing ahead in the final strides.

During her racing career Dial-A-Go-Go was owned by C. E. and Larry Swain, Circle Dot Ranch, San Antonio, Texas. Early in 1971, Mr. and Mrs. Ralph Brunner, Monroe, Wisconsin, purchased the nimble-footed little mare, and under their guidance she earned the final points needed for her APHA Champion title. She has to her credit two Grand Championships and three Reserve Championships, a Register of Merit in Western Pleasure, a Register of Merit in Racing, the title of Reserve National Champion Halter Mare in 1969, and an APHA Championship.

Dial is a blooded horse with an enviable performance

record on the track, in the halter shows, and in the performance arena. She is superbly built, daintily balanced, and completely self-composed. As so aptly put by Mrs. Brunner, "She is really a dream to ride and be around."

Because of an injury in the fall of 1971, Dial-A-Go-Go was no longer shown. She was bred and foaled a J Bar Junior colt in June, 1972. Her greatest moments of glory may be yet to come through her offspring, for Dial-A-Go-Go, graced by good foundation Quarter Horse blood, should produce an outstanding line of Paint Horses.

PART III **TRAINING**

10 USING THE PAINT HORSE

In the early pioneering days the horse was expected to do anything and everything asked of him. He was called on to pull a plow all day, cut a calf out of the herd at branding time, run a match race on Saturday, and carry the family to church on Sundays. A good, dependable horse who could do all that was required of him was a valuable asset to his owner.

Today the horse has an easy life—no more working from dawn to dusk performing any number of tasks. Specialization has entered the horse's world, as it has in many other fields. If a horse has an outstanding conformation and a gentle disposition, he is groomed as a halter horse for the show ring and sometimes never has a saddle on his back. If his ancestors were famous in the cutting or roping arena and he demonstrates a little extra cow sense, he is used exclusively as a stock horse to compete in the performance events. If his breeding shows a long line of winners at the race track and he himself has superior speed, he is trained as a race horse.

by George

My Painted Robin, National Champion Steer Roping Horse, Heading, and Grand Champion at Halter. Photograph by George.

Almost all horses of the light-horse breeds fall into one of three categories: halter and show horses, performance horses, and running horses. Paint Horses usually have some combination of speed, conformation, disposition, and performing ability. It is the contention of most modern breeders to breed, first, horses with ability—ability to perform in show contests or on the track—and, second, horses with conformation to show at halter. Regardless whether he is used in ranch work, in the rodeo arena, on the race track, in horse-show contests, or in parades, the Paint Horse has the substance to be a true do-it-all horse.

Several years ago an old horse trainer said that the Paint Horse has more endurance, tries harder, and sticks to a task with more determination than most horses of a solid color. It may be that the horses he worked with were exceptional horses, or it may be that he knew something about the Paint Horse that has long been overlooked. In all breeds of horses there are some whose dispositions motivate them to try, and succeed, at whatever job they are asked to do, while others do not try to learn anything except where the feed box is located.

The bloodlines are a key to a horse's ability. The horses that are in demand are the blooded horses with ability to show at halter and performance equally well. A blue-ribbon or grand-champion trophy will increase the value and improve the selling price of any Paint Horse or the colts produced by that horse. Breeders of Paint Horses have found, as breeders of other types of horses learned, that the best horses bring the best prices. Emphasis is placed on breeding along with showability. The Paint Horses that have that extra something more than color—the blood and the ability—are the horses that are bringing top price.

An exceptional horse of any breed with conformation and bloodlines of the very best cannot be expected to compete in today's contests without any training. A horse is not entered in the Kentucky Derby unless he knows what is expected of him at the track. The long-neglected Paint Horse is now being given a chance with attention, facilities, and proper training.

In the early rodeos and western shows the Paint Horse was always a crowd-pleasing favorite. He added color to the grand entry and led the parades, besides providing thrilling action in the bronc-riding, calf-roping, and cutting contests. One of the most spectacular bucking horses was War Paint, the Champion Bucking Horse for three years in a row, who upended scores of good bronc riders. He was the first horse to receive from the Rodeo Cowboys Association the silver-mounted halter naming him Bucking Horse of the Year, and he earned that award in 1956, 1957, and 1958. His 1958 record of twenty-eight starts with twenty-five buck-offs is one reason why he was around to thrill the crowds for over fifteen years.

Paint Horses have been the preferred mounts of many calf ropers of the Rodeo Cowboys' Association (RCA) and the International Rodeo Association (IRA). Dan Taylor for years roped off a top gelded son of Painted Joe, and Junior Robertson's Wahoo King was another calf-roping horse that was tough to beat.

As far as performance is concerned, color is only skin deep. The ability of a horse does not depend on his color but on the breeding and substance of the individual. As one saying goes: "You can't judge a book by its cover; neither can you judge a horse by its color."

The versatility of the Paint Horse is evident in the wide range of events in which boys, girls, men, and women may compete. The many youth and open events offered at the shows is responsible for a family togetherness that most Paint Horse people enjoy. The Paint Horse has become a major influence in developing healthy character in horsemen, young and old alike.

Youth activities are an integral part of the association. At Paint Horse shows youth classes in halter and performance events are almost always included. Awards such as the Youth Register of Merit in performance events and the Youth APHA Champion title increase the enthusiasm and competitive spirit among the younger set. The Paint Horse shows are designed with the "open" classes and youth classes so that Paint Horse owners can find more ways to enjoy their horses. While youth classes and awards are limited to all unmarried youth eighteen years of age or younger, the youth are eligible to compete in the open Paint Horse shows and provide some tough competition.

In 1966 a point system was set up in the APHA to provide a goal toward which exhibitors, owners, and breeders could work when competing their horses in these shows. Points are awarded horses based upon the number of entries in a class and upon the position in which the horse is placed (the Scale of Points for contests is given in Chapter 4). Registers of Merit, APHA Championships, Supreme Championships, and APHA Youth Championships are earned through the accumulation of points.

Paint Horses qualify for the Register of Merit when they have won at least ten points in any one event in approved APHA shows (see Chapter 4 for ROM qualifications). The performance contests (divided into five categories) that have been approved for the Register of Merit are:

Category I   Registered Barrel Racing
             Registered Pole Bending
             Registered Cow Pony Race
             Registered Cutter and Chariot Racing
Category II   Registered Reining
             Registered Western Riding
             Registered Working Hunter
             Registered Hunter Hack
             Registered Jumping
             Registered Trail Horse
Category III   Registered Working Cowhorse
             Registered Cutting and recognized Open Cutting Contests
             Registered Calf Roping and recognized RCA and IRA Calf Roping
             Registered Steer Roping and recognized RCA and IRA Steer Roping

Category IV   Registered Western Pleasure
                Registered Bridle Path Hack (hunt seat)
Category V   Racing

The leading sires and dams of Register of Merit Qualifiers from 1966 through 1973 are listed in Appendices 2 and 3.

11 THE HALTER HORSE

A halter show is a contest among well-bred horses to judge their beauty and conformation, where exhibitors display the quality, bloom, elegance, and disposition of their model Paint Horses. A halter show is also a good place to compare horses and a good place for browsing to learn about the breed.

To most horsemen the halter show is an inviting place. It has a strangely powerful attraction about it. In the lineup, when competition is keen and quality is important, the judging may be extremely tough. To the man with a beautiful horse this is compelling.

Showing at halter is no new story. Man has for years led his prized animal from the barn with only a halter and lead rope to receive the exclamations of praise of his friends and neighbors. For those millions of Americans who go through life without seeing a horse show and wonder what it is like to take part in this event, here is one individual's emotional experience when showing for the first time:

Junior Gelding Halter Class at the 1969 national show, Kansas City. Photograph by H. D. Dolcater.

We were lined up now, unmoving. My hands were sensitive to my horse's slightest quiver. Slowly the judge came closer and closer to stand there in front of me. My body became a vibrating thing. Out of the corner of my eye, I could see his deliberation. As he walked on by, discouragement surged through me. For fifteen minutes, although it seemed hours, the contest had raged, the judge carefully giving his attention to each horse alternately. When my strength began to wane, I saw the judge motion to me. I knew I must move—but how? My knees were weak and my hands were shaking. Finally, I suppressed my anxieties and tugged at the lead rope. Once out from the lineup, realization overwhelmed me. I had won my first blue ribbon!

In a Paint Horse show, after the horses enter the arena,

A 1971 Youth Halter Mare class. Photograph by Margie Spence.

they are led around the ring with only a halter and lead rope and are then lined up in front of the judge. Each horse is shown individually at a walk and trot and then returned to the lineup, where the judge carefully inspects each horse.

There are four very important general over-all qualities that a judge of a halter class at any Paint Horse show is required to look for: type, conformation, action, and disposition. Type refers to general outline, or shape and size. Conformation refers to muscular development, the detailed parts of the animal, and their relation to each other. Action can include alertness, soundness, and the way of traveling at the walk and trot. Disposition relates to manners, calmness, and obedience.

A grand-champion stallion, mare, and gelding are chosen from the first-place winners of each age class. A reserve champion stallion, mare, and gelding are chosen from the second

The get of Leo San Man in a Get of Sire class. Photograph by Margie Spence.

place winners in the Grand Champion Class and the first-place winners in the other classes.

One halter class specifically limited to the youth and devised to train them in the techniques of showing their Paint Horses is Showmanship at Halter. The class is judged on the condition, grooming, and trimming of the horse and neatness of the exhibitor's appearance. Apart from the fact that conformation does not influence the judging, the horse must be in good physical condition and well groomed. The showman must lead the horse correctly and must be able to settle the horse in position with his feet planted squarely under him. Emphasis is also placed on the exhibitor's politeness and sportsmanship.

It takes a good horse to be named grand champion at halter. The consistently successful horse is not merely lucky. He is well made. He is carefully groomed for the dramatic event. Not the least of the requirements is that he is well bred. His pedigree can be a clue to a horse's conformation, disposition

Josy Bar, leading dam of halter point earners, 1966–72. Photograph by Margie Spence.

and temperament. It will be rewarding to study in depth the pedigree of those Paint Horses who have been named grand champions. Even the harshest critics will have to say that Paint Horses look like Quarter Horses with color and are bred like Quarter Horses.

The Paint Horse with his classic style and colorful appearance may have "borrowed" his conformation from another breed, but the coat of overo or tobiano is his alone.

The first tabulation of the leading sires and dams of halter point earners was made in 1970. The charts in Appendices 4 and 5 list the horses that have sired or produced halter horses who have earned the most points in approved APHA shows through 1974.

12 THE CUTTING HORSE

The old-timers of the western range country remember with fondness and respect certain horses they rode while pushing cattle. Most of them have a story to tell about a horse that had real "cow savvy"—one that could separate brands and knew exactly which calf to cut out or one that could tell the difference between a calf with a brand and one without. These horses, legendary perhaps, evolved from an environment and heritage that admirably fitted them for cow work.

Almost any good cow horse that will watch a cow can be a cutting horse. He can be of any size, weight, or color, but to be a top cutting horse he needs an extra amount of this cow sense. The Quarter Horse has long been famous for his skill and intelligence in this specialized field. Years of working cattle have developed him into the most renowned cow horse in the world.

The original cutting horses were bred from the Spanish stock that spread across the Southwest in the early years. They were true cow horses in the sense that they possessed a bona fide talent for herding and holding cattle and cutting out yearling calves or bulls. A successor to these first Spanish range horses, the Paint Horse has a natural background for handling stock. He gets this instinctive comprehension of the nature of livestock as a normal endowment from his Spanish ancestry and from the recent addition of Quarter Horse blood in his veins.

Cutting began years ago during roundup on the open ranges. In actual ranch work the horse and rider moved into a herd, picked the cattle to be cut out, and drove them past the holders away from the main herd for branding. The kind of horse that rangemen wanted was alert, level-headed, and cooperative, valuable characteristics of a cutting horse.

The first known exhibition of cutting for money was held in Haskell, Texas, at the 1898 Cowboys' Reunion. During the first half of the twentieth century cuttings were a sequence in the rodeos and wild-West shows that traveled across the United States. The cutting contest became part of the western horse shows in 1946, when the National Cutting Horse Association was organized and official rules and regulations were set down for competitors.

In an arena cutting contest the horse takes the calf out of the herd and drives it toward the center of the arena. Turnback men force the calf back to face the horse. Without any help from the rider the cutting horse should hinder all efforts the calf might make to get back to the herd. A good cutting horse instinctively moves, follows, turns, and stops with the calf. Those that seem to sense what the calf is thinking and react naturally to outmaneuver it have a unique attribute—cow sense.

Paint Horse cuttings are designed to display the action and skill of the Paint Horse when put after cattle. Horses participating in this event are judged on their ability to separate and control a very active calf with the least disturbance to it and to the herd and on their naturalness to work entirely on their own without rider assistance. Good work comes through harmony between the horse and rider, but after the rider lets the horse know which animal to cut out, the cutting horse must establish control over the calf and do the rest.

Horses are penalized for creating any unnecessary disturbance, working on the fence, losing a working advantage, any help from the rider by reining or cuing, and letting a calf get back in the herd.

The American Paint Horse Association is an affiliate of the National Cutting Horse Association (NCHA). The rules of this association are used for all approved Paint Horse cutting contests, and Paint Horses showing and placing in a NCHA or Canadian Cutting Horse Association open show are eligible for points in the APHA.

The National Cutting Horse Association does not tabulate results according to breeds of horses, but it does furnish vital statistics to the APHA on all Paint Horses that compete in open or championship cuttings. The Open Cutting Horse Contests are open to all horses regardless of breed, age, sex, or color. Certificates of Annual Achievement are awarded to the top ten cutting horses each year based on one point per dollar won in NCHA-approved open cuttings. Also each year the NCHA presents a trophy to the Paint Horse designated by the APHA as the High Point Paint Horse in approved open cutting contests.

Paint Horses have competed in NCHA events since the very beginning of the Cutting Horse Association, and over the years a few could be found at year's end among the Top Ten. In 1973 the first registered American Paint Horse was honored as a World's Champion. In the open competitions Delta, through outstanding nation-wide performance, earned the necessary points to be declared and crowned the 1973 World Champion Cutting Horse Mare, a title she now bears with great distinction. Other trophy winners in the NCHA cutting contests are listed in Appendix 6.

Rhett Butler

Every Paint Horse is a product of his heredity and of his sur-

Edith's Dolly keeping her eye on a calf. Photograph by George. Courtesy Western Horseman.

roundings. Rhett Butler, a 1959 foal of two cutting-horse parents, was raised on a ranch in southeastern Texas, where cutting was a way of life. Before he was two years old he knew the essentials in the routine of handling cattle. He was one of those horses born with a natural cutting instinct and desire and eagerness to perform.

Rhett Butler was bred by Dr. Mack Daugherty, Houston, Texas, and is owned by his daughter, Mrs. Jim (Roann) Cartwright, Missouri City, Texas. His veins are filled with the blood of King (AQHA P-234), a foundation sire of Quarter Horses who has, through his get and grandget, established for himself everlasting fame. The top and bottom male line of Rhett's pedigree go back through B. K. Albert (AQHA P-48,115) and King

Albert to King. Rhett Butler's sire, Rex Albert (AQHA P-71,052), a well-muscled, solidly built horse by B. K. Albert, was used by Dr. Daugherty for working cattle and for general ranch work.

Rhett Butler's dam was Dixie Albert, one of the best Paint mares on the ranch by B. K. Albert. She was out of a black tobiano mare called Penny, who traces back to Joe Bailey (AQHA P-4) through her dam.

At 14.2 hands Rhett is not a tall horse. He weighs in close to 1,250 pounds and most of that is muscle, tempered like steel. He has a black tobiano coat that looks extremely good amid the solid-color horses at NCHA shows.

As soon as he had enough size, Mrs. Cartwright, a lightweight not even tipping the scales at 100 pounds, started riding him. He learned to travel quietly when working cattle out of a herd and to stay head to head with an active calf. Because of his alert eye and quick action, Mrs. Cartwright soon had him in the arena.

It has often been said that the smartest horses are true cutting horses, and Rhett Butler, though still young and pretty green at cutting, demonstrated convincingly that he was one horse that could outthink the cow. Roann Cartwright told of this amusing event and the novel performance by Rhett Butler:

We were at a practice cutting and the cattle were small and real sour. Everyone was losing cattle. The first calf I cut ran right down the fence and back into the herd. The next calf I brought out started down the same fence in about the same place. Rhett fell down to his knees flat against the fence and blocked the calf. Everyone started laughing, but I thought he had fallen down. The calf ran away from the fence and made a few fancy moves out in the middle of the arena and then headed back to the fence to test him again. Rhett had her number and went down on both knees again to block her. She turned around and ran by the two turnback men. Rhett had trained the calf.

Rhett Butler went on to become one of the top cutting horses in South Texas, in the Gulf Coast Paint Horse Association, the American Paint Horse Association, and the National Cutting Horse Association. He developed his own cutting style, but it did not include getting down on his knees.

Performance is one test of the worth of a horse, and no finer performance has been recorded than that by Rhett Butler over his seven-year career. He was named National Champion Cutting Horse and Reserve National Champion Reining Horse in 1964; the NCHA High Point Paint Cutting Horse for 1965, 1966, and 1968; and Champion All Around Using Horse of the Gulf Coast Paint Horse Association for five consecutive years, 1963 through 1967, for which he received a diamond-studded belt buckle.

Rhett Butler began competition in the NCHA in October, 1963, at the Brazoria County Fair Horse Show. He was entered at and won some of the largest open shows, including the Houston Livestock Show in February, 1965, where out of thirty-nine horses he tied for first-place money. For his notable performances over the years Rhett was awarded the NCHA Certificate of Ability #815 and the High Point trophy for three years, an honor that he shares with two other Paint Horses, Calamity Jane and Delta.

Roann Cartwright is a wise and experienced trainer. Her first horse, which she received when she was only six years old, was a Paint mare, Penny, granddam of Rhett Butler. For years Roann and Penny were a hard pair to beat at flag races, pole bending, and barrel races. She trained Rhett Butler in western pleasure, reining, halter, and cutting. He has a record at the Houston Livestock Show, one of the largest Paint Horse shows (326 entries in 1972), that still stood as of 1974. In 1963, the year of the first show for Paint Horses at Houston, he was Grand Champion Stallion at halter, first in reining, and first in cutting and was named Champion All-Around Using Horse of the show. This title he won again in 1964, 1965, and 1967.

Rhett Butler is not an APHA Champion, though if points

had been compiled from 1963 through 1966, he would be. On his tenth birthday in 1969, with hundreds of trophies, ribbons, belt buckles, and blankets, a fine cutting horse retired.

Sons and daughters bearing the Rhett Butler mark of distinction carry on today. Rhett Butler, Jr., doing a good job at the stud, is standing in Louisiana; Me-A-Butler, owned by Richard and Carol McPherrin, Yuba City, California, earned an APHA Championship in 1971; Well-I-Never, a gelding owned by Mickey Pillow, Jr., Baytown, Texas, is a Champion All-Around Youth Performance Horse in the Gulf Coast Paint Horse Association; and Rhett's Tara, a 1967 brown tobiano mare, has earned her Register of Merit in western pleasure.

13 THE ROPING HORSE

The cowboys of North America and the gauchos of South America learned their techniques of riding and their methods of handling cattle from the early Spaniards. For centuries cattle roamed the open ranges on ranches surrounding the Spanish settlements, and ranch hands drove them from pasture to pasture or rounded them up in the spring for branding.

When range-branding calves, the herd was first gathered together and the young calves cut out. Then a cowhand roped the calf and secured it for the branding iron. With no corrals or chutes to work in, roping was a necessity and one of the fundamentals of a ranch hand's job. The men who worked around stock developed, through years of experience and use, a skill with the rope and more or less "created" a horse possessing the valuable characteristics that have come to be associated with a rope horse.

During slack seasons the hands started holding contests to see which one could rope and tie a calf in the fastest possible time. This little bit of action grew into a competition of skill that today pays thousands of dollars annually to professional roping men.

In Paint Horse shows the horse is the contestant, not the rider. The *APHA Official Rule Book* lists these criteria for judging the performance of a horse in competition:

> *The horse will be judged on manners behind the barrier, scoring speed to calf, rating calf, the stop, working the rope and his manners while roper is returning to horse after tie has been made. . . .*
>
> *Breaking the barrier, or any unnecessary whipping, jerking reins, talking or any noise-making, slapping, jerking rope, or any unnecessary action to induce the horse to perform better will be considered a fault and scored accordingly.*

The calf-roping contests are held under usual rodeo conditions and standards with horses starting from behind a barrier. Horses are scored on the basis of 60 to 80 points, and the time required for the roper to throw the loop and tie the calf is not counted. The contestant is allowed to throw two loops if he is carrying a second rope tied to the saddle. If both loops are missed, the horse earns a "no score."

From a cowboy's point of view, the calf-roping horse is remarkable for its excellence and its astonishing versatility, and by any standard it is numbered among the world's greatest using horses. A good rope horse must be stout with good balance. He must be alert and quick to break to put the roper on his calf. He must have early speed to overtake the calf, a quick sliding stop to put the roper in position, and backing action to keep the calf immobile while the rider makes the tie.

Many professional ropers and trainers agree that rope horses are made, not born. Although certain stallions have proved themselves as progenitors of the characteristics that a good rope horse must possess, training is still a main consideration. Some Paint Horses with a Register of Merit in Calf Roping are Snip Bar, Yellow Mount, Bar Mount, Ceasar Bar's Dinero,

Nightwatcher, Skippetta, Red Mount, Yellow Mount's Pride, Chico's Doll, Skippa Streak, Poco Flicker, Pistol Bars, KoKo Bars, Baldy Raider, Missy Bars, Robin K, Rapid Ranger, Jackie Gill, Smokey Jack, Our Sir Prize, Bar Patches Reb, Mr. Twister, Pogo, and Blackeyed Sioux.

Chico's Doll

Chico's Doll is a sorrel tobiano mare. She was an ideal competitor in roping and reining events for nearly six years and received for her excellent performances five National and Reserve National titles. Foaled in 1963, she was bred and raised by Edward Monson, Kenedy, Texas, and trained for the arena by James Garrison, Kyle, Texas.

While bloodlines may not be the whole answer in getting a roping prospect, they are as important as the training provided. The know-how of a good rope horse must be obtained in competent training, but a trainer needs good blood to work with. Chico's Doll comes from a family of rope horses that trace back to one of the best, Joe Bailey (AQHA P-4). The sire of Chico's Doll is Esse's Chico (APSHA 1,629), who was by Flying Kite (APSHA 1,628) by Joe Bailey. Esse's Chico is a Register of Merit reining horse; Flying Kite is a proved breeder of working and performing horses; and Joe Bailey earned a reputation as a sire of some of the nation's top roping horses of the late 1930's and early 1940's.

The dam of Chico's Doll is Winedot, a sorrel tobiano mare, who won Reserve National Champion Produce of Dam in 1966. Nothing is known for certain of her ancestry, but as a number of people who knew her well have affirmed that "she had too much Quarter Horse conformation not to have some good blood from somewhere." Winedot produced two other good performance horses, both by Flying Kite: in 1964 she foaled Colonel George, and in 1965 she foaled Cowboy's Dream.

Chico's Doll was one of the best in the using-horse events.

Chico's Doll and trainer, James Garrison.

She had perfect body balance and the fire and competitive spirit that won for Edward Monson many roping and reining trophies. "She was dependable," he says, "and she rated a calf well."

Chico's Doll was named the 1966 Reserve National Champion Reining Horse and Reserve National Champion Calf Roping Horse, the 1967 National Champion Calf Roping Horse, and the 1970 National Champion Senior Calf Roping Horse and Reserve National Champion Senior Reining Horse. What is more, she has Registers of Merit in reining, roping, and western pleasure and three awards from regional clubs for All-Around Champion.

With the title of Champion All-Around Paint Horse of the Gulf Coast Paint Horse Club in 1966, the versatile little mare received for her owner a beautiful five-hundred-dollar diamond-studded belt buckle. She also finished up 1966 and 1967 as the Champion All-Around Paint Horse of the South Texas Paint Horse Club.

Now retired from the shows, Chico's Doll was bred for a 1972 foal to a AAAT son of Dividend (AQHA) by the name of Top Divi. A high-class running horse earning over $55,467.00 through 1971, Top Divi should prove to be a good cross for Chico Doll's first foal.

14 THE REINING HORSE

Ever since man began working livestock with the help of a horse, he developed greater speed and accuracy in the performance of his job through reining techniques. The action that a good reining horse can provide is almost equally important as the cutting and roping know-how of a horse in actual ranch work. But what, some may ask, does a reining horse have to do with a cutting or roping horse? The answer lies in the fact that these uses require a horse that is trained to make fast turns, skillful backups, and quick stops with the slightest touch of a rein. Nothing can replace the rhythmic coordination between man and horse that is essential to a relaxed performance on the range or in the arena. A reining horse is, simply, one that has been trained to move quickly with a natural grace and balance in performing any task for which he may be called upon.

The reining contests at the Paint Horse shows are designed to test the speed, willingness, ease, and neatness of the horse in following through the intricate stops, turns, and changes of leads in the patterns. In reining competition the horse does not work with livestock. In some respects the event is designed to judge his readiness for the sudden action that would be required of him in actual ranch work.

The horse gets his cue from the rider and should respond well. He should handle easily and have steady gaits and a smooth stop. He should be able to back, pivot, and roll over his hocks. The horse is handled with just reins only and not with the legs and knees. When he stops, he should do so smoothly with no bounce, and he should keep his head straight out and not up in the rider's face.

The APHA has four approved reining patterns. Any horse not following the exact pattern selected by the judge of the class will be disqualified. Scoring is on the basis of 60 to 80 points, with 70 denoting an average performance.

Most commonly judges mark against a horse improper change of leads, anticipation or hesitation, wringing of the tail, stumbling or falling, opening the mouth too wide, and backing sideways. Faults against the rider include changing hands on reins, losing a stirrup, and using any unnecessary aids, such as petting, spurring, quirting, or talking to prompt the horse to perform.

J B's Easter

J B's Easter is a 1959 chestnut tobiano mare, bred by Dale Schroeder, Eureka Springs, Arkansas, and owned by Joe S. (Sandy) Boone, Springdale, Arkansas.

From her sire she carries the blood of one of the old Quarter Horse foundation families—the Copperbottoms. This strain of Quarter Horses was replenished by Dexter (AQHA 193) through the success of R. L. Underwood as a breeder. To preserve this nearly extinct family, he followed the principles of line breeding and occasional inbreeding. The Underwood horses were a great combination of solid muscle and refinement, with beautiful heads and necks. They had their share of cow sense and could be depended on for long hours of hard range work.

Buddy Dexter, J B's Easter's grandsire, was sired by Dexter and was out of his half-sister, Little March. He was one of the best halter and show horses of his day, at one time beating Poco Bueno at the Fort Worth Livestock Show and winning ten other Grand Championships as well. One of Buddy Dexter's strongest points was his ability to transmit his favorable characteristics to his get. This is apparent in his most famous sons: Little Buddy Dexter, Cutter Bill, Buddy Day, and Smutty Bill, all AQHA Champions or Register of Merit horses. J B's Easter traces from her sire, Little Buddy Dexter, through Buddy Dexter to Dexter.

The dam of J B's Easter was a Paint mare of unknown breeding. She inherited her championship abilities, at least in part, from her sire. The Dexter horses were among the best performance horses—remember Cutter Bill, the World's Champion Cutting Horse. Little Buddy Dexter, by providing stiff competition in the working events, did all right for himself without setting any world's records. He developed into a good breeder, siring some excellent Register of Merit arena Quarter Horses and earned his place in a family where respect was gained by achievement.

J B's Easter began contesting in open horse shows before the American Paint Horse Association was founded. She was a smashing success, even in her youth, competing against horses of other breeds. As proof of this she has a trophy naming her the High Point Youth Reining Horse of the Ozark Quarter Horse Association.

By the time Paint Horse shows were established, J B's Easter had grown into a beautiful mare that was hard to fault. Her attractive conformation and gentle disposition won many halter classes and two National awards: Reserve National Champion Aged Mare in 1964 and a tie for Reserve National Champion Aged Mare in 1965.

Her talents did not end in the halter show by any means.

J B's Easter, owned by Joe (Sandy) S. Boone. Photograph by H. D. Dolcater.

Her performance record constitutes the best indication of her true value. J B's Easter had the speed, action, and perfect body balance that make up an ideal reining horse. In the tough competition at the national shows she displayed her expertise and gained two national reining titles: National Champion Reining Horse in 1965 and National Champion Senior Reining Horse in 1967. In the 1967 show she placed first, second, and first in the three go-rounds. An all-around champion and ideal of the breed, J B's Easter was awarded her Register of Merit in Reining in 1967.

As a broodmare she has produced three good colts—two by J B's San Bar, a Mister J. Bar–bred horse, and one by Painted Jewel. Still in excellent form, although, according to Boone, a "little too fat," J B's Easter was bred to a son of Cajun Creek (AQHA) for a 1972 foal. If her record as a producer of performing colts is as good as her record in the Paint Horse shows, her future as a great broodmare is assured.

15 OTHER PERFORMANCE EVENTS

Contests in western pleasure, western riding, and trail horse determine a horse's manners, ability, and good sense when riding for pleasure or performing ordinary chores on the ranch. All these classes require a demonstration of the horse's performance at the three gaits but differ in the additional routines that may be executed. All three classes require western equipment to be used and western apparel to be worn.

Western Pleasure, Western Riding, and Trail Horse

Horses in the pleasure class are judged on their ability to walk, trot, and lope on a loose rein without any unnecessary assistance or cues from the rider. Skillful changes of lead and simple obedience are essential. At the discretion of the judge additional work may be required of any horse, and, if he deems necessary, the class may be judged on conformation as well as performance.

Western riding is a test of the performance and character-

A Western Pleasure class at the 1970 APHA National Show in Amarillo, Texas. Photograph by H. D. Dolcater.

istics of a good, sensible ranch horse and one that can give a quiet and pleasant ride through open country and over varied obstacles. In addition to exhibiting his ability to walk, trot, and lope, the horse is expected to handle minor obstacles that might be encountered along any ride.

The trail-horse class is judged on the horse's manner of performance over obstacles, his response to the rider, his intelligence, his ability at the three gaits, and his conformation. Judging is based 80 per cent on work over the obstacles, 10 per cent on rail work, and 10 per cent on conformation. The gait between obstacles is at the discretion of the judge.

Six obstacles are used, four mandatory ones and two others

selected from the approved APHA list. The mandatory obstacles are (1) opening, passing through, and closing a gate, (2) riding over at least four logs, (3) riding over a wooden bridge or a log placed under a platform, and (4) backing the horse through an L-shaped course. A partial listing of optional obstacles includes (1) carrying an object from one part of the arena to another; (2) hobbling or ground-tying the horse; (3) putting on and removing a slicker, and (4) dismounting and leading the horse over obstacles not less than fourteen inches high or more than twenty-four inches high.

These classes are fun and interesting for both rider and spectator. They are designed to exhibit another talent of the Paint Horse as he follows his rider's bidding through the gaits and accepts each obstacle in his path readily, intelligently, and without excitement.

Working Cowhorse

The working cowhorse contest is a two-part event designed to judge these qualities in a western-trained Paint Horse: good manners, expertness of rein, fluency in lead changes, collected stopping, and herding and holding ability with one cow. To begin the event all the contestants enter the ring at a walk and move at a jog trot and slow lope upon request of the judge. The class is then retired, and each contestant returns to the ring to work individually.

The first half of the contest is a demonstration of reining. The contestant must execute reining pattern 4, a figure eight at a slow lope, twice around, during which fluency of gait is judged. The pattern then calls for a demonstration of sliding stops and quick turns in a run from one end of the arena to the other. After a short run to the middle and a third sliding stop the contestant must back and make a quarter turn to the right or left and then two half turns in both directions.

In the second half of the contest the horse is called on to show his skill in watching and turning a cow. One animal is

Poco Flicker, the 1974 National Champion Working Cowhorse. Photograph by Roger Graves.

turned into the arena, and the contestant is required to hold the cow at one end of the arena long enough to indicate that the horse is watching it. The cow is allowed to run down the side of the arena, during which time the contestant, to display his herding ability, is obliged to turn the animal twice each way against the fence. The horse must then take the cow to the center of the arena and circle it once each way. The horse is penalized if he loses the cow at any time. In this contest normal western apparel—hat, chaps, and boots—must be worn, and a stock saddle must be used, with a rope, or riata, tied to the saddle. These classes represent the greatest measure of a horse's intelligence as he reacts to the pressures of a true working situation. The good working cowhorse demonstrates his ability in a businesslike manner at reasonable speed while under the easy control of the rider.

Bridle-Path Hack (Hunt Seat)

One of the most colorful events at a Paint Horse show is the bridle-path hack class, in the past often termed English pleasure. The showmen in the ring are appropriately attired in riding coats of any tweed or melton for hunting and breeches that are generally white, cream, or buff. English boots and dark blue, black, dark-green, or brown hunting caps are required, as well as ties or chokers. Gloves are optional but preferred.

Horses are shown at a walk, trot, and canter both ways of the ring. The walk must be true and flat-footed in the pleasure class; the trot, brisk, with the rider posting; and the canter, smooth, collected, and straight on both leads. A hand gallop may be called for if there are no more than eight horses in the ring. After the gallop the contestants may be asked to halt and stand quietly on the rail with a free rein before lining up for inspection.

As in the western pleasure contest horses are judged on balance and smoothness at any gait and on their obedience when they are required to back and to stand quietly. Emphasis is also placed on suitability to purpose.

English tack appointments for the horse are mandatory. Saddles must be heavy and plain, leather-skirted, of English or forward-seat type. Regulation snaffles, pelhams, and/or full bridles, all with cavesson nosebands are required. In these classes western tack appointments are not allowed.

A popular event, especially for the young, the bridle-path

hack (hunt seat) is now included in most Paint Horse shows across the country, even in the West and Southwest.

Barrel Racing and Pole Bending

Two contests that test the speed and agility of the Paint Horse are barrel racing and pole bending. They are more recent additions to the western stock shows; however, barrel racing had been a popular event at the rodeos for quite some time. In addition to being a good test for the horse, these two events are fun and suitable for the young riders. Since they are timed events, the only requirements for a good barrel horse or pole-bending horse are speed, action, and maneuverability.

In the barrel race entrants compete in individual turn. The contestant may begin with a running start, and, as soon as the horse's nose reaches the starting line, timing begins. They are required to run a cloverleaf pattern around three barrels at the fastest possible speed without knocking over a barrel and return to the starting line. Touching a barrel with the hand or knocking over a barrel results in a five-second penalty. Failure to follow the course is a cause for disqualification.

Barrel races at the rodeos are usually run for money. At Paint Horse shows the winners receive trophies, ribbons, and performance points.

The pole-bending pattern is run around six poles, spaced at twenty-one-foot intervals in a straight line usually down the center of the arena. Each contestant begins with a running start and may go either to the right or to the left of the first pole to run the pattern. As is the case in the barrel race, if a pole is knocked over or touched by the rider's hand, a five-second penalty is added to the time. A horse is disqualified for failure to follow the prescribed course.

Sequoyah Chief

Sequoyah Chief does not have a fashionable pedigree as do

many Paint Horses today. Some horses are born to be great by the top blood that they carry, while others, like Chief, have to work hard most of their lives to achieve recognition. He is a 1959 bay tobiano gelding by a Paint Horse, Pocochice, and is out of a solid bay mare whose identity and breeding are unknown. It is of little importance who his sire or dam were, since performance is the main objective, and he has that. Sequoyah Chief is now an APHA Champion, five times a National Champion, and has three youth Registers of Merit to his credit.

Denver Weeks, Brookhaven, Mississippi, bred Chief and later sold him to Billy L. Smith, Natchez, Mississippi. In 1966 he was purchased for Patti Oswalt, Pineville, Louisiana, who could not have been over nine or ten years old at the time. For the next six years, wherever they went, the two of them were poison to all competitors in barrel-racing and pole-bending events.

Sequoyah Chief was tough, and he loved to run. It could even be said that he was a timed-event expert. Patti and Chief had a knack of weaving in and out between the poles, swiftly, without dislocating one pole and scrambling around the barrels with incredible balance. Through 1970 Chief had accumulated over 105 performance points, the greatest majority of which were in pole-bending and barrel-racing events.

The perfect balance of Sequoyah Chief was the key to many of his pole-bending and barrel-racing trophies. In 1966 he totaled a virtual "wipeout" of the pole-bending event at the national show by placing first in all three go-rounds and being named the 1966 National Pole Bending Champion. Another victory in 1967 earned him the National Champion Youth Barrel Racing trophy.

In 1970 he added the titles for National Champion Youth Barrel Racing and Reserve National Champion Youth Pole Bending. Again in 1972, at thirteen years of age, the story was repeated, and he won his fifth national award—Reserve National Champion at Pole Bending.

Patti Oswalt and Sequoyah Chief earned a great honor and gained admiration for the Paint Horse at the 1970 Louisiana

Four-H and FFA Light Horse Show in Baton Rouge, Louisiana. Competing against 227 youthful exhibitors riding Quarter Horses and Appaloosas, these two top performers won the award All-Around High Point Exhibitor. They earned a total of 119 points out of a possible 125. The next highest competitor, riding a Quarter Horse, earned 108 points. Paint Horses were accepted into the Baton Rouge Four-H and FFA show for the first time in 1970. In his first year competing against all other breeds, the Paint Horse rode off with the highest most prestigious award.

Sequoyah Chief has made a memorable name for himself in the APHA record books. He may lack the suavity of other great horses, but that has been more than offset by his talent and unrelenting determination.

Facing page: Sequoyah Chief and Patti Oswalt. Photograph by Margie Spence.

Margie Spence
©

16 PAINT HORSE RACING

Since colonial days running the quarter-mile has been the favorite pastime of the settlers of the rural areas and backwoods. Short-horse racing as a sport predates Thoroughbred racing in America by nearly one hundred years and began when the plantation owners "matched" their riding horses on the only tracks available—usually the village streets.

When the colonial gentlemen invested in the fashionable English horses that were more "enduring" and popularized a new, longer-distance race horse, the quarter-miler moved westward with the more common folks. Brush tracks were cleared through the virgin forests at crossroads and at the county seats. Short races were a part of every weekend gathering whenever two or three fast horses could be matched. Without the benefit of timing devices, gates, or chutes and standards to follow, the races were run from a flagged, "ask-and-answer," or lap-and-tap start. Under these conditions races were not always honorable, and often the most calculating jockey, and not the fastest horse, was the winner.

The early years were marked by many abuses in the unregulated matched races. Several methods were employed by both jockey and owner to gain every advantage, including race fixing, foul riding, doping horses, and catching the opponent off guard. There were no rules to follow except those set up by the individuals for the race, and there was no regulatory body to enforce them in any case. It was evident that an organization was needed to set rules, enforce them, and provide uniformity of competition.

In 1943 the first formal racing association was organized for the purpose of promoting and regulating the racing of horses at short distances. For seven years the association was known as the American Quarter Racing Association (AQRA). In 1950 it was incorporated into the American Quarter Horse Association as the Racing Division. The rules and regulations of the AQRA were patterned after the Jockey Club rules and adapted to quarter racing as necessary. Identification of all horses was as important as standardization of rules; therefore, the newly created organization required registration of every horse that ran on an AQRA track. Registration was open to any horse regardless of color, sex, age, or breeding. Probably the only association at that time that did not discriminate against horses because of color or breeding, the AQRA accepted Paint Horses for registration along with horses of all other breeds. In 1950, when the AQRA was merged with the AQHA, Paint Horses were no longer accepted or allowed to run on member tracks.

In those early days of quarter racing a dozen or more Paint Horses were providing stiff competition as they earned their place in AQRA history. Among the ranks of these performers the most famous horse was the legendary Painted Joe (his story is told in Chapter 18).

A little filly who was also a standout at the short-horse tracks in the middle 1940's was Little Nip. Her special flair for the short distances enabled her to defeat Miss Panama and Badger's Grey Lady in a thrilling three-hundred-yard race, in which she established a new track record in Tucson, Arizona.

Perhaps some readers remember a couple of other Paint Horses popular around the tracks in this era: Spotted Joe Reed and his sister Marylin (sometimes spelled Marilyn). This full brother and sister by Joe Reed (AQHA P-3) and out of Queen Clay by Joy by Jeff, both qualified for the Register of Merit in 1948.

Two splendid fillies foaled in 1946, running in the 1948 and 1949 seasons, were Speckled Dandy and Blue Streak. Speckled Dandy was a chestnut overo daughter of Hondo by the Thoroughbred Yankee Star by *Star Shoot. She earned a AA rating on the track and a Register of Merit in 1949.

Blue Streak, listed only as a Paint filly in the *1948 Year Book of the AQRA*, was by Red Man by Joe Hancock. In 1948 she set her record at the Las Vegas track and qualified for the Register of Merit.

Band Time, Jr., sired by Band Play and out of a mare by Grano de Oro, was another good running Paint Horse. He too showed top form in the 1948 and 1949 seasons, earning a Register of Merit in 1948.

Most horsemen who have more than a casual interest in the quarter race and who have attended a race or two over the years have a secret yen to own a running horse of their own. There is a thrill that cannot be equaled while watching a two- or three-year-old breezing down the track. A great many Paint Horse breeders have become absorbed in Paint Horse racing in the past few years, and interest in this sport is at an all-time high.

Not all breeders of Paint Horses expect their produce to be track horses. In fact, very few turn out to be "good" running horses. It is rare to find a horse with all the requisites of speed, stamina, balance, soundness, and courage that a prospective race horse must have.

Helen Michaelis once wrote: "Some say that a horse is as fast as the track, others say that he is as fast as the trainer makes him and still others say he is as fast as the jockey rides him.

Regardless of track, trainer or rider, the average fast horse gets his ability from his ancestors."[1] While speed in itself cannot be passed from one generation to another, the capacity for speed is handed down by heredity. The Thoroughbred has been bred for sustained speed for long distances. The Quarter Horse has been bred to run the quarter-mile or short distances with a quick burst of speed. Many breeders believe that the best way to ensure the capacity for speed in their Paint Horses is to crossbreed with the longer-legged Thoroughbred and obtain the staying qualities of this long-distance horse.

The right blood or pedigree makes a difference when breeding for speed. Since the capacity for speed can be bred in horses, it can be bred out by using the blood of horses whose background fails to show speed. A running horse needs a good conformation that will allow efficient operation on the track. He needs soundness, good legs, and sure feet. Above all, one of the most important parts of a race horse is his "motor," the organs and the way they function to give him propulsion power. Whether or not these and other qualities are best obtained through Thoroughbred blood is a decision left to each individual. With the activity on the turf steadily increasing and Paint Horse racing enthusiasts springing up all over, breeding for speed is a popular practice.

Crossing Thoroughbred blood with that of the Quarter Horse has become traditional down through the years, and this infusion in many instances has produced outstanding running horses. A similar cross using the Thoroughbred on Paint Horses has produced fast horses like Little Nip, Fast Time, Powder Charge, Bang Up 2, Misty Moon, Grey Wonder, and Chicka Charge.

In 1966 Paint Horse racing was organized in a classification system, and horses were graded according to their track time

[1]Robert Moorman Denhardt and Helen Michaelis, *The Quarter Horse*, II, 130.

on the same basis used by the AQHA. The standard distances for Paint Horse races are 220, 250, 300, 330, 350, 400, and 440 yards. Further to promote Paint Horse racing, in 1967 the Paint Horse Racing Division was set up to establish and maintain uniform standards for the sport. The rules governing Paint Horse racing are listed in "The Rules and Regulations of Paint Horse Racing" and are modeled after the rules of the AQHA. Until 1971 the APHA followed the Grading and Qualification Standards AAA, AA, A, and B for its determination of horses qualifying for a Register of Merit. Beginning on January 1, 1971, the APHA adopted the speed-rating system that is used by the AQHA on all approved quarter tracks that the association has rated. Horses are now given a speed index number, rather than a AA or AAA rating. Because the speed-index rating varies with track conditions, it is difficult to make a specific breakdown of the rating system. For information purposes the General Speed Index chart given in Appendix 7 indicates the speed-rating system as compared to the grading and qualifying standards.

Only races approved and recognized by the APHA will be considered for the awarding of points for championships or admission to the Register of Merit. It is necessary for a horse to earn ten points in racing to receive a Register of Merit. One point will be awarded for each race run in B time, or at a Speed Index rating of 60 through 69; two points for each race run in A time, or at a Speed Index of 70 through 79; four points for each race run in AA time, or at a Speed Index of 80 through 89; six points for each race run in AAA time, or at a Speed Index of 90 through 100; and eight points for each race run in Top AAA, or at a Speed Index rating of over 100. A horse must have run at least one race at a Speed Index of at least 80 (AA time) to qualify for the Register of Merit.

It is not enough, however, for a horse to run at a speed of 80 through 89 to earn the Register of Merit, which is the requirement of the AQHA. It takes at least two races, if one is run in AAA time (90 through 99), which earns six points, plus another race run in AA time for four points or two races run in A time (two points each).

In 1966, the first year of organized Paint Horse racing, only two horses earned the Register of Merit in racing. Seven years later, at the close of 1973, twenty-eight horses were ROM in racing.

One of the most encouraging developments in Paint Horse racing is the steadily increasing interest in futurities and maturities. The futurity is generally run by two-year-olds, and nominations are usually made early and horses kept eligible by subsequent payments up to the date of running. The purses are made up of all nominating and sustaining fees with occasional funds added to make the prizes more enticing. The futurities serve as an incentive for breeders to work continually to improve the quality of their stock.

The first Paint Horse futurity was run on August 1, 1964, at Midway Downs, Stroud, Oklahoma. The next year the Texas Paint Horse Club scheduled its first annual futurity on September 18, 1965, at Clear Fork Downs in Weatherford, Texas. Bar Patches, a sorrel overo stallion, owned by D. J. Bourassa, Freedom, Oklahoma, won the race, after winning a month earlier the second running of the Oklahoma Paint Horse Futurity at Stroud.

In 1966, Paint Horse races were held at four different tracks in Oklahoma, and an attempt was made to compromise with the American Quarter Horse Association on their ruling regarding mixed races. In Texas some twenty races were open for Paint Horses on the racing circuit. Race meets in Sonora, Bandera, Seguin, Brady, Fredericksburg, Junction, Goliad, Boerne, and New Braunfels were scheduled, giving racing enthusiasts more opportunities to prove the racing ability of their Paint Horses.

Further interest was sparked in 1967, when the Kansas Paint Horse Club held its first annual Paint Horse Futurity on September 4, 1967, and the first Colorado Futurity was run at the Centennial Race Track at Denver. The race at Denver was

Slow Danger, winner of the first APHA National Championship Futurity.

the first time for a Paint Horse Futurity to be held on a pari-mutuel track. The betting windows were more active during the Paint Horse race than during any other race of the day. The pari-mutuel race for Paint Horses at Denver brought invitations from other wagering tracks.

Futurities are now held in six states, together with a number of stakes races, derbies, and maturities. Efforts are being made to open races for Paint Horses in other states, including Arizona, Louisiana, and New Mexico.

Good purses are needed to attract horses, but more horses are needed at the tracks to get good purses. In 1966 the winner of the Oklahoma Futurity, Little Wahoo, received first-place money of $430 as the winner's portion of the purse. By 1973 the amount was over six times greater: the winner, Paul Bunyon, took home for his owners $2,706.

A steady increase can be noted in the average of total purses offered in the futurities over the seven-year period from 1966 through 1973. In 1966, when only two futurities were run, the average purse was approximately $1,000. By 1969 the purses averaged $2,200 for the four races, in 1971 the average had increased to $3,500, and in 1973 the purse for five futurities averaged $5,360.

The richest Paint Horse race, the "all-American futurity" of the Paint Horse breed, is the APHA National Championship Futurity. Race-day magic is very evident at all Paint Horse races, but at no time is it more apparent than on the day of the national-championship race. The good horses and good purses are combined to provide the kind of race that delights short-horse running men as never before. The first National Championship was run on August 30, 1970, at the Colorado State Fair Track in Pueblo, Colorado. The winner of the first championship race was a two-year-old sorrel overo, Slow Danger, by Lalito Canales (AQHA 209,834) and out of Crystal Eye (APHA 2022) by Slow Motion (AQHA 48,053).

The 1971 National Championship, held on October 23 at Stroud, Oklahoma, set a new high when eight horses ran for a total net purse of $7,348.50. Million Heir by Three Jets (AQHA 408,308) won the second Championship running, having taken the Oklahoma and Kansas futurities earlier in the year.

Well established in 1972, the National Championship Futurity went over the $10,000 mark for the two-year-olds. The winner, Party Gal, is a full sister to the winner of the 1970 stakes

Million Heir, by Three Jets, winner of the second APHA National Championship Futurity, Stroud, Oklahoma, October 23, 1971.

event. Her win made her the leading money-earning Paint Horse for 1972 with total earnings of $7,268.83 in official races.

Top Yellow (AAA), a superbly bred dun overo stallion by Top Moon (AQHA) out of Lady Yellow Jacket by Morehouse Yellow Jacket (AQHA) daylighted an eight-horse field to win

Party Gal, winner of the 1972 APHA National Championship Futurity.

handily the 1973 running of the National. In winning the fourth annual futurity, Top Yellow took home $4,474.03, to bring his earnings for the year to $10,801.78, the most ever earned officially in one year by a registered Paint Horse.

17 FAMOUS RUNNING HORSES

Since most breeders, owners, and trainers consider a race prospect on bloodlines, certain ancestral names take on great importance in a pedigree. Paul Crabb, Winfield, Kansas, breeder of Painted Jewel and other successful horses, had as much respect for good blood as anyone. He was known as a man who recognized quality in horses, and he raised some fine ones to prove it. Jet Dial and Babette, two proved producers of running horses, had all the qualities he or any other breeder of short horses could desire. His mating of these two popular horses brought forth Painted Jewel in the spring of 1964.

Painted Jewel

Painted Jewel's sire, Jet Dial (AQHA 216,980) was by Johnny Dial (AQHA 25,293) by Depth Charge and out of Leo Jewel (AQHA 53,665) by Leo (AQHA 1,335). Johnny Dial represents one of the important Quarter Horse bloodlines, and his effect on the Paint Horse appears to have been profoundly satisfac-

Painted Jewel, AA, ROM.

tory. He was the World Champion Quarter Running Horse of 1952 and topped the Leading Money Earners List for the year. A AAAT horse himself, Johnny Dial is the sire of a host of AAAT and AAA stakes winners.

Leo has always been admired for his influence on the modern short-horse, but his greatest glory has come through the excellence of his daughters as broodmares. Leo Jewel's good blood came rich from her sire, and she, a producer of running horses, passed on to most of her foals Leo's best qualities.

The sire of Painted Jewel, Jet Dial, has lived up to his breeding by giving to the racing world seven Register of Merit AQHA colts and so far one ROM APHA colt.

Painted Jewel comes from a long line of running horses both on the sire side and dam side. His mother, Babette, had a generous endowment of speed from the celebrated Painted Joe, and, by winning a number of match races, she gained a top-flight reputation on the tracks in her own right. It is in the stud, however, that she emerges with stature as one of the first and finest contributing dams to the modern Paint Horse.

Painted Jewel is a long-bodied, well-made chestnut tobiano. Everything about him is finely balanced, as if he were built for speed. He began his racing career as a two-year-old in 1966 and was a pretty popular horse around the track, winning nine firsts and one second out of ten starts his first season.

On August 20 at Midway Downs, Stroud, Oklahoma, Painted Jewel won the second heat of the Oklahoma Paint Horse Futurity Trials for 250 yards over four other contenders, only to come in second to Little Wahoo the following week in the finals. Both the trials and the finals were run in AA time of :13.79 and :13.71. Painted Jewel never lost another race. He took the Texas Paint Horse Futurity trials and finals in September, and on November 27 at Blue Ribbon Downs, Sallisaw, Oklahoma, he won the Southwest All-Age Paint Championship from such top horses as Boundin Lu Lu, Bar Boy, Aggie's Joe, Jim's Johnny Dial, and Joechief Bar. He received his Register of Merit in racing from the American Paint Horse Association in 1966 and is officially rated AA+.

In 1967 two other significant races were added to his record, making a lifetime record of twelve starts, eleven wins and one second. In July he won the Texas Paint Horse Derby, and in August he daylighted Bar Boy and Painted Rocket to win the four-hundred-yard Oklahoma Paint Horse Maturity at Little Dixie Downs.

Painted Jewel was owned and raced by Art Beall, Broken Arrow, Oklahoma, and Ray Conrad, Tulsa, as a two- and three-year-old. He was purchased in 1968 by R. H. Hefner, Jr., Oklahoma City, shown triumphantly at halter, and then sold to Bud and Betty Crump, Wynnewood, Oklahoma, in 1972, when Hefner dispersed his horses.

After two seasons Painted Jewel retired from the tracks. His striking qualities of conformation and disposition enabled him to embark on a show career that was as gratifying as his racing career. He was the Grand Champion at a number of big name Paint Horse shows, including the Houston Livestock Show on March 3, 1970, where he placed first out of a class of twenty aged stallions.

Painted Jewel entered the stud in 1968, siring such outstanding get as Painted Fashion, Jet Jewel, Painted Skipper, Barton Jewel, Mr. Doodle Bug, Tonto Jewel, Jewel's Chief, and Diamond Jim. His colts have done their part in spreading his fame; all of these and many more have been named Grand or Reserve Champions and are great performers at Paint Horse shows.

Powder Charge

Powder Charge was rich in the blood of many celebrated families of running horses. This sorrel tobiano stallion, foaled in 1965, was by the Thoroughbred Mr. Harrison (a winner of over $47,000 himself), who was by Alorter by The Porter and out of Miss Harrison by Wise Counsellor, Co-champion Two-Year-Old Colt in 1923. On the dam line Powder Charge was inbred to Three Bars. He was out of Sky Bar (APHA 1,053) by Skychief Bar (AQHA 66,329) by Three Bars. Sky Bar's dam was Jody Bar, who was by Skylark Bar by Three Bars. In addition to Three Bars, Powder Charge has another famous running ancestor on this dam line, Painted Joe, traced through Jody Bar's dam, Babette.

Sky Bar is the maternal source of other good running and performing horses. Her 1967 foal from the court of Top Bracket (AQHA) was Sky Top Bar, a AA ROM race horse; and her 1969 foal, Million Heir, also AA, by Three Jets (AQHA) was the winner of the 1971 APHA National Championship Futurity.

Powder Charge was bred by Paul E. Crabb, Winfield, Kansas, and was purchased by Mr. and Mrs. Cleon Cope, McAlester, Oklahoma, on June 4, 1966, at the Broken Arrow Horse Farm Sale. A new record was set for a yearling colt sold at public auction when the final bid of $3,150 was in.

One of the fastest AAA Paint Horses of all time, Powder Charge as a two-year-old won all four major futurities in 1967: the Texas Paint Horse Futurity at Austin, the Oklahoma Paint Horse Futurity at McAlester, the Kansas Paint Horse Futurity at Anthony Downs, and the Colorado Paint Horse Futurity at Denver.

On July 30, 1967, at Manor Downs, near Austin, Powder Charge set a new record for the 220, defeating Dual's Darling and Dual's Doll to win the Texas Paint Horse Futurity. His official time of :11.60 was AAAT, and the best time recorded at the track.

Powder Charge marked himself that year at the very top of the two-year-olds. He just could not be outrun, and he met and defeated some of the fastest Paint Horses: Miss Yellow Jacket, Squaw L, Miss Pana Rey, Blind Date, Donna Bars, Grand Manner, Miss Robin, and Mucho Peso. His lifetime record is nineteen wins out of twenty-one starts against Paint Horses, Thoroughbreds, Quarter Horses and Appaloosas. The winner of eight straight futurities and derbies, he was the first Paint Horse to run in official AAA time and has run AAA at 220, 250, 300, and 350 yards. He was awarded the Register of Merit in Racing in 1967.

Not only was he a champion of the quarter track, but Powder Charge had something else going for him—a good build with plenty of muscle and a kindly disposition making him easy to handle. It was no surprise then that he was very successful at halter, winning firsts in shows in Oklahoma and Kansas and three or four grand championships.

In March, 1971, after two previously unsuccessful attempts, Bud and Betty Crump, Wynnewood, Oklahoma, purchased Powder Charge from the Copes. In the words of Betty Crump:

We first saw the leggy weanling at the APHA National Show and Sale in Kansas City when Powder Charge along with a select group of mares and colts of Paul Crabb were first offered at auction. Our bid was turned down. At this time, Bud noted in his sale catalog, 'Good Race Prospect.'

At the time of the Broken Arrow Sale Powder Charge was developing into the "race prospect," but also showed the long hip conformation that we desire in our horses. Again, the Crump bid was unsuccessful as the Copes paid their record price for the flashy yearling.

After the sale we became friends with the Copes having the mutual interest, and Powder Charge rode to his new McAlester home in our trailer.

It was a long wait, from 1965 to 1971, but Bud Crump is a pretty determined individual. He was for years a real cowhorse man who carefully trained and rode many good ones in the rodeos and around the ranch.

Valuing his speed and smooth break, Crump started Powder Charge in arena work. An intelligent horse of unlimited potential, he seemed thoroughly to enjoy perfecting himself as a cowhorse and could have developed into one of the best. Most of the old roping and dogging horses that achieved the greatest glory were matched in short races from time to time. It was the short breaking speed—the ability to gain full momentum in a fraction of a second—that enabled a good roping horse to be a perfect match-race horse and a short-distance running horse to become a good rope horse.

The Crumps' breeding program was cemented with the addition of Powder Charge. In 1971 he was bred to forty-two Paint and Quarter Horse mares. Some of the finest, all owned by the Crumps, were Squaw L, Miss Yellow Jacket, Hank Kandy Bars (AAA), five National Champion mares, and many others that are AAA-rated or AAA producers.

Powder Charge died a young stallion in 1972. How extensive will be his influence on Paint Horses only the future will tell. As an indication, through 1973 he sired one APHA Champion, two ROM Qualifiers, and five starters: Blasting Cap, Do Say, Elusive Charge, Miss Powder Puff, and Painted Powder.

Bang Up 2

Bang Up 2 is a bay tobiano stallion foaled in 1967. He was bred by Carol A. Whitman, Carthage, Missouri, and purchased as a two-year-old by his present owners, Dr. and Mrs. John Owens, Durant, Oklahoma.

Those who hold the opinion that speed can be bred in a horse through the use of the right pedigree will approve of Bang Up 2's bloodlines. He is a son of Bang Up (JC 560,280) by Navy Chief by War Admiral by Man o' War. His dam was Painted Lydia (APHA 394) by Painted Joe.

No matter how one looks at it, Man o' War is an American phenomenon. In fact, in some regions, especially the bluegrass country, when race horses are mentioned, his name and competence are always recalled. He won twenty of his twenty-one starts, and these were all by open daylight. He set three world records, two American records, and three track records. Defeated only once (by a horse aptly named Upset), Man o' War had previously beaten him, and he bested him again in five races afterward. He retired in 1920 with over $249,000, the richest horse of his day. Man o' War sired an array of great horses, the likes of War Admiral, the Triple Crown Winner in 1937 and the Horse of the Year for 1937.

The name Bang Up shows up prominently in the ancestry of many outstanding running and showing horses in both the AQHA and the APHA. Before his tragic loss some years ago, he left his mark as a sire of Paint Horses through Bang Up 2, Joechief Bar, By Jingo, and Bon Bon. He has sired one APHA Supreme Champion, three APHA Champions, and four Register of Merit Qualifiers through 1971.

If speed was the desired goal, Painted Lydia was a logical cross on Bang Up. Although there is no record that she ever raced, Painted Lydia has proven herself in the stud and has passed along the extraordinary speed and quality of Painted Joe.

Judged in the light of breeding and performance, Bang Up 2 has done as much to enhance Paint Horse racing as any horse could. He always did his best and kept the family tradition by running an honest race every time. Beginning his career as a two-year-old, he won the four 1969 Paint Horse futurities in Texas, Oklahoma, Kansas, and Colorado. He received a Register of Merit in racing in 1969 and is now officially rated AAA.

In the first futurity of the 1969 season, run at Eureka Downs, Kansas, Bang Up 2 amply demonstrated his running ability. He won the second heat of the trials on June 8 and the finals a week later. Weather conditions on the day of the finals were good for skiing or sledding, but not for horse racing. On a damp and cold day and on a sloppy track the Bang Up horse ran a hard race to earn the right to enter the winner's circle and take home the winning purse.

On August 10 in the Oklahoma Futurity, Bang Up 2 met some of the strongest competition he had ever run against. On a fast track he won easily over Sky Top Bar, Miss Amigo Leo, Jo's Bid, Gold Doll, Dual's Doll II, Scatter Gun, and Katy's Little Bit in good AA time of :16.05 for the 300 yards.

During most of the 1970 and 1971 racing season Bang Up 2 suffered with a bad hock. In June, 1970, he finished second by a nose in the Kansas Paint Horse Maturity at Eureka Downs to the good contender Hank Kandy Bars. He came back in the sixth running of the Texas Paint Horse Maturity in July to win by three-quarters of a length over an eight-horse field, with Hank Kandy Bars finishing second. The 350-yard race was won in :18.52, AA time.

In 1971, Bang Up 2 lost to the Spoiler all maturity races except the first running of the National Championship Maturity at Stroud, Oklahoma, on October 23. The race, marred by fouls, was won by Spoiler, but, owing to an interference foul against Bang Up 2 when Spoiler weaved across the track into him, Bang Up 2 was declared the winner, and Spoiler was placed second. A hock bothered Bang Up 2 most of the year, and he rested through late 1971 and early 1972. In October and November, 1972, he made four starts and added two firsts and one second to his lifetime record, bringing the totals to seventeen starts, ten firsts, four seconds, and one third.

Like most horsemen, Dr. Owens feels that everyone has only one great horse in a lifetime, and for him Bang Up 2 has been his "great horse."

Spoiler

Spoiler's story began in the fall of 1965, when Raymond C. Surber, Chickasha, Oklahoma, purchased a 1964 bay tobiano filly, Painted Dream, from Ray McKammon, Spearman, Texas. Between the time of Surber's first phone call about the filly and the day he arrived to pick her up, she had got into some barbed wire and severely lacerated her right hock. Undaunted by this apparently crippling blemish, Surber recognized the quality shining through and bought her in spite of a possible handicap.

Tender care and skillful treatment from the Surber family were all that were needed for the filly's leg to heal. It soon returned to normal size, and only a small scar was visible. In early 1966 she was broken to ride and responded immediately to all training. At a Paint Horse show in April at Moore, Oklahoma, Painted Dream, shown by Deanna Surber (Mrs. Robert Foale), won the 1964 mare class, showmanship at halter, western pleasure, and barrel racing. At the end of her first show she was only a few points away from the high-point trophy award. Later in the year she was put into race training, and under the tutelage of the capable jockey Sonny King, Chickasha, she advanced quickly toward her debut on the track. In each of her two starts (one at Kiefer, Oklahoma, and the other at Stroud, Oklahoma) she placed third. She was not very impressive as horse racing goes, but she was catching on fast and could easily have had an excellent record the following season had she not been injured in the fall of 1966. For her good show record she was named the Champion Two-Year-Old Mare of Oklahoma, and Deanna won the All-Around Youth Award with her.

After the shoulder injury in late 1966, Painted Dream was bred in March, 1967, to Dream Man, a AAAT Quarter Horse by Go Man Go. Go Man Go was the World's Champion Quarter Running Horse for 1955, 1956, and 1957, and was one of the leading sires of money earners and winners through 1974. Dream Man himself has sired three AAA Quarter running horses.

The result of the mating of Painted Dream with Dream Man was a large, spirited colt foaled on February 9, 1968. He was given the name Spoiler. According to Deanna, "He was such a large colt that Daddy and my sister Betty had to help him into the world, but he was up on his own in no time at all. In fact, when he was only three hours old he severely kicked Betty."

Deanna, and her husband, Robert, were living at Moore, Oklahoma, and when Spoiler was six months old, he was weaned and moved to the Foale home. From the day he was foaled he was a stout, frisky colt. He had all the strong points of conformation, speed, and enormous physical energy that mark the typical running horse, but his early training and discipline were along the lines of a show horse. The Foales entered him in several shows as a yearling and disappointedly admit that Spoiler did not show very well. In the words of Deanna, "We made up our minds to show people that Spoiler could stand pretty and be a winner—in the winner's circle on the race track." That he has done.

With speed from both parents and grandparents Spoiler was destined to run. When he was eighteen months old, Deanna and Robert began saddling him and driving him. He was soon ready for race training and was moved to Chickasha, where Sonny King could gallop him regularly.

Sonny had helped train and condition Dream Man and became very devoted to Spoiler. He often said the Spoiler would be AA as a two-year-old, and AAA at three. Sonny brought Spoiler to the winner's circle six times in 1970. The only two futurities that Sonny won in his many years of jockeying were won on Spoiler—the 1970 Kansas Paint Horse Futurity and the 1970 Texas Futurity. This is not to say that he did not win many races; he did. But winning a futurity is something special to any jockey or trainer. His untimely death by a fall from a filly he was galloping at La Mesa Park, Raton, New Mexico, on August 10, 1970, deeply saddened Robert and Deanna. Deanna volunteered for the job as jockey for Spoiler. She was well qualified, having competed from the time she was fifteen in all-girl rodeos in such events as bull riding, bareback riding, roping, and goat tying. She and her sister Betty tied for the state championship in bull riding in 1966.

Spoiler won the Kansas, Texas, and Oklahoma futurities of 1970, earning a AA Register of Merit in the Kansas finals on June 20. He placed second to Slow Danger at Pueblo, Colorado, in the first running of the National Paint Horse Championship on August 30. At Pueblo, for unknown reasons, Spoiler broke out of the gates two lengths behind the pack. At 250 yards he was catching and passing horses but finished one and one-half lengths behind Slow Danger, to win second-place money.

He continued his winning way in 1971, having what is probably a first in Paint Horse racing history—a woman jockey. Deanna had now completely accepted her new role, galloping Spoiler and thirteen or fourteen other horses every other day and jockeying Spoiler to the winner's circle in six races during 1971. Two of his six wins were in official AAA time: an open race at Eureka Downs, where he won by a length of daylight over the AAA Appaloosa What's Up Ghost; and the 350-yard Kansas Paint Horse Maturity, where he again won by a length.

Spoiler's racing career has been a thrilling one. He has run against some veterans and has put down to defeat most of the top Paint Horses at one time or another. He has run in several unofficial, mixed races and has defeated My Breeze Bar, Breezing Marie, and Hy Time Bob, all AAA Quarter Horses.

Of the twenty official APHA starts he has fourteen wins, five seconds, and one third. He was named the Oklahoma Running Horse of the Year in 1970, 1971, and 1972, and has a AAA rating and a Speed Index rating of 94. His earnings total over $13,900 for the four years he raced.

The Paint Horse racing world lost one of its greatest sprinters when Spoiler died of a ruptured major blood vessel near his heart following the running of the Texas Paint Horse Maturity at Ross Downs on September 16, 1973. It was his first official race that year and, tragically, his last.

PART IV **PAINT HORSES FROM
THE PAST**

18 PAINTED JOE

There can be little argument that Painted Joe has greatly influenced the modern Paint Horse and contributed immeasurably to the advancement of the Paint Running Horse. All one needs to do is analyze the bloodlines of the most popular running horses to see this fact.

Like many early-day foundation Quarter Horses whose unrevealed past was cause for speculation about their true breeding, Painted Joe's ancestry was uncertain and incorrectly recorded for a number of years. During the time that he raced in the old American Quarter Racing Association, he was believed to be by a son of Joe Bailey (AQHA P-4) and out of a Thoroughbred mare, breeding unknown. These were the bloodlines that went into the AQRA records and the pedigree used by breeders who registered his sons and daughters. One reason for this misunderstanding could have been the fact that Old Joe Bailey's home was at Gonzales, Texas, about eighteen miles south of Luling, where Painted Joe was broken as a yearling and where he first raced against sons and grandsons of Old Joe Bailey.

175

When the APHA got in touch with Owen E. Lay, Sealy, Texas, breeder of Painted Joe, some years ago, it was learned that his sire was not a horse by Joe Bailey but a Quarter Horse named Rondo Joe owned by Lay.

Rondo Joe is of the blood of two founding Quarter Horse sires, Traveler through Little Joe and Sykes Rondo on his dam side. Rondo Joe's sire was Grano de Oro, who was by Little Joe by Traveler.

Grano de Oro was a fine bay, and fast, who resulted from the union of Little Joe and Della Moore. Ott Adams raised three colts from this cross. In 1923, Della Moore foaled Aloe, a beautiful sorrel filly; in 1925 she dropped Grano de Oro; and in 1927, bred back again to Little Joe, she foaled Joe Moore. When still a young colt Grano de Oro was sold to John Dial, who raised him and then sold him to Meador Northington, Egypt, Texas. Grano de Oro was as fine a horse as Joe Moore, but he did not receive the acclaim his brother did, possibly because Joe Moore was bred more extensively and outlived Grano de Oro by a number of years.

The Sykes Rondo mare bred to Grano de Oro to produce Rondo Joe was a brown Quarter mare that Herman Habermacher had given to Lay. She was by a son of the old sire Sykes Rondo and was the kind of mare that usually raised a good colt. In 1935, Lay carried his mare to Northington's ranch at Egypt and bred her to Grano de Oro.

The following year this brown mare, whom everyone called the Habermacher Mare, foaled a sorrel colt that was given the name Rondo Joe. He did not become as well known as most of the horses of the Little Joe line because he died as a three-year-old of a tumor that had developed in his back from an injury the year before.

The story of Painted Joe's dam began in the early 1920's, when Lay purchased a Paint stallion from a man in Sealy, Texas, who had acquired him as a colt a few years earlier. His origin was unknown, but Lay guessed him to be of Thoroughbred blood because he was fast; yet he was ideal for match racing since his looks misrepresented his ability. Lay owned at that time a blaze-faced, stocking-legged racy little mare called Lizzy whose background was also a blank. He bred his Paint stallion to Lizzy, and she foaled a well-made filly with a lot of white. He named her Painted Lizzy. Several years later Painted Lizzy was bred to Rondo Joe, and in the spring of 1939 she foaled Painted Joe on the Lay ranch at Sealy.

In the same year Lay bred Rondo Joe to two other Paint mares, a Paint half-sister of Painted Lizzy and another Paint mare that he had purchased from Northington. All three mares had Paint colts the following year. Painted Lizzy's colt was Painted Joe, the best of the lot.

Painted Lizzy foaled three other colts while Lay owned her, but only one lived. In 1942 she was bred to a son of Rondo Joe (the Paint colt out of her half-sister that was bred to Rondo Joe the same year as Painted Lizzy). In 1943 she foaled another horse colt that colored, but he did not have the speed of Painted Joe, and as a two-year-old Lay sold him to Tan Croaker, Orange, Texas, for $150. After Croaker gelded him and trained him in cutting, he became a highly valued cutting and working horse.

In 1946, Painted Lizzy was taken to the court of Flying Bob at Richmond, Texas. She was bred to Louisiana's famous race horse, and Lay was hoping for another "running machine" like his Painted Joe. Painted Lizzy did her best, only to foal a solid-colored colt the following year that lived only ten days. Lay bred the mare back that year, and after the next colt also died, he gave her away. To his knowledge Painted Lizzy did not have another colt.

Painted Joe was a strong, healthy colt. He showed considerable speed as a weanling, but Lay was not immediately moved to make a race horse out of him, although he admitted that there was a pretty solid background of running blood. He first broke Painted Joe to ride and tried to rope calves on him. Joe could explode from the chute and had the speed to overtake

The immortal Painted Joe as a three-year-old in a photograph taken on February 17, 1942. His appearance was usually ragged and lean, but he made his impression as he crossed the finish line.

the calf, but, Lay says, "He was too rough in the chute and he'd run right over a calf." Painted Joe just was not interested in cattle.

About this time, and in a way by chance, Lay discovered that Painted Joe could run. Some of his friends had come by his ranch with a smooth little race mare. They galloped her a few times, measured her tracks, and were glorying in the length of her stride. After they left, Lay, wanting to see what Joe could do, gave him a run down the dirt road. He put the tape on his tracks and found his stride to be twenty-four feet, extremely good when compared with the twenty-two-foot stride of the race mare.

He soon began to run Painted Joe in some of the local arenas against neighboring roping horses. Joe's first run on a track was in 1941 at the Johnson Grass Patch Track, near San Antonio, where Lay matched him against a two-year-old black stallion. That first race was certainly a thrilling one and probably the most talked about for some time.

For the race Lay hired a young black jockey who rode for Boyd Givens, Gonzales. He told the jockey to be sure not to hit Joe in the flanks because he was still bad about pitching. After breaking from the chute (gates were not yet used at the track), the jockey must have forgotten the warning. As the black stallion broke and headed down the track, he instinctively brought the bat down alongside Painted Joe's hip. For a few seconds there was bedlam in Painted Joe's movements. When the boy brought the bat down again, Joe suddenly pitched and almost started bucking. The jockey had a difficult time staying in the seat and grabbed at everything he could to stay on. Finally he regained his balance and heard Lay's voice telling him to bring the bat down across the shoulder. Although the black horse was nearly thirty yards out front, Joe settled down to racing and did not stop until he passed the black and won the 220-yard race by two good lengths. All the horsemen of South Texas who were there that day talked about the spotted horse that bucked halfway down the track and still won the race.

Never before had Lay been so aware of Joe's eagerness to run. After that first race, he turned him over to Boyd Givens and Newman Low, who were to run him and split the winnings with Lay.

Back in the early 1940's county fairs were usually occasions for horse races, and the county tracks were the proving ground for some of the outstanding Quarter Running Horses that made a mark in the AQRA. Painted Joe too spent his early racing days match racing at the county-fair tracks before advancing to the official tracks and organized racing. For his second race, Givens, Low, and Lay took Painted Joe to the county fair at Mason, Texas. He was matched against a horse called Little Bill Wade for 220 yards. With two-to-one odds against him Joe started slow but made up the difference with his tremendous stride. For him winning was a simple matter of running faster once he got in high gear.

They then moved to Junction, Texas, where the fair was just beginning. There Painted Joe was matched against a fine race mare named Mae West who belonged to a deputy sheriff, John Cowan, Cuero, Texas. Mae West was a stylish little mare and hot on the tracks. Fame had not yet come to Joe, and Cowan and his backers thought that winning looked easy. But Painted Joe was undefeated and had no intention of changing his status that day. He took one look at the track and then went about the business of chalking up another win. Cowan, who had done a little bragging earlier, went away somewhat embarrassed and sold Mae West the next day.

Lay moved to Orange, Texas, in late 1941, and Givens and Low took Painted Joe to Gonzales to continue his conditioning and training. In January, 1942, Givens talked Lay into selling his spotted horse, and the ownership of Painted Joe was transferred to Givens for $375. Most of the race meets were getting underway in Arizona, and Givens and Low loaded up their new horse and another fleet-footed match horse, Little Joe, Jr., and headed for the Arizona tracks.

At Cortaro, Arizona, Painted Joe was matched against Betty Lou, a daughter of the famed Joe Bailey. Owned by Tom Clark, Betty Lou was a smooth, fast filly with quite a reputation. Givens diligently worked Joe toward the coming event and was justified when he daylighted the mare by three lengths. He knew that he had a prize package in his colt, but he sold him to Clark for $2,500, an amount that was pretty persuasive in those days.

Clark already had a match in mind for his new horse, a match that not every horse could hope to win. Painted Joe was put up against the 1941 World's Champion Quarter Running Horse, Clabber. Like good wine, Painted Joe was getting better and better with age. He proved it as he ran every inch of the way. He was too much for the "Iron Horse," and he outdistanced Clabber to the finish line, much to the delight of his owner and the spectators on the rail.

After racing under the joint ownership of Clark and Roy Adams, Painted Joe was sold to Vernon Goodrich, Maxwell, New Mexico, sometime in 1944 or early 1945. For years Goodrich was known in the Southwest as a tough bronc rider before he began handling race horses. He and his jockey took Joe to Oklahoma and matched him about nine times in the summer of 1945. As usual, when a horse gains a reputation for winning against all comers, it becomes harder and harder to get a race. The biggest rivalry of the season was the race at Lawton, Oklahoma, often called the "binder-twine affair." The contestants were Painted Joe, Grey Badger II, and Grey Eagle. Grey Badger II by Midnight, Jr., once held the world record for 220 yards and was a truly outstanding sprinter. It was the kind of race that was a real display of Painted Joe's talents. He exploded from the start, lined out like a rocket, and did not stop until he won the race over the two grey Quarter Horses by a good length.

Not convinced that a Paint Horse could actually outrun the favored Grey Badger II, his owner arranged a rematch between Joe and Grey Badger II. The first rematch turned out to be a "no race" when a mix-up occurred at the gates, although Joe was first to the finish line. A lot of money had been bet on this race, and it was rematched again, this time at Borger, Texas. Painted Joe was again first out of the gate and led all the way, to win by almost the same distance as the first race.

His fame had spread and developed into a virtual mystique,

making competition so scarce that Goodrich left for Chicago with Painted Joe. With luck he worked up a race against a Thoroughbred mare that was on a winning streak. When all the bets were made—and there were plenty of them—Goodrich had covered over three thousand dollars. The race was run the next day—but it proved to be Painted Joe's last. Running in extreme pain, he really had to put his heart into it. Blessed with incredible courage and great muscular powers, he passed the Thoroughbred mare at the quarter pole and held on to win the race. As he limped off the track, everyone knew that it was the end of a glorious track career for Painted Joe. He had pulled his hip down and could never run again.

Goodrich moved him back to Oklahoma, where he stood at stud for the next two years. In 1950 Goodrich sold the horse to John Jensen, Enid, Oklahoma, who kept him for stud until 1952 and then sold him to Tom Clark, Tucson. Sometime between 1952 and 1959 Clark sold him to Dave Miller, Mammoth, Arizona. As has been the case with a number of the more famous Quarter Horse stallions, Painted Joe met with an untimely and careless death. While on Miller's ranch he was turned out with a band of mares, and in the pasture he evidently ate some mesquite beans that had become toxic from the rains. And so it was that, at the age of twenty, the great Painted Joe died.[1]

By no means was Painted Joe infallible, for like all true campaigners he had his on and off days. Many of the horses he outran in turn beat him to the finish line. Of his countless number of races only those feats that are most vividly remembered were recounted here.

Painted Joe was a regular fixture at the Quarter race meets in 1942, 1943, and 1944 at the Moltacqua and Rillito tracks in

---

[1]Sam Ed Spence, "Painted Joe—The Spotted Man o' War," *Paint Horse Journal*, January–February, 1970, pp. 6–8, 14, 39, 40. Summarized in part by permission of the author, the American Paint Horse Association, and the *Paint Horse Journal*.

Arizona and at a few in California. While racing on AQRA tracks in 1944–45, he was owned by Vernon Goodrich, as listed in the 1945 *Year Book of the American Quarter Racing Association.*

Melvin Haskell, secretary of the old AQRA, wrote of Painted Joe in the 1943 *Racing Quarter Horses Year Book:*

> *Here is a most unusual thing—a Paint that can really run! His muscle is heavy and carried well down toward the hock— he looks like a horse that would run best a 3/8 mile. Strangely enough he is dynamite out of the gate and has won most of his races at distances under a quarter. He shares the Track Record for 300 yards.*

Lacking the conformation and grooming of today's Paint Horses with their aristocratic build and bearing, Painted Joe would provide no competition in any halter class. He was built for speed, and in that he was not lacking.

Officially rated AA (the top racing classification at that time, which would generally be equivalent today to a speed index in the 90's), Painted Joe outran many top Quarter Horses including—besides Clabber and Grey Badger II—Chicaro, Cowboy, Miss Bank, Squaw H, and Bartender. At the close of 1943 he was among the horses selected as the Top 20. To become one of these elite, a horse had to run the 440 within one second of the track record time or hold a track record at a shorter distance. The American Quarter Racing Association recognized a track record on a straightaway course, from a closed gate and a standing start. Painted Joe set his track record in 1942 as a three-year-old at the Moltacqua Track, Tucson, for 300 yards, catch weight, in :16.2.

The AQRA qualified a horse as either a Quarter Running Horse or a Celebrated American Quarter Running Horse according to his record on a recognized track. A horse classified in Grade A or better was considered a Celebrated American Quarter Running Horse, and his name was added to the Register of Merit.[2] Painted Joe ran in AA time officially at four distances, 300, 350, 400 and 440 yards, and is listed in the 1945 *Year Book and Register of Merit* of the American Quarter Racing Association as a Celebrated American Quarter Running Horse.

Best Times Recorded by Painted Joe

Yards	Time
220	:12.8 (track record, :12.6)
300	:16.2 (track record)
350	:18.6 (track record, :18.4)
400	:20.8
440	:22.8 (track record, :22.6)

In his lifetime Painted Joe must have sired hundreds of colts. Proper honor has never been given to him in the stud because so many of his get had no means of proving their parentage, and all his good colts that could be traced were gelded when young. During the 1940's and especially in the 1950's, after Joe was retired and used exclusively in the stud, he fathered a number of valuable colts. But Paint Horses were not then popular among most horsemen, and little effort was made to keep track of them or record their bloodlines. A few of the more fortunate colts went to men interested in good horses, no matter what their color, and most of his get that were foaled in the late 1950's and have been located are registered in the APHA.

Painted Joe's daughters have served as the link to the blood of this famous old horse. While most of them have produced progeny that are worthy of the family name, Babette is the mare whose influence is so great that she has often been called the *grande dame* of the Paint Horse breed.

A complete list of Painted Joe's get cannot be given for the reasons given above. Some of his known sons and daughters are

[2]Melville H. Haskell, *The Quarter Running Horse* (1945).

Painted Joe, Jr., Painted Joe's most famous son.

Babette, Painted Lydia, Geronamo, Painted Joe, Jr., Joe II, Jo
Jo V, My Joleen, Copper, Painted Model, Joe's Painted Girl,
Painted Beauty, Joe's Line Up, Joe's Painted Lady, Painted
Bess, Painted Jan, Painted Millie, Painted Breeze, Painted Bad-
ger, Cowboy's Painted Gal, Painted Three Bars, and Spotted
Lena.

Painted Joe, Jr.

Painted Joe, Jr., has been called a legend in his own time, and
rightly so, because the likes of him are seldom seen. He moved
into the spotlight as a young colt and through his seventeenth
birthday he was still running, defeating top horses, and doing it
in AAA time.

A sorrel tobiano gelding, Painted Joe, Jr., resembles his sire in many ways and inherited his quick burst of speed. He had every reason to be a good running horse: his dam was a dark bay race mare named Red Bird by the Thoroughbred Spearhead and out of an Oklahoma match race mare, Itchy.

Foaled in 1949 on the Cal Allison ranch near Ada, Oklahoma, Painted Joe, Jr., has lived his entire life there when he was not racing. For the first few years of his life he spent a lot of time in transit, moving from track to track. Complete records have not been kept on his races, track times, or total winnings. Because he is a Paint Horse, he was not allowed to run at most of the major tracks after the AQRA had been merged into the AQHA as its Racing Division. He was matched at the brush tracks or raced in open races at a few of the official tracks. Allison remembers that out of fifty-four races Painted Joe, Jr., won fifty and came in second in the other four.

He ran his first race as a four-year-old. It was a close match against a roping horse owned by Vance Runyan, Sulphur, Oklahoma. Painted Joe, Jr., came in second. After that disappointing start, he raced with almost 100 per cent success at tracks throughout Oklahoma, Texas, Kansas, and Missouri. Once clocked unofficially at Anadarko, Painted Joe, Jr., ran the 220 in :11.9, which would have broken the world record in quarter racing—220 yards in :12.1. His most spine-tingling race was the one he ran as a seventeen-year-old on September 12, 1965, at Ross Downs, Texas. He had always been good, and on this day the old campaigner set a new track record in AAA time for the 330 in :17.04.

At the age of twenty-one this immortal was still as fit and sound as ever when he entered the 350-yard event for three-year-old and older horses on June 21, 1970, at Eureka, Kansas. The seven-horse field was made up of three Paint Horses and four Appaloosas. After all the horses had crossed the finish line the Paint Horses took the win, place, and show positions. The ageless Painted Joe, Jr., was the sentimental favorite of the spectators as he broke the gates and led until the final strides.

Placing second over a field of three- and four-year-olds, he was beaten only by Flying Earl, an overo gelding owned by H. B. Johnson, Shreveport, Louisiana.

Joe II

Joe II was Painted Joe's 1943 son out of Anita by Ben Hur by Rainy Day. His second dam, Nellie Gray, was by the Thorough-bred Uncle Jimmy Gray. All combined, they gave him a pretty good background of speed. He was bred while Painted Joe was owned by Tom Clark, Tucson, Arizona, and was gelded as a yearling.

Joe II's track records were recorded at the Rillito Track, Tucson, where in 1947 he beat his sire's record for the 220 in the fast time of :12.5 (AA). He was good at the short distances and was not often raced at the 400 or quarter-mile. Earning a respectable name for himself and his sire, Joe II was awarded a Register of Merit from the American Quarter Racing Association in 1946.

Babette

The daughters and granddaughters of Painted Joe are among the finest producers of the breed. Babette, a 1944 foal, was a brown tobiano whose dam, a Thoroughbred, has been untraced. It was only natural that she should run, which she did with fair success. Although she held no records and was not regularly seen at AQRA tracks, she could cover the ground in good AA time matched horse against horse. After a number of years of racing she was retired and assigned an even more rewarding role in life. It is in the stud that she achieved the greatest glory, and, no matter how one measures her, on the track or as a producer of outstanding Paint Horses, she was in all respects a great mare.

While owned by Ralph Gardiner, Babette was bred to Sky-lark Bar by Three Bars in 1954 and 1955, and foaled Josy Bar

Babette, the grand matron of the Paint Horse breed, in a photograph taken when she was twenty years old.

and Jody Bar, two individuals that are counted among the best contributors of Paint Horse stock by the luster of their produce.

In 1958, bred to Skychief Bar, a full brother to Skylark Bar, Babette foaled Crazy Joe, a sorrel tobiano that was later gelded. The following year, 1959, she foaled another colt from Skychief Bar, who was given the name Only Chance. Because he did not color, he became a fair race horse on the quarter tracks in 1961 and 1962, earning a AA rating with the AQHA.

Later sold to Paul and Carolyn Crabb along with her two daughters, Josy Bar and Jody Bar, Babette was bred to Jet Dial in 1963 and the following year foaled her only other registered Paint foal, Painted Jewel. In 1965, Paul Harber, Jenks, Oklahoma, purchased Babette, Josy Bar, Jody Bar, and a grand-

Jody Bar, the good-producing daughter of Skylark Bar and Babette.

daughter, Sky Bar, who was out of Jody Bar and by Skychief Bar.

Josy Bar, Babette's 1955 foal, is described as a glossy chestnut tobiano, of adequate height and put together as well as any Quarter mare. She has no performance record, and with her excellent record of production none is needed. Her name in a horse's pedigree stands for true quality. Five proud sons and daughters that speak well for their dam are Bar Joe, foaled in

1963; Joechief Bar, foaled in 1964; Bon Bon, foaled in 1966; King Bee, foaled in 1967; and Merry Thought, foaled in 1971. Through 1973 her foals had won one Supreme Championship, three APHA Championships, eight Registers of Merit, and a total of 304 points. She was the Leading Dam of Halter Point Earners, Performance Point Earners and Register of Merit Qualifiers for three consecutive years and still retained the number position as Leading Dam of Halter Point Earners for the period 1966–73.

Jody Bar, a 1956 chestnut tobiano, has also done a magnificent job in the stud. Her first registered foal was Sky Bar in 1961, followed by Bright Bar in 1962, High Jinx in 1966, and Painted Fashion in 1968. Bright Bar was the National Champion Three-Year-Old Mare in 1965 and Painted Fashion, by Painted Jewel, is a Superior Halter Horse with over fifty halter points to her credit.

Babette died in 1966 of natural causes at the age of twenty-two. The production and personal accomplishments of this grand old mare and her daughters is documentary evidence of their value as broodmares. Their influence on the performance records of the Paint Horse breed will long be felt.

Painted Lydia

If an order of importance were to be established of Painted Joe's daughters, the second on the list would be Painted Lydia. She was a 1958 foal, a sorrel tobiano, and was out of a Quarter mare, R Q's Queen. Painted Lydia was a good-looking individual and was considered a tough calf-roping mare to beat in her younger days. Probably her top colt is Bang Up 2, the AAA winner of the Texas, Oklahoma, Kansas, and Colorado futurities in 1969. Other foals that have helped maintain her reputation by their superior performance are Painted Van (1960), Painted Bill (1961), and Miss Painted Ship (1964).

Painted Van, a very smooth, fast horse, left little to be desired as Painted Joe's grandson. He was a gelding owned by

A 1959 pasture scene of some daughters of Painted Joe with foals on the Robert Q. Sutherland Ranch, Kansas City, Missouri. Courtesy Robert Q. Sutherland.

C. A. Whitman, Jr., Carthage, Missouri, and was matched skillfully until his unexpected death in 1965. One of the most exciting races of his career was a match between Painted Joe, Jr., and Painted Van in 1964 at Pawhuska, Oklahoma. Even though Painted Joe, Jr., was the first to cross the finish line—and he no longer in his prime—it was the kind of race that was a real display of the Painted Joe talent.

Painted Lydia was purchased by Bang Up 2's owner, Dr. John Owens, in 1969, and was bred to his Quarter Horse, Joe Queen (AQHA 36,183), for a 1972 foal. Joe Queen, once owned by Audie Murphy, Hollywood, California, is AAAT rated and coholder of the two-year-old record for 330 yards, which he established in 1954.

19. **LITTLE NIP**

The pages of quarter-racing history are filled with names of great and exciting horses. A list of these equine stars reads like a list of *Who's Who* in the Quarter Horse world. In their midst from time to time have been some horses, rather lightly quarter-bred, which possessed practically all the most valuable traits of a Quarter Running Horse and showed consistent high class during their careers. Of course, a Quarter Running Horse was, in the beginning, any horse of early speed whose best distance was anything less than a half a mile. Most of these horses, at least by the time short-horse racing was organized, were called Quarter Horses regardless of their bloodlines. There were few that were *true* Quarter Horses and who got their speed without benefit of Thoroughbred blood.

One outstanding sprinter who had a natural endowment of running blood and yet was never looked upon as a "Quarter Horse" because of her color, was a little Paint Horse from Houston, Texas, known as Little Nip. She was bred by Harold Willy, Houston, and foaled in 1944.

Little Nip's sire was Whymefo, a chestnut Thoroughbred foaled in 1939, by Fortunate Youth by Lucky Hour and out of Palia by Prince Pal. Whymefo is not as famous a running horse or sire of short-horses as other Thoroughbreds. His pedigree is rich in the blood that has produced some fast long-distance horses, and he is deserving of more recognition for the good horses he sired by infusing this blood into a number of Quarter Horse mares. There were superb performers among his get, evidenced by the seven Register of Merit race colts bearing his mark of quality registered in the AQHA.

The dam of Little Nip was Hut Sut, a Paint mare who was somewhat short on stature, standing about thirteen hands. It would be hard for those who did not know her to believe that she was a better dam than her appearance would indicate. She was foaled in 1939 and died in late 1966 at the age of twenty-seven. Regrettably, her ancestry remains a mystery, but to judge from her produce record, she must have had some good breeding not too many generations back. By giving to the world two outstanding running horses and three producing daughters, she has passed the supreme test of her worth as a breeder.

Little Nip was Hut Sut's first foal. One year later, in 1945, she delivered Little Beaver. He was a solid chestnut without Paint Horse markings, by Kai Finn, a Thoroughbred tracing back to the imported Ogden. Little Beaver made his start on the AQRA tracks in 1947. His two-year-old record out of six starts was two wins, one second, two thirds, and one unplaced. Both wins were at 220 yards, and at Del Rio, Texas, on October 23 he defeated Flit and Booger H in :12.5, to be admitted to the Register of Merit.

Like his dam, Little Beaver was a small horse. The 1948 *Quarter Running Horse Yearbook* describes him in this manner: "He looks like a Shetland pony but he runs like a race horse." Although he may have lacked the size of other horses that dominated the field, he lacked neither courage nor spirit and was rated high up in his age division. Little Beaver, unbeatable at the short distances with catch weights, won three of his

Little Nip in 1947, when she was owned by W. W. Morrow. Courtesy Quarter Horse Journal.

starts in 1948, improved his time for the 220 to :12.4, and was rated AA at two distances.

Hut Sut has three daughters registered in the APHA. In 1957 she was bred to Three Bars and foaled Hut Sut Bars the following year for Maurice Martin, Pawhuska, Oklahoma. A good filly that did not color, she was registered as breeding stock with the APHA. Hut Sut Bars is the dam of two Register of Merit running Paint Horses, Boundin Hut Bars and Flash Thru Bars, full brothers by the thoroughbred Bounding Thru.

Hut Sut's 1959 foal was Miss Kitty, a bay tobiano filly by the Thoroughbred Black Sambo. She, too, is a good-producing broodmare who enriched Paint Horse racing with Johnny Osage, winner of the 1964 Oklahoma Paint Horse Futurity.

There is no complete record of all Hut Sut's produce. She was in her prime in the 1940's and 1950's, years before the APHA was organized, and pedigree records were not maintained. Only those foals that were later registered or performed on AQRA tracks are cited above.

Her first daughter, Little Nip, was a very racy-looking yearling. She grew into a streamlined, long-bodied filly of fine appearance with a good head and four clean, straight legs that appeared to be designed with speed in mind. Loudly marked with white, she had tobiano characteristics about the body and legs, but her bald face was a distinctive overo characteristic. In all probability, her dam, Hut Sut, carried both color genes, the result of earlier crossbreeding of Paint Horses in her background, because two of her daughters were registered tobianos and another, Hut Sut Bars, has produced two clearly marked overos by a solid Thoroughbred.

By the time Little Nip reached the recognized tracks in May, 1947, Willy had sold her to F. C. Davis, also of Houston, and she already had quite a reputation in East Texas as a match-race horse of incredible speed who could not be outrun at short distances.

In her first start at Del Rio on May 2, 1947, Little Nip finished second to Pep in a field of six horses three years old and up. She ran in AA time of :17.5 and pushed Pep to set a new track and world record for the 330 in :17.3.

On June 15, 1947, at Arrowhead Park, Houston, one of the treats of the day was a special matched race between Little Nip and Woven Web (also known as Miss Princess, the World Champion Quarter Running Horse of 1946–47, 1947, and 1948). Little Nip, trim and vibrant, ran extremely well, to come in second only to Woven Web, and once again she forced the winner to a new track record of :18.5 for the 350 yards.

In 1947 the Houston Paint, as Little Nip had become known, started six times on recognized tracks; she won two races, was second twice, and went unplaced twice. Before showing up at Albuquerque, New Mexico, on October 5, 1947,

Little Nip at Del Rio, Texas, October 26, 1947. She ran the 440 in AA time of :22.8 and defeated eight other top horses. D. Clark up. Courtesy Quarter Horse Journal.

she had been purchased by W. W. Morrow, who the following year became manager of Fairview Park Race Track in Alpine, Texas.

At Albuquerque, the little Paint, now accustomed to running with a field of horses, recorded her first win on a recognized track over ten other good A horses. One thing that could be said of Little Nip, "she sure could run pretty," and as she came in three lengths ahead of Albert H, Blue Stone, Wonder Lad, Gold Nuggett, Black Bessie, Cowboy Gypsy, Tony C, Little Rainy, Sug, and Texas Boy, she certainly looked pretty.

The Fall Meet in Del Rio got underway about the middle of October. Morrow entered Little Nip in only two races, one

Little Nip setting a new track record for 300 yards at Tucson as she defeats Badger's Grey Lady and Miss Panama on January 31, 1948. Courtesy Quarter Horse Journal.

for 250 yards and the other for 440. The first weekend she did not run her best and went unplaced as Texas, Jr., established a new track and association record.

In her second race, on October 26, 1947, Little Nip was back to her usual style and had quite a day running against some veterans in the quarter-mile race. She won by a length over Loretta D, Bob Shade, Liberty Girl, Mariposa, Hyglo, Jap, Free Silver, and Hoddy and established her best time for the 440-yard distance in :22.8, carrying 111 pounds' weight. Her time for this race was exceeded during the season by only one other three-year-old. At the close of 1947, Little Nip had the best record of any three-year-old filly and was admitted to the Register of Merit.

In 1948 she ran only two AQRA races and improved her time in each race. When she was ready to run, she gave it all she had and either won the race or forced whoever beat her to set a new track record. Another example of this was a 350-yard handicap at Tucson on January 18, 1948. Little Nip broke on top, as usual, and led for the first 220 yards, but Miss Steamship, a much larger and longer-striding mare, overtook Nip and won, driving in the last thirty yards. Little Nip's time of :18.3 beat the old record; however, Miss Steamship in a powerful finish was caught at :18.2 to take the win and establish a new track record. Also running and coming in third and fourth were B Seven and Miss Bank.

On January 31, 1948, Little Nip was entered in a handicap with Badger's Grey Lady and Miss Panama for 300 yards. If any one race stands out as the most memorable of her career, certainly it would be this one. It was a clean race run by three great Quarter running mares—but it was Little Nip all the way. Under the guiding hands of her jockey, the little Houston Paint who loved to run covered the 300 yards in the record time of :15.9, beating Badger's Grey Lady by a neck and Miss Panama by two lengths. She turned in a fine performance and established a new record at the Tucson track. As she limped off, it was feared that on this last day of January, 1948, Little Nip had run her final race. It was a thrilling one, yet a tragic one.

Best Times Recorded by Little Nip

Year	Track	Yards	Time	Rating
1947	Del Rio	330	:17.5	AA
1947	Del Rio	440	:22.8	AA
1948	Tucson Rodeo Grounds	350	:18.3	AA
1948	Tucson Rodeo Grounds	300	:15.9	AA (track record)

She was retired through the remainder of the year and was reported to be bred to Hard Twist. There is no record that she ever foaled, and since she showed up at the track in 1949 for one race, it is believed that she did not produce a colt. The *Quarter Running Horse Yearbook* for 1949 lists Little Nip with one start, but in all probability she no longer had her form, and her career as a race horse ended when she pulled up lame the year before.

Little Nip met many of the great short-horses at one time or another and defeated most of them, sometimes more than once. She was victorious over Miss Bank, winner of the 1947 New Mexico State Championship; she defeated Miss Panama, holder of the World Record for 330 yards and winner of the 1948 Speed Championship at Tucson; and she outran B Seven, holder of two track records in 1948.

In 1947 Little Nip and Little Beaver were in different age divisions; however, if Little Nip had been able to run in 1948, this brother and sister might have had the opportunity to meet on the track. Both of them were fast breakers and good at short distances. Who knows which head might have pushed over the finish line first?

Badger's Grey Lady, a prominent race horse around the tracks for four or five years, had the misfortune to meet with Little Nip and Little Beaver on separate occasions. Each time she tasted the dust from the heels of Hut Sut's two offspring, losing by a neck in each case. In fact, the Grey Badger horses have always lost out to Paint Horses. Badger's Grey Lady's sire, Grey Badger II, tried three times to take Painted Joe, and it just could not be done.

Little Nip was a great performer who ran with her heart in it all the way. Although her career was short, she did much to enhance the reputation of Paint Horses as running horses and proved that there were some worthy of the title Quarter Running Horse.

20 **FAST TIME**

Few Paint Horses were running on the short-horse tracks from 1930 through 1940. Of this small number only one or two achieved any distinction to be rated among the best performers. Paint Horses generally were not looked upon with much favor and were seldom given a chance to prove their ability. Those that did get to the tracks and gave a good account of themselves in defeating some high-class Quarter Horses were never forgotten by those that came in second best.

A Paint Horse standing out as one of the all-time greats was Fast Time, a brilliantly colored sorrel overo gelding whose performance was in keeping with his name.

Foaled in 1930, Fast Time was raised in Mullins, Texas, by a man known only as Kemp. He was purchased as a three-year-old by Oscar Schnaubert, Hobbs, New Mexico, his owner-trainer for the six years he raced, from 1933 through 1939.

Fast Time was sired by Fleeting Time, a chestnut Thoroughbred by High Time by Ultimus. His dam was a Paint mare whose ancestry was never known for certain. She apparently

Fast Time, in a typical finish, winning a $10,000 race at Caliente, Mexico, April 23, 1939.

never raced but was a producer of running horses, having foaled three colts by different Thoroughbreds, and all three were good race horses.

Fast Time's sire, Fleeting Time, gained recognition in the Southwest as the sire of Nellene, who produced Joe Reed II, the 1943 World's Champion Quarter Running Stallion. Through 1934 Fleeting Time's sire, High Time, had sired the winners of 1,127 Thoroughbred races with total earnings of over $1.54 million. He was the leading sire in 1928; the leading sire of juveniles in 1927, 1928, 1932; and the second-leading sire in 1933. His most valuable colt was High Strung, the leading money earner of 1928, who won $153,900 that year and established a track record for the Pimlico Futurity, running the mile in 1:39.

Fleeting Time's dam was British Fleet by another standout Thoroughbred, Great Britain. Even though some may feel that he was lightly bred on his dam side, with such good blood coming from his sire, it is no surprise that Fast Time was a horse of great courage and tremendous speed.

Before Schnaubert purchased Fast Time in 1933, he had a sorrel, bald-faced horse named Little Wonder that was a pretty fair roping and dogging horse. Because of a lengthy illness Schnaubert was unable to ride Little Wonder for some time. He happened to be at a small show one day when some of the boys got up a match race. He entered Little Wonder, never anticipating that the horse could respond with any amount of speed. The little horse burned up the grass and won the race handily, to Schnaubert's jubilation. After this first good showing, Little Wonder was raced all over the country and was never outrun.

"We must have run Little Wonder twenty or thirty times," recalled Schnaubert, "and one day Cecil Locklear, my jockey, commented that he didn't know of a single horse that could outrun 'Wonder' unless it was a Paint Horse his dad was training at Goldthwaite, Texas. I laughed at Cecil, but decided we ought to have a look; so the next day we hooked up my trailer (just in case) and drove to Goldthwaite."[1]

It was a fateful trip, because Schnaubert had the opportunity to see Fast Time run, and he looked pretty terrific doing the quarter of a mile in 23 flat carrying 138 pounds.

Fast Time was a colorful, well-formed horse, not lacking in size or energy. He stood about 15.2 and weighed a trim 950 pounds in racing condition, which is the condition Schnaubert kept him in while he owned him. Speed was evident in his conformation: he had a long belly, trim feet and legs, and flat muscle, plus good wind and a good stride.

The price on him was $500. Taking a long second look, Mr. Schnaubert reached into his pockets and started counting. After he was settled in his new home, what could be more natural than to match the Paint Horse against Wonder? In a fast sprint amid no fanfare Fast Time outran Wonder—just as he did most other horses he met for the next six years.

[1]Oscar Schnaubert, "Fast Time," *Paint Horse Journal*, March–April, 1967.

Schnaubert, now convinced he could put Fast Time on the tough ones, loaded him up and drove to Seguin. This is how he described Fast Time's first race:

His first hard race was run in Seguin, Texas, in November of that [1933] year. He looked like a cinch to win, going three-eights of a mile, his odds were good. He closed at eighteen to one, and I put five hundred dollars on his nose.

He left the gate in front and opened five lengths in the first quarter, then broke down and came in third. I lost the five hundred dollars and he walked on three legs all the way to the barn. I couldn't lead him from the stall for four days and he was lame for five months. At that time I broke him to the stock saddle, for he had never been ridden off of a race track or with a stock saddle. When he was well I started racing him again. I froze his foot with Menthol Crystals and Ether. He ran better and faster and was never badly lame again."[2]

Schnaubert began touring the country with Fast Time and winning races from then on. Before taking him to New Mexico and California, he raced him across the state of Texas, in Pecos, Odessa, Junction, Sonora, Fort Stockton, Alpine, and any other town that had a track. His injury of the previous November did not slow him down, and his form seemed better than ever. He was the fastest horse Schnaubert had ever trained and the fastest horse that a number of the competitors ever met.

Since no track records were kept, only a guess can be made of the number of races Fast Time won. Chances are good that the number would be in the hundreds.

In 1937, Schnaubert and Fast Time went to California. Schnaubert said:

I matched him nineteen times from Visalia, California, to Caliente, Old Mexico. I lost one race in Visalia, California.

[2]Oscar Schnaubert, "Fast Time," *Texas and Southwestern Horseman,* March, 1964.

If a horse ever beat him I would match the race over and win.

He ran a match race with a horse owned by the president of the bank of Mexicali, Mexico. I won about eighteen hundred dollars that day.

I matched him against a horse called Pure Gold in Kent, Texas, once. The horse was from El Paso; the match was a quarter mile, lap and tap, for thirty-five hundred dollars. I imagine that ten or fifteen thousand dollars changed hands that day.

Running out of competition in Mexico, Fast Time and Schnaubert started home. On the road to Prescott, Arizona, Fast Time was seriously injured when, owing to a quick stop, the horse in the rear of the trailer slid into him. The frightened Fast Time jumped out of the trailer and cut an eighteen-inch gash in his stomach. The cut was sewed up and treated by a veterinarian, and after a three month's rest Fast Time had healed completely.

By that time he had gained himself such a deadly reputation that no one would challenge him in a match race. His consistent speed made him a legendary figure, and the names Oscar and Fast Time were well-known by all short-horse racing men.

Fast Time must have been guilty of poor behavior on occasion. Schnaubert said, "He was pretty mean sometimes and I would have to ear him down to put a jockey up on him." He was willing and courageous, but never a horse that could be pushed around.

Fast Time could run any distance from 200 yards to a half-mile and broke track records at all distances. On one occasion he was even matched against an automobile for 300 yards and won. He was hard to lap and tap in most races but perfect out of a gate. In fact, he was never beaten away from a gate.

Schnaubert has said that Fast Time won over $100,000 during his six-year track career. His richest race was the $10,000 match at Caliente, Mexico, on April 23, 1939, a lap and tap on a polo field for 400 yards, which he won in twenty-two seconds flat.

Late in 1939, Schnaubert sold Fast Time for $1,000. He went to Arizona and in his later years was ridden after cattle around Yuma. He had become crippled in the hind ankle and was too badly lamed to run.

At the time Fast Time was racing there was no AQRA and no AA or AAA ratings. Those who knew him well say that he could run in AAA time and would have earned the top rating if he had raced in later years.

21 CALAMITY JANE

Cutting horses do not have to be large horses, nor do they need a long line of excellent bloodlines. One of the best all-around cutting horses was Calamity Jane, a little mare who stood close to fourteen hands and looked as if she weighed no more than 950 to 1,000 pounds. She made up for any lack of size with her determination and special flair for working cattle.

Bred by Ira Riley, Snyder, Texas, Calamity Jane was foaled in 1949. When registered in the APSHA, her sire was given as Pal by Joe Clegg (AQHA 419). This may be an error in listing, for the AQHA *Registry* indicates that the registration number 419 is "George Clegg, dun horse, foaled 1939, bred by Bert Benear, Tulsa, Oklahoma; owned by Benny Binion, Dallas, Texas."[1] George Clegg was by Tommy Clegg by Sam Watkins by Hickory Bill. His dam was Lady Coolidge by Yellow Jacket— all good foundation Quarter Horse stock. Riley later said that Calamity Jane's sire was a Palomino stud raised by Binion, but

[1]*Official Stud Book and Registry of the American Quarter Horse Association*, Vol. 1.

after twenty-five years he could not remember the horse's name.

Doyle Riley, one of Ira Riley's sons, says that Calamity Jane's granddam on her sire's side was known around Snyder as Sweatpea. She too was quality quarter-bred and was by a dun horse owned by Doyle Riley's uncle. On the subject of Calamity Jane's bloodlines he could add nothing more, other than that he knew she came from some good-blooded stock that had a solid background of association with cattle and that she lived up to her heritage because she "took to livestock like a duck takes to water."

Calamity Jane's dam was a stock-type black tobiano mare, who some say came into Texas from New Mexico. Like so many other Paint Horses of that time when no records were kept, her bloodlines cannot be traced. Very likely she had some infusion of Quarter Horse blood, for she bore a striking resemblance in her general conformation to this breed. Ira Riley could not shed any light on her parentage. He said that he traded with a county judge for her when she was still a fairly young mare for the "kiddos" to ride to school and never thought too much about her pedigree.

It has been difficult to trace with any safe degree of accuracy the ancestry of a large number of the earliest Paint Horses, particularly the Paint mares. While most breeders of twenty and thirty years ago were quite selective in their breeding practices, they were not record keepers. The sire, his sire, and his grandsire were known in most instances, but little attention was given to the maternal side of a horse's pedigree. The lack of historical information on the lineage of many individuals has caused confusion among breeders and has perplexed those who rely on some genetic basis for planning their breeding programs.

The black-and-white mare, who later became Calamity Jane's dam, was, according to Riley, "a wonderful mare. She showed breeding and good color." He continued:

She was the mother of eight colts, all Paints but one—three fillies and five horse colts. I kept two of her colts, a bay and

a black, which were her third and fifth colts. Both of them
were good cutters out of a roundup. I know of one other colt
that was entered in contests. His name was the Riley Paint
and he was owned by D. M. Cagdell, Clairmont, Texas.

Calamity Jane's dam was not only a good broodmare but
also a good horse under saddle. She had a gentle spirit and an
easy rein, two characteristics that were sufficient to endear her
to the Riley family, especially the children. She could be ridden
by anyone, whether working around the ranch or carrying the
younger Rileys to school. Fortunately, she passed on her gentle
disposition and easy handling qualities to most of her foals.

In 1949, Riley moved from Texas to South Dakota. When
he left, he gave Calamity Jane, a young filly then, and her
mother to his grandson to raise. About two years later, in
another horse trade, she went to Gerald Hart, a Texas horseman who has spent a good part of his life saddling some of the
really good ones. He broke her out to the stock saddle and
started her in cutting. From the time he first put her after livestock, the gifted little mare appeared to know all about cows
and how to handle them. When she was three years old, Hart
began showing her in National Cutting Horse Association
competition.

One of the first real cutting-horse men to own Calamity
Jane was Bob Burton, who was then living at Arlington and now
lives in Mansfield, Texas. He tried to buy her from Gerald Hart
for one thousand dollars after seeing her work in a show at San
Antonio. Hart was willing to sell, but he must have had a better
offer than Burton's because he let H. R. Burden, Ennis, Texas,
have her instead and even delivered her to Burden's ranch.

Not too many months later Bob Burton got another opportunity. He said:

It was sometime late in 1954 and I was buying cattle at the
time when Mr. Burden told me about a little Paint mare he
had that he sure would like to sell to me. I already knew the

Pony Express Relay Station, *by R. E. Carothers. The original is in the BMA Tower Collection, Business Men's Assurance Company, Kansas City, Missouri.*

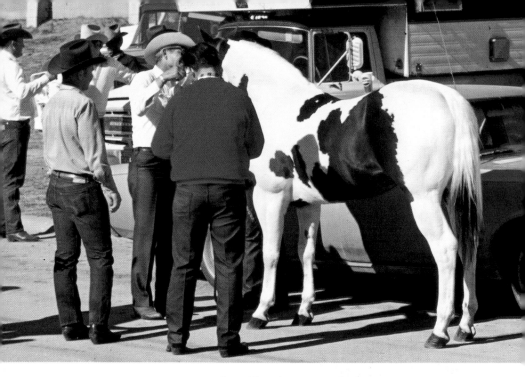

A stallion inspection.

Quarter Horse broodmares with Paint foals.

Copper Bar—a typical American Paint Horse by a registered Quarter Horse (Half Bar) and out of a cropout, registered Paint mare (Copper Penny). Photograph by Bob Bullard.

Mares and foals in a pasture on the Doug Edwards Ranch, Ryan, Oklahoma.

The overo color pattern—Bandit's Squaw.

The tobiano color pattern—Cherokee War Chief.

Strawberry Lasan, a horse with blue (glass) eyes.

A cropout Paint Horse—Wildfire by Flit Bar (AQHA), dam Bar V Fanny (AQHA).

Rhett Butler, holder of three high-point trophies

from the National Cutting Horse Association.

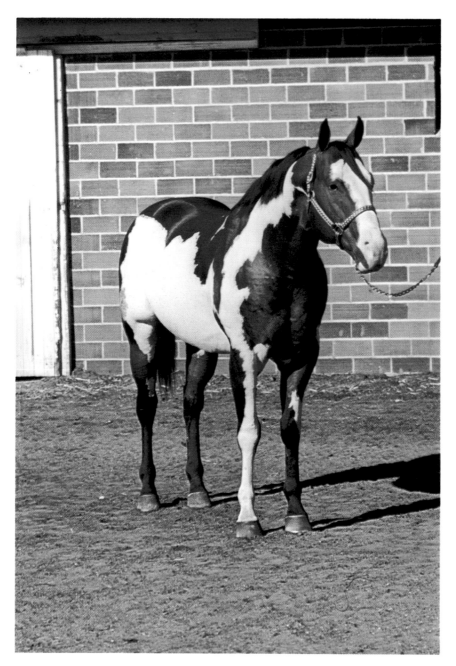

Flying Fawago by Yendis (AQHA) and out of Tango Scooter (AQHA).

218

Tinky's Spook executing a perfect stop in a reining pattern.

Bang Up II, a AAA Paint Running Horse.

Saddling for the 1970 Texas Paint Horse Maturity.

Powder Charge (AAAT), winner of all four major futurities in 1967.

Yellow Mount, leading sire of APHA Supreme Champions.

221

Spoiler, leading money earner in Paint Horse racing from 1966 through 1973.

Painted Lasan, Double R Ranch, McKinney, Texas.

Joechief Bar, a Supreme Champion.

Skippa Streak.

mare he was talking about and I knew she had not been win-
ning much. Since I had seen her after cattle, I figured she
wasn't being worked right and took her on home with me. It
didn't take long to find out how to get along with her and
where everyone had been making mistakes.

Bob Burton was a cutting-horse trainer in the best sense of
the word. Perhaps the outstanding Quarter Horse that he trained
and became famous in the NCHA was Hollywood George—or
it may have been Nancy Bailey, depending on who is doing the
reminiscing. There was a special kind of relationship between
Burton and a cutting horse. He could make a fair cowhorse out
of any animal that showed even the slightest interest in cattle.
Although he rode Calamity Jane very little—his daughter Judy
at the age of thirteen took over the riding and showing—he had
spent enough time with her to make her a top performer.

With few exceptions all the great cutting horses have had
available to them the best possible training. Training alone,
however, cannot make a top cutting horse. Other essential
characteristics are necessary: intelligence is one; performance
is another, and the right kind of conformation is yet another.
Calamity Jane possessed an abundance of all these qualities.
She had a kindly disposition and more intelligence than some
human beings. She was quick and easily learned what was expected of her. She had the maneuverable speed for rapid
changes in pace and direction. She could dodge as sharply as
any calf, and it was evident that cow savvy was bred into her
because she knew her business. And, her conformation—sound
legs and feet, strong back and croup, and alert ears—was one
of her greatest assets in working cattle.

Many cowhorses have all the above qualifications, and
yet Calamity Jane was somehow different from all of them. Her
size, naturally, put her in a different class, and her color sepa-
rated her from other horses. She was a beautiful tobiano,
sporting a rich black-and-white coat and four almost identical
white stockings to her knees in front and to her hocks in back.

The kind of cutting horse a trainer dreams about riding, Calamity Jane had class, action, and plenty of color.

Among the ranks of Paint Horse performers few have known overnight success. Calamity Jane began cutting in 1952, ten years before formation of the APHA, and was only allowed in open cutting-horse competition of the NCHA. The AQHA did not permit unregistered Quarter Horses to compete in registered cutting contests even though NCHA rules were used. She was shown for nearly three years in NCHA competition, but she was not regularly a winner. Then, after her purchase by Burton, she suddenly moved into the spotlight. By 1956 she had won some of the largest shows, including the ones at Vernon, Dallas, Hallettsville, Fort Worth, Odessa, and Tucson.

Burton remembers the Tucson show well:

> *The purse was an unusually large one and horses were plentiful. Little Calamity put on one of the finest cutting exhibitions that most of us ever witnessed. Her talents really came together at Tucson. She won a first and a third and paid for a new in-line trailer on that one trip.*

He recalls another of her spectacular feats, a matched cutting against Hollywood George following a show in Fort Worth:

> *Edgar Brown who owned Hollywood George wanted to match them and he got covered pretty quick with some good-sized bets. There are people who doubt the ability of a Paint Horse on the grounds that they are a Paint Horse. In my opinion, both horses were remarkable. I had ridden and trained them both. Some believed Hollywood George was the best cutting horse of his day, and to tell the truth he was good. Calamity, though, was developed to a peak of perfection. Her performance when she won the match was her best. She proved, at least in this case, that the qualities of a great performer are not affected by color.*

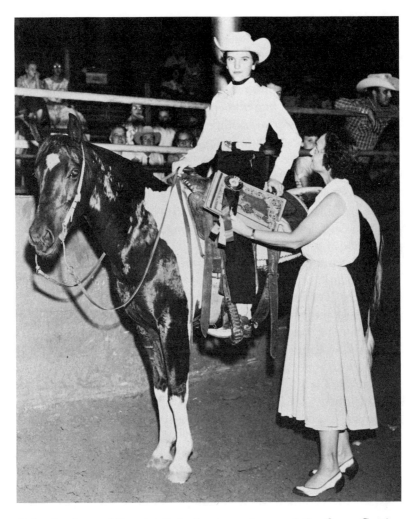

Calamity Jane, ridden by Judy Burton, winner of the Open Cutting Horse Contest, Dallas, Texas.

In 1957, Calamity Jane led the nation for the first nine months, but owing to illness in Burton's family he could not enter her in competition the last three months, and at year's end she was in sixth position among the leading money earners for 1957. She was awarded the NCHA Certificate of Annual Achievement #237 for her entrance into the Top Ten and received the bronze award in 1957 for having won in excess of $10,000 in contests approved by the NCHA.

In 1960 she was the recipient of the Silver Award from the NCHA for earnings in excess of $20,000. The bronze and silver awards are bestowed upon horses for money won in National Cutting Horse Association Approved or Championship Cutting Horse contests only. Calamity Jane had earnings of $20,369.73 at the end of her ninth year in cutting competition.

About 1959, Burton sold Calamity Jane to an Allen Riley, Refugio, Texas (not the Riley from Snyder who had bred her). Riley in turn, let Edgar Brown, Orange, Texas, have her. Then she came into the ownership of Tommy Arhopulos, Bryan, Texas, who later registered her with the APHA. Arhopulos, a skillful hand with a cow pony, was riding some of Brown's horses at the time. He knew a lot about horse sense from his wide experience in their handling. There was no question in his mind that she was one of the best cutting horses in the country that could be purchased, even at twelve years of age. So, he bought her.

In 1962 with her new owner she was one of four Texas cutting horses to fly to Washington, D.C., and then to San Francisco to compete in two of the biggest cutting-horse events. On October 21 at the Municipal Airport in Phoenix, Arizona, Cutter Bill, Mertz Scooter, Cha Cha Frisco, all owned by Rex Cauble, Crockett, Texas, and Calamity Jane were loaded into their custom-built stalls on the plane. The following day they arrived in Washington, D.C., where they participated in the NCHA Championship Cutting at the International Horse Show. It was the first time that western horses and cutting horses were included in the horse show, and all four of the Texas horses made it to the cutting finals.

In order not to miss the world-famous cutting show at the Cow Palace, the quartet of horses boarded for San Francisco on October 25. Arriving in San Francisco in top condition, they took part in the Grand National Livestock Exposition, and Cutter Bill won the cutting event.

When the American Paint Stock Horse Association was organized in 1962, Calamity Jane was the first mare registered in the association, and was given the number APSHA 21 (the first twenty numbers were reserved for stallions).

Soon after its organization, the APSHA became affiliated with the National Cutting Horse Association for the purpose of recognizing and rewarding Paint Horses of outstanding cutting ability. For her fine performance in 1962, 1963, and 1964 Calamity Jane won the first three National Cutting Horse Association affiliate trophy awards presented by the APSHA as the High Point registered Paint Stock Horse in approved NCHA contests.

In 1963, at fourteen years of age, Calamity Jane won over $1,100, ending her career in 1964 with two more shows. Her accumulated lifetime earnings total $24,591.16 in NCHA open and championship cutting contests.

The last honor bestowed upon this little champion was to be selected the first Paint Cutting Horse in the National Cutting Horse Association Hall of Fame. The most apropos summation of her worth as a cutting horse was made by Burton when he said, "She was the biggest little mare that ever hit Texas."

Having a magnificent career behind her, Calamity Jane retired to the Arhopulos ranch in Bryan. In 1971, at twenty-two years of age, she looked as good and as sound as ever. She had been bred the year before and produced a perfectly formed colt, but it died the day it was born. This was the only colt she had ever foaled, and Arhopulos bred her back with the hope that in 1972 she would bring a colt so the memory of Calamity Jane would forever live on. At this point in her life, however, Calamity Jane was unable to raise a foal. Although she hardly fulfilled expectations as a broodmare that her admirers hoped, there is still a feeling of respect for a great mare, and she is living out her remaining years in peace and tranquillity on the grassy pastures of the Arhopulos Ranch.

22 WAHOO KING

If a Hall of Fame for Paint Horses were to be established, one of the first names to be entered therein should be that of a truly great roping horse, Wahoo King. Those who have seen him work have said that he possessed the finest action of any roping horse of his time. To quote the man who owned him most of his life and rode him all the way to the top, Junior Robertson, "He was the best roping horse I ever owned."

Robertson, Waurika, Oklahoma, is a man who admires good horses, no matter what their color. Despite the fact that back in the 1950's, when Paint Horses were scoffed at, he always had a few around his barn and one a little finer than most that he used roping and dogging. A pretty well-known rodeo contestant in the Rodeo Cowboys' Association at the time, Robertson would take some guffawing about his Paints, but when he rode again and again into the prize money, those who "horse-laughed" would have to agree that his pony always did his part.

For quite a few years Robertson roped off a Paint gelding

he called Agate. He says that Agate was a real horse under saddle. He worked some of the major rodeos and won most of his money on the back of the big Paint. Robertson had a lot of confidence in Agate, and when the horse became crippled, he started looking around for another Paint Horse to replace him. One winter day in late 1958, as he was driving by Charles Champion's Quarter Horse ranch north of Ardmore in good Oklahoma horse country, he found just the horse. There in the corral was a sorrel overo yearling about sixteen or seventeen months old with the solid build that most ropers look for in a roping prospect.

The yearling colt, later named Wahoo King, came from good Quarter Horse foundation stock. His sire, Illini King (AQHA 43,195), a King Ranch–bred horse, was a reliable cowhorse and a good sire of working and performing horses. Among his get are three AQHA Champions and eight ROM Arena Quarter Horse colts.

The mare who foaled Wahoo King in 1957 became known a few years later in the APHA as Pocohontas. She was supposedly of Oklahoma Star breeding, but the identity of her sire and dam could not be learned. Af first glance she did not appear to be a show animal, but a good horseman would note that she had plenty of quality all the way through. She had an extremely good head, a long hip, and a lot of breeding from somewhere. She was the right kind of mare for the job she had to do, and as a breeder she improved the quality of American Paint Horse stock by the excellence of her produce. Her registered Paint foals include three National Champions: Wahoo King, J Bar Junior, and C-Note; and three others equally well bred: Shady Lane, J Bar's Day Money, and J's Johnny Reb. In 1966, J Bar Junior and C-Note stood side by side to win for Pocohontas the title of National Champion Produce of Dam.

On the day that Robertson stopped to look at Wahoo King, he tried his best to buy the colt and his mother. Unfortunately, the two Paint Horses belonged to Mrs. Champion, and she had no desire to sell them at that time. The gelding was being

Wahoo King, 1957–67. Photograph by James Cathey.

trained to become her personal mount, and the mare had been bred to one of the Champion's Quarter Horse stallions.

At that time Wahoo King was a colt with plenty of size and a lot of character. He had the muscling and good forelegs that were essential to a rope horse for increased stability when stopping and turning at any rate of speed.

Being unable to purchase the two Paint Horses, Robertson bought a Quarter Horse gelding named Tehuacana. He was a well-made individual that had won Grand Champion at several AQHA shows. Not completely satisfied with his horse, because he still yearned to own the young Paint Horse at Ardmore, Robertson worked with Tehuacana to get him ready to haul.

But, as luck would have it, the following spring, in 1959, Charles Champion rode over to the Robertson ranch to talk up a horse trade. It seems that the Paint gelding was "too much horse" for Mrs. Champion to ride. "He was one of those nervous, alert kind of horses," said Robertson, "and it just takes time with a horse like that." The trade was made on the spot— Champion's two Paint Horses for Robertson's Quarter Horse gelding.

With the horse tradin' complete, Wahoo King was moved to Waurika. He spent an easy first summer at the ranch; he was ridden just a little then turned out in the pasture until October. By fall it was time for him to earn his oats and hay. There is no discounting the importance of good breeding and good training to get a top rope horse; both are essential. When working the rodeos, a cowboy is competing for money and he wants a horse under him that he can depend on, one that knows his business during the strenuous competition.

To get the training he needed, Wahoo King was sent up to Herb Dalton's ranch at Duncan, Oklahoma. There were few hours of idleness here and no pampered horses either. After several months of breaking from the box, following a running calf, perfecting the stop, and working the rope, Wahoo King showed his true ability. Because he had, among other things, split-second coordination and a quick-breaking speed, he easily developed into a good rope horse. Robertson has said, "He had such terrific power and speed coming out of the box he was sometimes hard to ride." It took a real rider to stay aboard when he broke, and in the business of roping calves a quick break was as important as a fast tie.

Wahoo King was introduced to the rodeo in the spring of 1960. Time after time as he came off the field covered with lather and arena dust, he appeared to be as much at home as he was back at the ranch. His performance was conclusive evidence of his sound quality and good training.

In 1962, when the American Paint Stock Horse Association was getting started, Wahoo King was entered in every show that was held. When he went to a calf roping, he wore his everyday work clothes. Underneath, though, was an over-all high-class quality of Paint Horse with a beautiful show-ring conformation. At halter he always stood first in his class, and, with the exception of the 1960 Fort Worth Livestock Show, he was Grand Champion Gelding at every show he attended. In 1964 he became a National Champion by taking the Aged Gelding class at Hutchinson, Kansas.

Robertson showed and roped on Wahoo King until the middle of February, 1965, when he sold him to Monroe Tumlinson, Lampasas, Texas, another of the formidable RCA calf ropers. The two cowboys had known each other for years and were friendly competitors at most of the rodeos. Although he had never actually roped on Wahoo King, Tumlinson valued his competence and only two days after he bought him won a second in the day money in the calf-roping event at the San Antonio Livestock Exposition and Rodeo.

In 1966, Tumlinson, riding Wahoo King, finished as one of the RCA's Top Ten ropers. Therefore, the final proof of whether or not he was a real rope horse was disclosed in his last full year of rodeo competition.

Another world champion roper four-time runner up, Glen Franklin, rode the Paint while Tumlinson owned him, and he, too, won a great deal of money every time he stepped into the

Wahoo King and Monroe Tumlinson, Fort Madison, Iowa, Rodeo, 1965. Photograph by Ferrell Butler.

saddle. Franklin has ridden a number of good horses on hundreds of rodeo fields and is a qualified judge of rope horses. His admiration for Wahoo King was plainly expressed when he said that he would liked to have owned him himself.

The year 1967 looked like another championship year for Tumlinson, until the day Wahoo King suffered a fatal injury as he shot out of a roping box. Like most great horses Wahoo King was an ideal blend of performance, conformation, courage, and personality. He was an authentic representative of the breed and, for certain, one of the best rope horses of all time.

PART V **THE GREAT SIRES**

23 MISTER J. BAR

Years ago when man began breeding and raising horses, he designated horses of exceptional ability as "great" horses. Today there are many "great" horses, but what measurements are used to determine the degree and quality of greatness? Only comparisons of a horse's general physical qualities, his performance or running ability, and his sire records with those of other horses can determine the degree of greatness.

Generally speaking, a Paint Horse of good blood, conformation, and disposition that has made a contribution to the APHA record books through his personal performance ability and has produced excellent progeny that have likewise proved successful at performance or racing is a great horse. He becomes a great sire by producing good horses out of mediocre mares and superior ones from good mares.

All the modern Paint Horse sires represented in this chapter are great sires and important contributors to the Paint Horse breed. They are worthy individuals of some of the finest Quarter Horse and Thoroughbred blood and have sired champion working, running, and performance horses. These celebrated sires, whose names appear in so many pedigrees of honored present-day horses, will always be remembered as prominent foundation sires of the Paint Horse breed.

An article in the *Ranchman* stated the following:

> *In the beginning of any venture there always must be someone who is first. Junior Robertson, Waurika, Oklahoma, probably comes nearer being the first breeder of American Paint Stock Horses than any person that could be mentioned. When Rebecca Tyler first conceived the idea of an American Paint Stock Horse Association, the first person she turned to for advice and encouragement was Junior Robertson, because she knew of his great admiration for the Paint Stock Horse and because he bred them and rode them and rodeoed on Paint Horses when he bore the brunt of much good natured kidding by the other contestants.*[1]

One of the most successful Paint Horse breeders of the country and a remarkable exhibitor of fine Paint Horses, Robertson spent many years calf roping and bulldogging with the RCA. He owns a service station and restaurant at the junction of Highways 81 and 70 just east of Waurika. His place of business, known as "Junior's," is a gathering place for horsemen—a place to eat, swap gossip, and catch up on the latest horse news. One mile east of the truck stop is the Robertson Ranch, complete with paddocks, working arena, and grounds. It is here that one can meet Mister J. Bar, a sorrel overo stallion whose name appears on the top sire line of a large number of the finest Paint Horses.

Mister J. Bar was bred by J. W. Kromer, Vinson, Oklahoma, and foaled in 1961. His sire, Jamina Pondfly 2 (AQHA 98,924) was by Pondfly by Pondie. Pondfly was out of Shielfly by Blackburn (AQHA 2,228). Most breeders of Paint Horses

---

[1]"Junior Robertson—First of the Paint Stock Horse Breeders," *Ranchman*, August, 1962, pp. 21–22.

and Quarter Horses will recognize this side of Mister J. Bar's pedigree as some of the best Waggoner breeding. For years the 3D Waggoner Ranch, of Arlington and then of Vernon, Texas, bred, raised, and owned good-blooded stock that had the know-how to do more or less everything asked of them.

Jamina Pondfly 2 was foaled out of Jamina Adair (AQHA 25,564), whose sire, King George, was a grandson of the Old Sorrel, the foundation sire of the King Ranch.

The dam of Mister J. Bar is Minnie, a Paint mare who goes back to Three Bars and Joe Reed (AQHA P-3). Her sire, Iron Bars, is a AAA son of Three Bars and is a AAA producer of AQHA running horses. His get have done equally well at the horse shows, as evidenced by the six AQHA champions he sired through 1971.

Minnie's dam, a Paint mare, is distinctly remembered by many old-timers as one of Joe Reed's fastest daughters. In all respects she had every right to be a good track performer, for the blood of Joe Blair (a Thoroughbred) and Della Moore was preserved in her through her sire.

In 1959, Minnie had foaled Squaw Man, a sorrel overo with a solid athletic body and over-all smooth lines. One of the top geldings around at that time, he won Grand Champion Gelding at the Fort Worth Livestock Show in 1967 and 1969 and Reserve National Champion Senior Gelding at the 1967 National Show. He is an APHA Champion and was the high-point gelding and reining horse in both Texas and Oklahoma in 1968.

Robertson purchased Mister J. Bar in 1963. After making a deep and close study of the breeding and performance records of Mister J. Bar and his ancestors, he was convinced that this stallion's blood would be of everlasting beneficial influence to the Paint Horse breed. Even when he was a two-year-old colt he had the ingredients of greatness that became manifest as the years unfolded.

Mister J. Bar is a dignified and alert individual who inspires both affection and admiration in those who have seen him and

Mister J. Bar. Photograph by Margie Spence.

have competed against him. He is an artful blending of conformation and performance, and he cut quite an appearance at Paint Horse shows. He looked like a halter horse, which he was; and he performed like a true rope horse, for which he was exactly suited. He had the quick breaking speed, the smoothness of action, and split-second coordination, with a pro to teach him the mechanics. For reasons very clear he was spectacularly successful.

When asked about Mister J. Bar's ability, Robertson had this to say: "Mister J. Bar came to this earth with cow in him. He's probably the best scoring horse that I ever rode. I can't remember him ever giving me a minute's trouble in the box. And he's well mannered—not that I've gotten after him much. He's just that way."[2]

Because he was contesting before the American Paint Horse Association was formed and the Performance Department established, complete records of Mister J. Bar's accomplishments are not available. If they had been recorded in the books of the association, many more Grand and Reserve Championships would be listed under his name, and many firsts in calf roping would be listed to his credit. Even so, Mister J. Bar is the holder of five national championship titles: 1964 Reserve National Champion Three-Year-Old Stallion, 1965 National Champion Aged Stallion, 1965 National Champion Roping Horse, 1966 National Champion Get of Sire, and 1967 National Champion Get of Sire.

During the past ten years at least a dozen good Paint stallions went through the Robertson's paddocks, but Mister J. Bar's position is secure. Because of his excellent record as a potent Paint Horse sire, Mister J. Bar will, no doubt, always stand as the senior sire at the Robertson Ranch. In 1975, as a fourteen-year-old, he is still a very active horse and can show the young ones how to work a rope.

[2]Junior Robertson, as told to Jane Pattie, "Take Your Rope Horse Slow!" *Horseman*, March, 1967, pp. 21–25.

After a successful showing as a performance horse and halter horse, Mister J. Bar has surpassed all expectations as a sire. Some Paint Horses seem to be endowed by nature with the ability to stamp their get with uniformity and ability. Mister J. Bar is one of those sires. His sons and daughters show his same traits and excellent conformation, and eight of them have testified to his greatness as a sire by earning their APHA championships.

A 1964 son, J Bar Junior, is a bright sorrel overo stallion and a replica of his sire in refinement, excellent conformation points, and lengthy muscling. His dam was Robertson's top producing mare, Pocohontas (APHA 38). She and her produce are discussed in Chapter 22.

When J Bar Junior was less than forty-five days old, Rebecca Tyler persuaded Robertson to sell him to her. He did, though with some reluctance, because J Bar Junior was the first Paint colt that he had raised. Mr. and Mrs. Ralph Brunner, Monroe, Wisconsin, subsequently purchased him, and he has made his home at the Dairyland Paint Farm ever since.

From his weanling days on, J Bar Junior was shown with much success, age and competition considered. He was one of those horses that was skillful in a number of events in an above-average fashion. At the 1968 National Show in Oklahoma City, he received his first national award when he was named Reserve National Co-Champion Aged Stallion. In 1969 he was shown only a few times, but, thanks to his attractive build and bearing, he won all three go-rounds of the aged-stallion class over seventeen entries, to earn the title of National Champion Aged Stallion that year. He has been Grand Champion many times, he has received Registers of Merit in competition in western pleasure and reining, and he is an APHA Champion.

J Bar Junior, no longer in the proving class as a sire, has been getting some very good foals in the past few years. Among them one cannot overlook the following: J Bar's Josie, Jr.'s Honey Moon, San Bar, Miss Gold Bar, Jr's Baby Doll, Milady J-Bar, Miss Dawn Bar, Jr's Snowflake, and J Bars Dutchess.

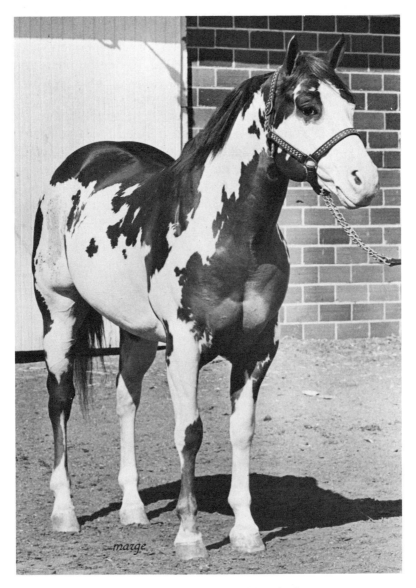

J Bar Junior. Photograph by Margie Spence.

Certainly one of Mister J. Bar's finest sons was C-Note, a sorrel overo stallion, and a full brother of J Bar Junior. In the spring of 1965 the grand old foundation mare Pocohontas again foaled a handsome colt of great potential. He was purchased as a two-month-old by Jim Smoot, Gainesville, Texas.

Today there are many horses that make fine records and stand out remarkably, but how many can equal the record set by yearling C-Note in 1966? Shown thirteen times at halter, C-Note placed first on all thirteen occasions and established an unprecedented record when named Grand Champion at seven shows and Reserve Champion at three shows over all aged stallions. One of his grand championships was received at the large 1966 Houston Livestock Show. At the National Show in Baton Rouge in the same year he was named the National Champion Yearling Stallion.

C-Note earned a Register of Merit in western pleasure and his APHA Championship in 1969. He was beginning to earn quite a reputation as a sire when he met a premature death on January 30, 1971, from a ruptured intestine. Although he had been bred to only a few mares, his get are deluxe show horses. One of his sons, C-Note's Playboy, was named the 1969 National Champion Yearling Stallion at the national show in Kansas City, and another elite son, C Note's Champ, was selected out of a class of twenty-nine, the National Champion 1970 Stallion at the 1971 national show.

Much success has come from the mating of Mister J. Bar to Pocohontas; however, he breeds equally well to all types of mares. Red Wine (APSHA 95) is another good Paint mare, once owned by Robertson, who delivered Cimmaron Badger and Buffalo Gal before joining the court of Mister J. Bar. Red Wine is the kind of mare who puts all her desirable qualities in her foals. If her mating with Mister J. Bar had produced only one outstanding foal, she would have been praised for her worthy contribution. But two of her sons have already become APHA champions in the short history of the APHA. J Bar Flash, a sorrel overo, is her 1964 foal and is owned by Victor

C-Note, 1965–71. Photograph by Margie Spence.

Roquette, Coloma, Michigan. Her 1966 son, J Bar Desperado, now deceased, was sold to J. Jay Simons, Fort Lauderdale, Florida, as a weanling. Both J Bar Flash and J Bar Desperado are APHA champions and hold a Register of Merit in western pleasure. Other get that became big names in show business are J Bar's Lady Bug, an APHA Supreme Champion, and J Bar's Sundial, J Bar's Sweet Thing, and J Bar's Sweetheart, all APHA champions.

Mister J Bar is a prolific sire and has fathered an enviable number of excellent horses, most of whom have commanded much attention both in performance and at halter. His progeny include some of the most versatile horses in the country. They have been put to nearly every performance test, and through their records of achievement Mister J. Bar has become the second Leading Sire of APHA champions and the second Leading Sire of Performance Point Earners for the period 1966 to 1973. Because of the blood of a fabulous stallion, combined with the wisdom and integrity of Robertson as a breeder, the name Mister J. Bar stands as a truly great Paint Horse sire.

24 **YELLOW MOUNT**

The 2J Horse Farm at Iowa Park, Texas, is the home of many outstanding Paint Horses, but none brought it more fame than Yellow Mount. Since his purchase by Mr. and Mrs. Stanley Williamson in 1966, this stallion has greatly improved the quality of 2J Horse Farm stock and Paint Horse stock in general nationwide. This speaks well for the Williamsons, who have devoted their time and talent to raising Paint Horses of the finest quality and have shown many to APHA championships.

Reared in the farming and ranching country around Wichita Falls, Texas, Williamson began showing livestock at the age of thirteen while a Four-H club member. In 1936 he showed the Grand Champion Angus Calf at the Texas Centennial Fair. He now has ranches in North and South Central Texas. He was selected by *Who's Who in the Southwest* for 1971.

As early as 1962 with a little prompting from his wife and youngest son, Williamson became interested in raising Paint Horses. It is interesting to note that the horse farm was named the 2J by Williamson for his wife, Jodie, and son, Joe Howard, the "two J's." In 1962 they bought their first registered Paint Horse, a mare for Joe Howard, and began looking for a stallion to be the pillar of the 2J breeding program. It took nearly four years for them to find a Paint Horse that showed all the promise of becoming their "ideal" sire. The stallion selected was a dun overo Paint Horse, Yellow Mount, who had just been named the 1966 National Champion Two-Year-Old Stallion.

Yellow Mount was sired by Tetrak Scooter (AQHA 154, 479) by Cripple Mount by Gold Mount. Gold Mount (AQHA 2,078) was the sire of the famed Bright Eyes (often designated Maddon's Bright Eyes), a 1946 AAA sprinter who held three racing titles: World's Champion Quarter Running Horse in 1949 and Champion Quarter Running Mare in 1949 and 1950. Bright Eyes also coheld with Monita the titles Champion Quarter Running Mare and World's Champion Quarter Running Horse in 1951.

Cripple Mount was not one of Gold Mount's fastest colts, and there is no record that he ever raced. He was good in the stud, siring three Register of Merit running colts, three AQHA champions and four Register of Merit arena horses.

Yellow Mount's dam, Lady Yellow Jacket (APHA 1,907) was by Moorehouse's Yellow Jacket (AQHA 13,220) by King George, who goes back to Old Sorrel. Lady Yellow Jacket was out of a Moorehouse Paint mare of Yellow Wolf breeding. There is good Quarter Horse foundation blood on both sides of Yellow Mount's pedigree, and, as has often been reiterated in this book, blood is the one thing that must be considered in any breeding operation.

Bred by Bill Hitson, Santa Rosa, New Mexico, Yellow Mount was foaled in 1964. He was first owned by Jack Bruns, Muleshoe, Texas, who purchased the little colt and his dam a few months after foaling. Bruns gave Yellow Mount special attention from the day he brought him home. His debut at the Paint Horse shows was made in 1965 as a year-old colt. By the time he was in his second year, he was successful in compiling ten grand championships and four reserve championships out of the fourteen times he was shown at halter. In performance classes Yellow Mount placed first eight times and second once in junior western-pleasure events. That year he was named the National Champion Two-Year-Old Stallion and Reserve National Champion Junior Western Pleasure Horse at the association's National Show in Baton Rouge, Louisiana. He had accumulated the necessary halter and performance points through October, 1966, to qualify for the first APHA championship. Following the national show, the Williamsons purchased Yellow Mount for a record price of ten thousand dollars, the highest price ever paid for a Paint Horse at that time.

In 1967, Yellow Mount was placed in race training. While he received no acclaim on the straightaways, in his first race Yellow Mount showed that he had plenty of speed. Out of his three official starts he is credited with one win, one second, and one third.

On August 20, at Little Dixie Downs, McAlester, Oklahoma, Yellow Mount won an open Paint Horse race for 300 yards, defeating Hi Song by a neck, followed by Dial-A-Go-Go and Home Brew. He was officially rated AA in the Texas Paint Horse Maturity, earning a Register of Merit, and again in the Texas Paint Horse Derby for 350 yards he ran AA time. In a mixed race with Quarter Horses at Ross Downs near Grapevine, Texas, Yellow Mount was clocked in AAA time, but it was not an official APHA race.

Throughout 1968, Yellow Mount was used in the stud. Returning to active performance in 1969, he was put in roping and reining training. Under the capable hands of Lanham Riley and then Vicki Adams, Yellow Mount earned enough points for the Register of Merit in these two events and won the 1969 National Champion Senior Roping Horse title. Vicki began preparing Yellow Mount for barrel racing in the summer of 1970. It was his first-place showing in a class of nine barrel-racing horses at Loveland, Colorado, on August 15, 1970, that produced the final points needed for the Supreme Champion award.

There is no doubt that Yellow Mount has made a tremendous contribution to the APHA record books. Since beginning his show career in 1965, he has received the following titles or awards:

1. *Supreme Champion #2*
2. *APHA Champion #1*
3. *1966 National Champion Two-Year-Old Stallion*
4. *1966 Reserve National Champion Junior Western Pleasure Horse*
5. *1967 National Champion Three-Year-Old Stallion*
6. *1969 National Champion Senior Roping Horse*
7. *1971 Reserve National Champion Get of Sire (Tied)*
8. *1972 National Champion Get of Sire*
9. *1973 Reserve National Champion Get of Sire*
10. *1974 National Champion Get of Sire*

Yellow Mount has a disposition and temperament that is even and reasonable. He has run the barrels, been roped on, and followed the trail-horse pattern in the same show, calmly and surely and has either won or placed high in all events. Several trainers have ridden Yellow Mount and other 2J horses and have only praise for their varied abilities. Joe Howard Williamson is a superb showman, having trained and shown four National and Reserve National champions in the Youth Division and three APHA champions. He has won Youth National championships in reining, western pleasure, showmanship and youth breakaway roping.

The breeding program of the 2J Horse Farm is a combination of conformation, disposition, and potential working ability. Williamson's judgment in the matching of high-quality mares with Yellow Mount will provide many present and future breeders with the fundamentals of Paint Horse breeding stock.

Facing page: Bar Mount, 1968–72. Photograph by Margie Spence. Courtesy Paint Horse Journal.

marge

More than six years were spent collecting the 2J broodmare band, which includes five National and Reserve National Champion mares, Quarter mares of the blood of Three Bars, Top Moon, Skippety Scoot, Black Easter, Johnny Dial, Bright Bar, Leo, and Joe Moore. A few Jockey Club mares are included in this highly selective breeding operation.

The ability to pass on his favorable characteristics is manifested in his get, since over 50 per cent of his colts are "show colts." His sons and daughters are showing and performing in all parts of the United States from New York to California. They are versatile horses in the sense that they are not bred for any specific performance. They are consistent winners and APHA champions in all events.

Listing the get of Yellow Mount seems a bit like calling an honor roll of Paint Horses. The most impressive ones may be Bar Mount, Red Mount, Lady Brush Mount, Yellow Mount's Pride, Yellow Jo, Yellow Bonnet, Yellow Sonnet, Bright Socks, Bright Yellow, Chicka Mount, and Yellow Pages.

A supreme champion is made much of these days, and when he happens to become the sire of a supreme champion, it is certainly a very noteworthy event. Proper honor must be given to one horse who may be unique among Paint Horses since the APHA began. Yellow Mount is the sire of not one but three American Paint Horse Supreme Champions. Within a single year, 1972, Bar Mount, Yellow Mount's Pride, and Red Mount passed every halter and performance test to earn this very respectable title.

Bar Mount was a 1968 foal whose breeding is without reproach. His dam was Miss Half Bar (AQHA 75,444) by Three Bars out of a Paint mare by Revenue. Miss Half Bar is also the dam of APHA Champion Chicka Mount. Bar Mount was an extremely beautiful animal. His rich sorrel overo coat and smooth body lines completed the picture of a perfect Paint

Facing page: Lady Brush Mount. Photograph by Margie Spence.

Margie Spence ©

Horse. When he was two years old, he was purchased by Fred Adam, Wilcox, Nebraska, who carefully readied him for the public eye. By the time he was four, he had an APHA championship, five Registers of Merit and a supreme championship. Tragically, Bar Mount was killed in a trailer accident while traveling to the national show in August, 1972.

Yellow Mount's Pride is a 1967 bay tobiano gelding, big-hearted, and a delight to be around and to ride. His dam was a tobiano Paint mare by Iowa Lou Cody (AQHA 145,779), which accounts for his color pattern. He is a typical Yellow Mount colt in skill, wisdom, and durability. His eventful life includes winning a national championship in Junior Barrel Racing, an APHA championship, and a supreme championship.

Almost simultaneously the third Yellow Mount colt to win the supreme championship got his talents together and stepped into the hallowed hall reserved for the special few. This was Red Mount, a 1968 sorrel overo stallion owned jointly by the 2J Horse Farm and Jimmy Willis, Summerville, Georgia. He is a National Champion at halter and has Registers of Merit in calf roping, reining, trail, barrel racing, and western pleasure.

To round out the list of champions, two others that cannot be overlooked are Lady Brush Mount, an APHA Champion and the Reserve National Champion Yearling Halter Mare in 1970; and Yellow Bonnet, an APHA Champion and the 1972 National Champion Aged Mare.

Yellow Mount is a very popular horse. He has been used as the subject of commercial sculpture; his picture appears in feed-company advertisements, on calendars, and in needlepoint pictures. But above all he has emerged in the stud with stature as a sire comparable to the best of any breed of horse.

25 JOECHIEF BAR

On April 6, 1964, a stout sorrel tobiano colt was foaled on the Paul Crabb breeding farm near Winfield, Kansas. This little colt, Joechief Bar, was "all horse," and was destined for greatness in APHA record books.

He is one of those fortunate horses to be an heir in an illustrious family line. His sire, a very popular Thoroughbred stallion, Bang Up (JC 560,280),[1] had established a fine record as a sprinter on the eastern tracks before retiring lame. Bang Up, owned by Paul and Carolyn Crabb, was later lost in a barn fire but left many well-known offspring, particularly in the Paint Horse breed.

Joechief Bar's mother is the Leading Dam of all time, Josy Bar (by Skylark Bar by Three Bars and out of Babette by Painted Joe).[2] She has been one of the most important contrib-

[1]For further information on Bang Up, see Chapter 17.
[2]For further information on Josy Bar, see Chapter 18.

utors to the breed, and her foals have elevated her to a greatness that is richly deserved.

An examination of the bloodline charts shows that Joechief
Bar carries a good deal of Thoroughbred blood—that received
from his sire, that received through his dam from her Three
Bars breeding, and that received from his granddam, Babette.
In conformation he typifies the Quarter Horse–Thoroughbred
cross with a long bottom line; good, clean, flat bone; and
straight, slender legs on a well-muscled, athletic body.

Late in 1965 Paul and Carolyn Crabb dispersed their
horses, selling a number of the best Paint Horses, including
Joechief Bar, to the late Art Beall, Broken Arrow, Oklahoma.

At that time in the quiet little southern town of Port Gibson, Mississippi, the Mott Headley family had been carrying on
a serious debate. They wanted and needed a royally bred horse
to cross on their band of broodmares. Unanimously the family
came to an agreement that Joechief Bar was one horse whose
ancestry combined some of the finest blood available for im-
proving the quality of foals on the Headley Ranch. In this they
were right, and in the years to follow they never had reason to
regret their choice.

Mott Headley, his father before him, and his grandfather
before him, had been raising Paint Horses for over half a century. In the late 1890's Grandfather Headley went to Port Gibson with the first Paint Horses. They were rugged Indian ponies
of considerable size, akin to the Spanish horses that had swept
wild and free over the American plains. Used for riding, plowing
and general ranch work, these hardy Paint Horses possessed a
good balance of quality and durability. Through the years the
horses were crossed on Quarter Stock Horses and have improved generation after generation until they are now some of
the finest Paint Horses around. The best broodmares on the
Headley Ranch today are direct descendants of those original
Indian ponies.

The purchase of Joechief Bar was, in the beginning, to
have been a syndicated purchase by Mott Headley and nine

other Mississippi Paint Horse breeders. For one reason or another arrangements were never completely worked out for the purchase price and for the stabling and training, and in the end Joechief Bar came into the ownership of the Headleys alone. In April, 1966, when the trip was made to the Art Beall Ranch to pick up the horse, the two-year-old Joechief Bar did not appear to be as promising a horse as they had believed. But Headley, with his good eye for a horse, could see underneath the surface a diamond in the rough. Joechief Bar had a fine, clean head; plenty of muscle; and perfect balance in his movement. A little grooming, graining, and working could bring out all the details of body and build that are a delight to a horseman's eye. There was no doubt in his mind about the horse or his potential, and Joechief Bar was moved to his new home in Port Gibson without further ado.

Mott Headley, Jr., began the expert breaking and training of the colt, who seemingly enjoyed the attention and care he was receiving. In October, 1966, at the APHA National Show in Baton Rouge, Louisiana, the hard work bore fruit when Joechief won his first three halter points.

Along with his good looks Joechief Bar showed that he possessed considerable speed, a speed that may be attributed to his strong Thoroughbred heritage. In late 1966, when the show season was over, the young stallion was sent back to Oklahoma for race training. He cooperated wholeheartedly in this strange experience, and after six weeks on the straightaways he made a pretty good showing. Although he would never break any track records, he was good at three hundred yards. Of his two starts, he won one and went unplaced in the other. A good indication of his racing class was given in a three-hundred-yard race for two-year-olds at Blue Ribbon Downs, Sallisaw, Oklahoma, on November 20. Running like a well-oiled machine that day, Joechief Bar led Bar Boy and Jim's Johnny Dial over the finish by a good one and a half lengths.

Happy that their horse proved he was a pretty good sprinter, the Headleys took Joechief back to Mississippi. Mott, Jr., said,

"My life's ambition does not include owning the World's Champion running horse. I'm satisfied just owning the World's Greatest Paint Horse."

Through 1967 and 1968 the younger Mott introduced his horse to various performance events and began accumulating halter and performance points. With his natural endowment of speed, Joechief Bar easily won barrel races and pole-bending events at several A-rated shows. At other times he demonstrated his ability in reining and western pleasure. In November, 1968, having a total of 14 halter and 17½ performance points, he was named the twenty-second American Paint Horse Association Champion.

While Mott, Jr., was attending Mississippi State University earning a Bachelor of Science degree in animal science, he found it difficult to travel to the shows every weekend. Being an intelligent and understanding horse, Joechief Bar helped in every way he could by winning an abundance of points at each show. For instance, in February, 1970, at the Dixie National Paint Horse Show in Jackson, Mississippi, he turned in his most dazzling performance. He stood first in his class out of ten aged stallions and then became the Grand Champion Stallion of the show; he was first in pole bending out of fifteen entries; first in reining out of twenty entries, first in barrel racing out of eighteen entries; and fifth in western pleasure out of thirty-six entries. Small wonder he was soon to become the APHA's third Supreme Champion.

Joechief's life, from the day he moved to the Headley Ranch, was one of hard training and hard work. During the daylight hours, when he was not in the arena learning a new performance event, he was out riding after cattle. He was and is a horse who could do it all. Had he been temperamental or rank, he could not have been such a consistent winner. Besides, he never lost interest and was always ready to do his best. It took but one more year of arena work for the final reward. On March 28, 1971, the title of American Paint Horse Supreme Champion became his.

In working his way up to Supreme Champion, Joechief Bar earned Registers of Merit in barrel racing, western pleasure, working cowhorse, pole bending, and reining. He became a prime figure in American Paint Horse history by winning the first register of merit to be awarded in the working-cowhorse event. Upon receiving his supreme title, he had compiled 34 halter and 64½ performance points, and had been named Grand Champion Stallion at 13 Class A shows.

All five Headley sons are good exhibitors and skilled horsemen. Mott, Jr., the oldest, has been riding and showing for many years. David Headley, the next in line, is writing his own record book, with many firsts in western riding, barrel racing, and pole bending in both open and youth events. In 1971, after several momentous performances during the year, he won High Point Youth and High Point Overall Rider in Mississippi. Mark Headley moved into the spotlight with a Joechief Bar colt and won a first in Youth Halter Geldings with Chief's Moore Bars at the September 7, 1974, Port Gibson, Mississippi, show.

As a sire of Paint Horses, Joechief Bar is one of the best. From all indications he appears to be a strong breeder in color, conformation, intelligence, and ability. The family that he began includes Joechief's Image, Joe's Star Snip, Joechief Bar Junior, Joe Mac, Joechief Bar's Pride, Chief Dakota Bars, Joechief Bar Bee, Joe Roan, Vaquero Bar, and Jolene Bars.

One of his oldest and finest sons, Joechief's Image, is a 1969 foal, owned by Robert Shanks, Marthaville, Missouri. He blossomed at an early age and as a weanling stood Reserve Champion at the 1970 Dixie National Show in Jackson, Mississippi. He has been exhibited in recent years and has always been in top form. In May, 1972, showing extremely well at Lincoln, Nebraska, he was named the 1969 Midwest Regional Stallion Champion, and in 1973 he became an APHA Champion.

The second of Joechief Bar's sons to become an APHA Champion is Chief Dakota Bars, 15.3 hands and weighing thirteen hundred pounds. In 1974 he was named the Three-Year-

Joechief's Image, owned by Robert Shanks, Marthaville, Missouri.

Old National Champion at Halter and National Champion Junior Roping Horse.

Joechief Bar Junior is a gelded son who inherited from his sire a rare combination of intelligence and action. He has stood Grand Champion Gelding at some large shows, including the ones at Natchez, Mississippi, on August 28, 1971, and at Edwards, Mississippi, on June 11, 1972. He has won for young Perry Luke youth halter and youth western pleasure events in shows all over Mississippi and Louisiana.

Joe's Star Snip, a 1970 colt, was not shown as a yearling, but when he did appear in 1972, he was a leading competitor with firsts in western riding and junior reining at such large shows as the Mid-South Paint Horse Show in Memphis.

Joechief Bar is a great horse and a great sire who well deserves the honors he has achieved and whose record in the stud is a tribute to the Paint Horse breed.

26 DUAL IMAGE

In the spring of 1961, Slow Motion (AQHA 48,053) and Dangerous Girl by Danger Boy II (AQHA 48,052) produced a stud colt with all the priceless qualities that are the marks of greatness. This sorrel overo colt was named Dual Image. He was a hard-twisted, eye-catching little horse with stylish conformation and a way of traveling that caused people to turn their heads and take a second look.

The Paint Horse and Quarter Horse breeders of the Southwest need no introduction to the sire of Dual Image. He is a Quarter Horse that not only made a name for himself on the track but also has been a beneficial influence to short-horse racing stock. Slow Motion was a 1947 foal of Jack Lary, Jr., and Dolores G. by Joe Moore. He was raced at tracks in South Texas, particularly in and around Del Rio, and was officially rated AAA. In 1950 he became coholder with Stella Moore of the three-year-old world record for 330 yards.

Of Slow Motion's Quarter Horse colts to race, Canales Black, a AAA sprinter, is probably the one whose name would first come to mind. Of his producing daughters (AQHA) Monina, AA herself, gained recognition as the dam of Lalito Canales (AAA), winner of the 1964 Endurance Sweepstakes at Columbus, Texas, for 440 yards. All totaled, he has sired eleven Register of Merit race colts registered in the American Quarter Horse Association.

Slow Motion stands out as another of the great Quarter Horses to become famous as sires of outstanding Paint Horses. He provided, among others, Dual Image and a full sister, Crystal Eye (APHA 2,022). A good, sound mare whose influence on Paint Horse racing has been tremendous, Crystal Eye produced Sentimiento, AAA; Slow Danger, winner of the 1970 APHA National Championship Futurity; and Party Gal, winner of the 1972 APHA National Championship.

Through his dam, Dangerous Girl, Dual Image is the grandson of Danger Boy II and the great-grandson of Coldstream, a Thoroughbred. During 1945, Danger Boy II was rated AA on AQRA tracks, and in one of his starts that year, he set a track record at Eagle Pass, Texas, for 400 yards under catch weight at :20.9. He has sired twenty-one AQHA Register of Merit running horses, including Lalito Canales, mentioned above. It is through his daughters, Dangerous Girl, Dangerous Miss, and Parr Lady, that his speed and good blood are being perpetuated in the Paint Horse breed.

Dual Image was first owned by Carl Vickers, Corpus Christi, Texas, who sold him to Jack Archer, also of Corpus Christi, in February, 1964. Under Archer's guidance Dual Image became a consistent winner whether in a race or in a halter class. He did his best every time he went out and was one individual who made coming in first look easy.

During the three years he was owned by Jack Archer, Dual Image was raced at several tracks in Texas. On October 10, 1965, as a four-year-old he ran a match race at La Bahia Downs, Goliad, Texas, with On and On for 350 yards. He won the race easily in :18.3. This is good AAA time, although it is unofficial, because rules for Paint Horse racing were not established by

Dual Image.

the association until 1966. In recent years he was computer-checked and received a Speed Index rating of 95.7 to 440 yards.

In 1967 Dual Image became the APHA's first "triple-crown" halter winner, taking Grand Champion Stallion at the three big stock shows in Fort Worth, San Antonio, and Houston. He had previously won Reserve National Champion Aged Stallion at the 1966 National Show in Baton Rouge, Louisiana.

It was in 1966 at a Paint Horse show that Larry Swain, San Antonio, saw Dual Image for the first time. He began showing Dual for Jack Archer a short time later, and the more that he was around the horse the more he liked his sleek refinement and refreshing willingness. In February, 1968, Larry Swain succeeded in buying Dual Image for the Circle Dot Ranch, San Antonio, Texas.

The Circle Dot is a father-and-son ranching operation covering 180 acres with both C. E. Swain and his son, Larry, working to build up a Simmental cattle herd. The Swains became interested in Paint Horses when the elder Swain's daughter, Pam, outgrew ponies in 1960.

Soon after Dual Image moved to the Circle Dot, he was put in western-pleasure training under Jim Daniels. In 1969 at his first western-pleasure show at the San Antonio Livestock Exposition, Dual placed second out of a class of twenty-six horses. Pam Swain, who was sixteen years old at the time, began to ride him, and with his calm disposition and fine handling qualities she was soon showing him. Pam said, "My method of showing and training Dual is a very simple one. I just let him know what I want him to do, and he does it. He tries his best to please me, and I'm very satisfied with the results."

In June, 1969, Pam and Dual, in their second western-pleasure event, placed second out of a very large class. In his first two shows alone he acquired a Register of Merit in Western Pleasure. After the National Show in Kansas City, Missouri, Dual Image had enough performance points to complete his APHA championship.

By then Dual Image was ten years old, at an age when most

stallions have long since been retired to the stud. But Pam kept working and riding him. In 1971, after thirty days' training in English pleasure, Dual won the National Championship in Senior English Pleasure at Tulsa, Oklahoma. Again, having been shown in only two shows, he was awarded a Register of Merit in English Pleasure.

Pam has said that Dual has the ability and coordination to do everything. She added, "He's smart and he likes to win." He proved this with the forty western-pleasure points, twenty English pleasure points, and thirty halter points acquired in the three years she showed him.

Dual Image's breeding record is very good. He has a host of notable colts on the ground that are well enough put together to please the most discerning eye. By following a carefully planned breeding program, each of his get has the blood to qualify as a show, working, or running prospect. Some of the Paint Horses that carry his deep, rich blood are Dual's Doll, Dual's Darling, Painted Image, Hollywood Image, Dual's Bugs, Miss Dual Image, Dual Motion, Dual Stream, Dual's Doll II, Snow King, Master Charge, Tag A Long, Dual Spots, and Dual's Nightmare.

One of his oldest sons is Snow King, a 1964, predominantly white, sorrel tobiano. His dam, Christie Girl (APSHA 775), of King Ranch blood, is a tobiano mare; so Snow King became one of the overo-tobiano crosses that resulted in a color pattern of both characteristics. His body and leg markings are of the tobiano pattern, and his face is bald—a distinct overo characteristic.

Snow King was shown briefly in his youth. He was used almost exclusively for several years as a pasture-breeding horse in South Texas, and sired a long line of horses that include Lucky Image, Texas Special, Overo Jay, Painted Chick, Snow

Facing page: Dual's Doll II, owned by Chris Coffin, Miami, Florida.

Diamond, Snow Miss, White Mischief, My Snow Princess, Snow Bailey, Paleface Image, and J's King.

Presently owned by the J Bar D Horse Ranch, High Point, North Carolina, Snow King continues to breed well, getting colts that help carry on the heritage of his influential sire.

Dual Image has many exceptionally fine daughters. No list of his get would be complete without mention of three daughters that did their share of campaigning on the tracks in Texas and Oklahoma. The sisters, Dual's Doll, Dual's Darling, and Dual's Doll II, are distinctive in being but three steps away from My Texas Dandy. Dual's Doll and Dual's Doll II are full sisters, and their dam, Miss Hi Tex, is by Hi Tex (AQHA 27, 422), who is by the great My Texas Dandy.

In the 1967 futurities Dual's Darling and Dual's Doll, owned by Jack Archer at the time, brought respect to the name of their sire. The two-year-old Dual's Darling earned a AA rating at Manor Downs in her first track appearance, and Dual's Doll earned an A rating that day.

Dual's Doll II ran in the 1969 futurities in Kansas, Oklahoma, and Texas. On the whole she gave a good account of herself, running against the top two-year-olds. She was much more at home in the show arena and has excelled splendidly at halter and in western pleasure. A model Paint Horse, as many of the leading judges have attested, Dual's Doll II stood Grand Champion at some very large shows and was the 1970 National Champion Three-Year-Old Mare at Amarillo, Texas. She earned a Register of Merit in western pleasure in 1971, and since her purchase by Chris Coffin, Miami, Florida, has become an APHA Champion and has won for Chris the APHA Youth Championship award.

Another trim and statuesque mare commanding attention wherever shown is Miss Dual Image. Foaled in 1966, she built her early reputation at halter by standing Reserve National Champion Weanling Filly in 1966. Winning her class at such shows as the 1968 Houston Livestock Show has helped her maintain a true mark of excellence as a halter mare.

Honorable mention should be made of a son, Dual Spots, with Registers of Merit in western pleasure and reining; and Hollywood Image, a daughter, like a chip off the old block, has a computer Speed Index rating of 95 at 400 yards.

Great horses of whatever breed, ancestry, or strain are, almost without exception, excellent in the stud. Because of his contribution of fine foals Dual Image stands in distinctive company as a great American Paint Horse sire.

27 Q TON EAGLE

The names Q Ton Eagle, J. D. Hooter, and the Lazy H Ranch, Lecompte, Louisiana, have become synonymous with the growth of the Paint Horse breed. In a few short years the Lazy H became one of the foremost Paint Horse breeding operations. To a large extent the success of the Lazy H is due to Hooter's efforts to breed quality Paint Horses with the conformation to show at halter and an all-around ability to perform.

Having a great desire to find a Paint Horse stallion to become the foundation of the Lazy H breeding program, J. D. and his brother, J. M. Hooter, were absorbed in a most intense search in late 1963 and early 1964. In 1964, J. M. Hooter found a stallion with promising credentials and immediately telephoned his brother, asking him to purchase the three-year-old at the upcoming sale at Broken Arrow, Oklahoma. A tragic automobile accident near Amarillo, Texas, took the life of J. M. Hooter before the brothers could get together again.

On June 8, 1964, J. D. Hooter fulfilled his brother's request and traveled to Broken Arrow for the specific purpose of buying Q Ton Eagle at the Art Beall Paint Stock Horse Sale. Q Ton Eagle was bred, raised, and consigned to the sale by Quention Foster, Broken Arrow, one of the early breeders of stock-type Paint Horses. At the time the $7,200 bid for the stallion was considered by some an extremely high price for a Paint Horse, but he has shown by his performance and his progeny that he was not overpriced for his value. Hooter's competitive bidder was George Hall, Jenks, Oklahoma, at $7,100. Nine individuals bid, and four of them continued the bid past $6,000. At the same sale Hooter purchased what proved to be one of his best broodmares, Little Speckled Hen, and her stud colt by Lee Bars.

Q Ton Eagle is a very highly regarded Paint Horse stallion who has contributed much to the Paint Horse. He is a sorrel tobiano with a beautiful quarter-type head; deep, powerful muscles of the thigh, stifle, and gaskin; and a style about him that shows his good Quarter Horse breeding. He is by Freno (AQHA 62,306) by My Texas Dandy, Jr., by My Texas Dandy. The dam of Freno was a Gill Cattle Company mare No. 71 by Bear Hug.

Before we go any further, a few words should be said about the My Texas Dandy horses. It is an accepted fact that My Texas Dandy himself was not much of a race horse. He had the breaking power and early speed to make an impressive start, but he would not go the distance. His progeny, however, were far-famed for their records on the short-horse tracks, and because of their success his name has been set down in Quarter racing history. To list a few of his most distinguished money earners, there was Clabber, Texas Jr., Ginger Rogers, Hot Shot, Texas Star, Little Texas, Texas Dandy, and My Texas Dandy, Jr.

Q Ton Eagle's dam is Q Ton Dixie Alpha by Bear Cat (AQHA 3,501). Q Ton Dixie Alpha has put into her foals a classic characteristic that gives an indication of what lies further back in her ancestry. One of her daughters, Q Ton Stormee, was a leading dam in the APHA with the most halter point

Q Ton Eagle at the time of his purchase by J. D. Hooter (right) from Quenton Foster (left) June 8, 1964, Broken Arrow, Oklahoma. Photograph by Wayne C. Hunt, Tulsa.

earners through 1971. Her foals are likewise good under saddle. Their excellent showing in various performance events has placed her in fourth position as a Leading Dam of Register of Merit Qualifiers.

With a pedigree tracing back to My Texas Dandy and Bear Hug (also a good sprinter on the Quarter tracks), one would think that Q Ton Eagle would have been sent out to try his running ability. He had the good legs and sound feet, the breeding, and the heart to run. He even had the speed to overtake a calf and the quick mobility to whirl through the reining patterns, but not enough to last the distance.

He was trained instead in the performance events and developed into a very good pleasure and reining horse. He seemed to enjoy the working events and did well in roping and cutting, as well as in western pleasure. Q Ton Eagle was entered in all the shows in Louisiana, Texas, Oklahoma, and Mississippi during the middle 1960's. He was never unplaced in the halter classes, and has been named Grand Champion at some of the largest APHA shows. Because the Performance Department of the APHA was not formed until 1966, most of Q Ton's accomplishments have not been recorded. He has the distinction of having won six national championships. He was named National Champion Aged Stallion in 1964 and again in 1966. Also in 1966 he was named National Champion Senior Reining Horse and Reserve National Champion Get of Sire. In 1968 and 1969 he added the title National Champion Get of Sire.

The achievements of Q Ton Eagle are overshadowed only by the accomplishments of his get. Through 1973 he had sired one Supreme Champion, six APHA Champions, fourteen National and Reserve National Champions and fifteen Register of Merit Qualifiers. Since the true value of a sire lies in his ability to perpetuate his characteristics in his offspring, then the performance and halter records of his get are evidence of this stallion's prepotency and would fill page after page of this book.

Miss Q Ton Eagle, a 1963 daughter and the first of the Q Ton line to receive a national championship, was twice named National Champion at Halter—in 1964 and 1967. She won Grand Champion Mare at the "Big Three"—Fort Worth, San Antonio, and Houston—in 1968, and was first in western pleasure at many of the major shows.

Another outstanding daughter is Lady Q Ton Eagle, owned by Bud and Betty Crump, Wynnewood, Oklahoma. She was

Lady Q Ton Eagle. Photograph by Margie Spence.

National Champion Mare at Halter three different years, 1965, 1966, and 1970, and has won many western-pleasure classes.

Other national champions by Q Ton Eagle are Q Ton Sonnyboy H, the 1965 National Champion 1965 Stallion; Pet's Q Ton Eagle, the 1969 National Champion Junior Cutting Horse and 1971 and 1974 National Champion Senior Cutting Horse; Q Ton Jumping H, the 1970 National Champion Two-Year-Old Gelding; Rio's Q Ton H, the 1970 National Champion Junior

Q Ton Eagle's Supreme Champion son, Gill's Q Ton. Photograph by Margie Spence.

Reining Horse; and Koko Bars, the 1970, 1971, and 1973 National Champion Senior Reining Horse and 1972 Reserve National Champion Senior Reining Horse and National Champion Senior Roping Horse.

From the first tabulation of a leading-sires list in 1970, Q Ton Eagle completely dominated every category for four years. He was the Leading Sire of Halter Point Earners, the Leading

Sire of Performance Point Earners, and the Leading Sire of
ROM Qualifiers from 1966 through 1973.

Q Ton Eagle's Supreme Champion son is Gill's Q Ton,
owned by Chuck and Genie Bloomquist, Castle Rock, Colorado. He is a 1966 sorrel tobiano carrying the same perfection
of body and limb as his sire. In 1972, his peak year of showing,
he earned his supreme championship after compiling this very
impressive performance record: 169 performance points; Registers of Merit in western pleasure, English pleasure, steer
roping, working cowhorse, reining, western riding, trail and
barrel racing; and 12 Grand Championships and ten Reserve
Championships. He is one of the most natural working horses
in action and top caliber when it comes to the using-horse
events.

Q Ton Tonette, owned by Margie Hahn, Denver, Colorado,
was the first of Q Ton's get to become an APHA Champion.
She was soon followed by Pet's Q Ton Eagle, owned by Hooter's
Lazy H Ranch; Gill's Q Ton, owned by Chuck and Genie
Bloomquist, Castle Rock, Colorado; Q Ton Firelight H, owned
by Cindy Pettibone, Pleasant Grove, California; and Okie Q
Ton H, also owned by Hooter.

Q Ton Eagle has had a tremendous influence on the Paint
Horse breed. His sons and daughters are built very much like
him and have inherited his striking conformation and ener-
getic temperament. He is a great breeder of color, averaging
from 1964 through 1971 approximately 86 per cent Paint foal
production. This percentage varies from year to year, with a
low of 50 per cent one year to a high in 1971, when Q Ton's
colt crop was 98 per cent Paint. Hooter is well pleased with
these results, from the standpoint of color as well as personality
and ability, in Q Ton's progeny.

As a Paint Horse breeder Hooter has a profound interest
in the betterment of the breed. His philosophy, "You've got to
match the horse with the right individual," has proved to be a
worthwhile rule to follow when choosing broodmares to mate
with Q Ton Eagle. At one time eighty registered Paint and

Quarter mares of some of the best bloodlines roamed the Lazy H. Little Speckled Hen and her 1962 daughter, Flying Gale, were two of his top mares, along with Miss Tadepole Red H, Pet H, and Jumpin Jerry. Such outstanding mares as these, and a number of other good ones, have produced by Q Ton Eagle progeny that earned through 1973 a total of 432 halter points and 881 performance points.

In the first ten years of APHA history no other stallion in the breed sent so many winners to the shows. The get of Q Ton Eagle will continue to show at halter and performance and may prove him to be a Leading Sire through another decade.

28 PAINTED LASAN

Painted Lasan, a sorrel overo stallion foaled in 1963, is a product of superior parentage. On both sides of his family is the breeding of a host of great horses long since immortalized in the history of the Quarter Horse breed. The son of Calhoun's Lasan (AQHA P-67,958) and Magby's Van (AQHA P-98,754), Painted Lasan traces back to Joe Reed, Bert, Zantanon, and Peter McCue.

Calhoun's Lasan resulted from the union of Leo San and Betty Bert, who was by Bert, Jr., by Bert. Leo San was by Leo by Joe Reed II by Joe Reed. Calhoun's Lasan piled up a number of performance and halter points during his show years and in 1964 was named AQHA Champion. His stud career is no less magnificent. He sired two AQHA Champions, seven ROM arena horses, two ROM running horses and two APHA Champions, Painted Lasan and Strawberry Lasan. Painted Lasan is a copy of his versatile sire and is passing down to present-day Paint Horses the same fine performance traits.

On his maternal side Painted Lasan goes back through

Magby's Van to Chico Chief (AQHA 24,113), who was by Chico, a good son of Zantanon. Her granddam on her sire's side, Fay Stinson, was by Chief (AQHA P-5) by Peter McCue.

The recessive overo genes apparently were concentrated in both Calhoun's Lasan and Magby's Van because in 1961 they created Jonie's Santoni, another crop-out Paint foal. Calhoun sold Jonie's Santoni as a two-year-old for five thousand dollars, a substantial price at the time, considering the newness of the breed. She had won three grand championships and one reserve championship in four shows, including the Top Mare award at Fort Worth and the Reserve title at Houston in 1963.

Painted Lasan is a powerfully smooth horse with heavy muscling and perfect balance, standing approximately fifteen hands and weighing around 1,250 pounds. He has an excellent disposition and is well mannered around people and other stock.

When Ralph and Dorothy Russell, of the Double R Ranch, McKinney, Texas, purchased Lasan in February, 1965, they found that he was a horse that could "get out and do." Giving him their best training, they took him to all the shows that had the toughest competition. A steady and consistent winner, Painted Lasan always gave a brilliant performance.

In his first showing Lasan placed first out of a class of thirteen two-year-olds at Alexandria, Louisiana, in March, 1965. After a very successful show year, he received the High Point Two-Year-Old Stallion of the Year award in both Texas and Oklahoma.

During 1966, Painted Lasan was shown at eighteen shows approved by the APHA and won eighteen firsts under eighteen different judges. He was named the High Point Three-Year-Old Stallion of the Texas Paint Horse Club, the High Point Three-Year-Old Stallion of Oklahoma, and the High Point Western Pleasure Horse in Oklahoma. In October, Painted Lasan won all three go-rounds of the national show to be named the National Champion Three-Year-Old Stallion. Having accumulated thirty-one points in halter, western pleasure and cutting, he became the second APHA Champion—all in 1966. It was a memorable year for a remarkable horse.

The Russells have always been great enthusiasts of the cutting horse. Although they started Lasan in western pleasure, it was not long until they discovered that the horse had an inherent talent for cutting. For the next several years, with the best cutting training available to him, combined with his own intelligence, dexterity, and levelheadedness, he made a top cowhorse. His ability as a cutting horse has been confirmed by his excellent record at Paint Horse cuttings, including the one at the 1967 national show, where he won Reserve National Champion Cutting Horse. He looks good in the arena and has plenty of natural action to get the job done.

Painted Lasan is an extraordinary individual in his own right, and under the rein of Ralph or Dorothy Russell, he is well-nigh unbeatable. Through 1971 he had a total of 132 APHA points and had earned Registers of Merit in cutting, western pleasure, barrel racing, and pole bending.

No two trainers have worked harder, pulled further, or had more first-place winners than the Russells. In fact, a Paint Horse Show is not a Paint Horse Show if these two wonderful showmen are not there. There is no disputing the fact that Ralph and Dorothy Russell are unexcelled at showing a horse. Each one has a unique technique at fitting and showing a horse that only a few horsemen or horsewomen possess. They can actually help a horse perform and can get everything out of a horse that is in him. People who know the Russells will agree— they know their business. Some of the Paint Horses that owe their APHA Championships, Registers of Merit, and first-place wins to the training and showing they received from the Russells are Painted Lasan, Bandit's Banner, Blind Date, Lasan's Conchita, Bon Bon, East Gold, Bandit's Ann, By Jingo, Bueno Bandit, Kniss' Nifty Boy, Liz Shoshone, Tuff Cat, Babby Skit, and Paint Siss.

Ralph Russell has many years of close association with horses and cattle. When he says that the Paint Horse is just about the best all-around horse he has worked with, he means it, and he should know what he is talking about. He likes a horse that is tough, yet intelligent and quiet, and one that can do what is asked of him. And he has worked plenty of them that fit this description.

Raising top Paint Horses is the goal of the Double R breeding program. To the Russells is due much credit for establishing the American Paint Horse breed on Quarter Horse bloodlines. Another good example of their philosophy is Bay Bandit (AQHA 55,402), a 1954-foaled Quarter Horse, strong in Traveler blood on the top and bottom sides, who is standing at the ranch along with Painted Lasan. Bay Bandit has descendants in the Paint Horse breed that are outstanding at halter and in all activities—cutting, reining, western-pleasure, and timed events. Bueno Bandit, an APHA Champion, stands out as one of his finest offspring with Registers of Merit in four different categories of arena work.

Painted Lasan is rated highly as a sire because of the kind of colts he gets. They are streamlined and clean-boned. They have action and tremendous amounts of energy. With an abundance of good blood in their composition, his get have every possible advantage.

Lasan's Ann, foaled in 1968, is a beautiful sorrel tobiano and a real looker. While a young filly, she was named National Champion Weanling Mare at the 1968 national show. She is owned by Carl Mertens and J. E. Rosenbaum, El Paso, Texas, who proudly display her at every opportunity.

Loretta Lasan, a 1970 mare, made it clear that she was one of Lasan's best daughters by winning her class in nine consecutive shows, including the 1971 Fort Worth and Houston livestock shows. Lasan's colts are never without muscle, and Loretta certainly has her share in all the right places.

Still another pair of Lasan's daughters that show well are Lasan's Sana, a Superior Western Pleasure horse; and Lasan Soul Sister, who is ROM in Western Pleasure. These and other Painted Lasan daughters will probably be heard from in the

Lasan's Ann, by Painted Lasan. Photograph by H. D. Dolcater.

future through produce that contribute in a large measure to the glory of Painted Lasan.

Ralph and Dorothy worked Lasan hard for a couple of years after they acquired him, and he was bred to only a few mares before his fifth birthday. Even so, through 1974 he had sired eighteen winners and point earners and seven Register of Merit qualifiers in arena work. In the 1971 and 1972 Paint Horse shows the names of Lasan's sons began to appear under

"Show Results" in the *Paint Horse Journal*. Lasan's Man is a good example of a top youth-show gelding. After climbing the ladder from third at Fort Worth to second at San Antonio, he won his class at the Houston Livestock Show in 1971. He was started in performance and now has a Register of Merit in Trail.

One of the better Paint Horses in halter competition is St. Lasan. A 1970 foal, he has met some of the best equines in conformation classes and has many first-place awards, specifically grand-champion titles at the 1972 Edwards, Mississippi; Harrah, Oklahoma; and San Augustine, Texas, shows.

Lasan's Black is one of the excellent arena horses. To his credit are ROM's in Western Pleasure, youth English Pleasure and Youth Reining. In 1974 he was named Reserve National Champion Youth Reining Horse under Rosy Russell's guiding hand.

Other colts pulling down firsts in their halter class and in the performance events are Cee San, Lasan's Patch, Lasan Paul, and Dandy Lasan.

Painted Lasan, joining other great sires in a decade of outstanding horses, is leaving a legacy of remarkable offspring. The galaxy in which they shine is no longer sparsely populated, and, as quality becomes more and more apparent, the valuable characteristics of his get show up prominently.

29 SKIP HI

Skip Hi, the first and most important Wiescamp-bred Paint Horse registered in the American Paint Horse Association, was foaled in 1959 at Alamosa, Colorado. He is a sorrel tobiano with the disposition, beautiful head, good wither, long hip, and deep muscle that characterize most Wiescamp horses. With few exceptions all the Paint Horses from the Wiescamp establishment are excellent in conformation and well marked with color and their breeding is tops.

H. J. Wiescamp is very nearly a living legend in the Quarter Horse, Thoroughbred, and Paint Horse industries. He has bred, raised, traded, sold, and auctioned horses for over thirty-five years. Wiescamp knows horses. In the early 1930's he raised and sold polo ponies, hunters, jumpers, and cavalry horses that were a Quarter type out of Thoroughbred mares. Then he purchased Nick Shoemaker. By crossing his Thoroughbred mares on this new Quarter Horse sire, he was able to produce the qualities in his horses that fitted his requirements. Times have not changed too much today. His horses still have a lot of Thoroughbred blood and a good Quarter Horse conformation, but wisely he has maintained the integrity of the breed.

Although Wiescamp breeds uniformity, he also breeds color. He has said many times, "I don't want a horse *without* color. An old man told me one time—who was very successful in the horse business—the first thing you have to do to sell a man a horse is to get him to stop and look. If he doesn't have anything to look at, he won't stop. . . . I like a yellow [palomino] horse, a buckskin or a sorrel horse with a lot of white on him. The last color I want is brown. I want a horse with refinement— but he has to have color."[1]

Skip Hi has the refinement, the color, and the blood. He was sired by a blaze-faced, stocking-legged, sorrel Quarter Horse, Skipper's Lad (AQHA 36,881), by Skipper W. by Nick Shoemaker. His dam was Miss Helen by Plaudit (AQHA 1,657). Skipper's Lad is a horse of considerable merit who has many get and grandget that are AQHA champions. He is now gaining a reputation as an excellent Paint Horse sire.

Wiescamp followed his outcrossing philosophy to good Thoroughbred blood when he bred Skip Hi's mother, Sky Hi, to Skipper's Lad. Sky Hi is a sorrel tobiano mare by Advantage, a tight-twisted kind of Thoroughbred with what would be considered a good Quarter Horse conformation.

Skip Hi belonged to Larry Wiescamp, Alamosa, at the time he was registered in the old American Paint Stock Horse Association in 1962. As a colt on the ranch he was carefully handled, broken to ride, given some working education, and, when he grew older, used in the stud. About the time his second crop of colts were on the ground, the great upward surge in Paint Horse popularity was felt, and horse-conscious people from far and wide went to Alamosa for horses bearing the Skip Hi name.

Somewhere down the line Skip Hi's reputation as an excellent sire reached the ears of Terry and Karen Overmyer, El-

[1]Bob Gray, "The Wiescamp Horses . . . and How They Got That Way," *Western Rider's Yearbook for 1967*, 21–32.

more, Ohio. They did some horse-trading business and made themselves the owners of one of the best Paint Horses to come out of Colorado. While residing at the Ja-Le Stables, Skip Hi was used in the stud and with great success for the Overmyers, who reported 90 per cent colored colts out of sorrel mares.

Sometime in late 1969, when Skip Hi was ten years old, he was sold to Jo-An Soso, Live Oak, California. She used him the following spring to service the Overo Acres mares, and, when her operations were dispersed, Skip Hi was purchased June, 1970, by his present owner, Lynn Henry, Montgomery Creek, California.

Lynn Henry and his wife, Christine, live in northern California on a beautiful mountain ranch of 160 acres. He is president of a bank in nearby Burney by vocation but a breeder of fine Paint Horses by avocation. Born and raised in Loup City, Nebraska, surrounded by livestock people, Henry has had close association with horses all his life. From the time he was seven years old, he has always owned a horse. He was riding bucking horses at fourteen and said, "I rode very few gentle ones until about 10 years ago when I quit as a result of back surgery."

His surgery was quite serious, and he was told that he would never walk again. After proving the doctors wrong, he began riding horses once more and raising a few Quarter Horses. He says that he was never quite satisfied with the results and began looking at Paints.

He was impressed by the stallion Skip Hi, which he considered to be the finest-looking horse he had ever seen. Skip Hi stands just over fifteen hands, weighs about eleven hundred pounds, is well muscled, and carries a fine, clean head. Henry has found Skip to be a perfect gentleman, although he had the reputation around Sacramento of being vicious. At the time he bought Skip, Henry was told not to try to ride him. Being a bronc rider who had bucked out many young colts in his earlier years, he saddled him right away. Henry said, "He acted a little silly for about two minutes but then he settled down and hasn't acted up again."

*Skip Hi, owned by Lynn Henry, Montgomery Creek, California.
Photograph by Mary Ann Czermak.*

Skip Again, by Skip Hi. Photograph by Margie Spence.

To prove to the people around Sacramento that Skip Hi could be easily handled, Henry spent some time teaching him the leads and then entered him in a pleasure class at one of the shows. Skip went perfectly, but Henry confessed that he made a few mistakes.

"He likes people," said Henry, "and will do anything asked of him, quietly and efficiently, but he prefers not to have any affection. If he thinks he is going to be petted he will take a step or two away if he can do it politely. If not he will tolerate it."

Skip Hi does not have a performance record. Since formation of the APHA Performance Department he has been used in the stud. He had won a few points in halter and reining in Ohio, but they were won in the early days of the association. The mark of any good stallion is his prepotency as a sire, and Skip Hi has shown through his get that he is indeed a sire.

At the time Henry bought Skip, he had only one Paint mare and two Quarter-bred mares. During 1971 he added to his breeding stock and now owns daughters of Lucky Blanton (who foaled to Skip Hi in the spring of 1972), Texas Dandy, Legal Advice, Wilsons Yellow Dunn, and Topper. He also has a granddaughter of Rowdy, two double granddaughters of Sugar Bars and two daughters of Glennbarred, all registered Quarter Horses. Jo-An Soso bred twenty to twenty-five mares to Skip Hi in 1970, and so in 1971 a good number of extremely fine colts were foaled in central California.

Some idea of Skip Hi's success as a sire can be gained by reviewing the history of one stallion he sired, Skippa Streak. The life story of this APHA and National Champion is told in Chapter 30.

Other of Skip Hi's better-known sons are Skip's Lad, Skippa Rope, Skipover, Skip-A-Dollar, and Butch Cassidy Hi. Most folks in Colorado would say that Skip's Lad was as good a progenitor of Paint Horses as his sire. He was responsible for Skip's Dude, Skip's Wonder, Skippa Hank, Skip Cash, Skip's Pride, Skiparado, and Skip Mount.

Skipolator, a 1967 sorrel tobiano mare owned by Kenneth Crull, Jr., Monticello, Indiana, was the second of Skip Hi's get to become an APHA Champion (Skippa Streak was the first). She was the High Point Reining, Western Pleasure, and Trail Horse in both Indiana and Michigan in 1970 and is a magnificent performer in all events.

Skippa Rope, owned by Karl and Sandy Spielmann, Wray, Colorado, is a versatile 1968 stallion. After a couple of years of

Skipolator, APHA Champion. Photograph by Margie Spence.

performance, which was of the highest level, in 1973 he became APHA Champion No. 267.

Skip-A-Dollar, a palomino tobiano from Tacoma, Washington, was one of the Pacific Northwest's best stallions. He was the High Point Halter and All-Around Champion Horse of the Washington Paint Horse Club in 1969.

Skipover is one other high-point Paint Horse that earned a Register of Merit in western pleasure. In 1968 he received the High Point Performance Stallion award from the Rocky Mountain Paint Horse Club.

Most of Skip Hi's daughters that are in the stud are wonderful breeders. The influence of these high-quality mares on Paint Horse pedigrees has been a continuous benefit. Some of his best producers are Skip Lady, Skip Along, Skip O'Gold, Skip After, Skip Away, Skip Shi, Skip's Flash, Skip Satin, and Skipity.

Skip Lady's contributions as a broodmare cannot be ignored because of foals like Skiparado, Skip's Pride, and Skip Again, among others. Skip Again, her 1966 foal by Skip Hi, is a sorrel tobiano mare bred, raised, and shown by Larry Wiescamp. By 1971 she was Register of Merit in western pleasure, an APHA Champion, and a National Champion at halter.

Judged in the light of his breeding, individuality, and sire record, Skip Hi is surely one of the greatest stallions of the Paint Horse breed. His get have made him a Leading Sire of Register of Merit Qualifiers, Halter Point Earners, and Performance Point Earners for seven straight years; and from all indications their performance will keep him high on the lists for many years to come. Unquestionably the Paint Horse is richer for his influence.

30 SKIPPA STREAK

Most of the greatest Paint Horse sires of the first decade of the breed's history, such as those discussed thus far, were sired by a Quarter Horse or a Thoroughbred. Even the best Paint Horses of earlier years, Painted Joe and Spotted Joe Reed, are sons of outstanding Quarter Horses tracing directly to the foundation sires. Their dams were either Quarter-bred mares or Paint mares of Quarter Horse or Thoroughbred bloodlines. This fact was important to the future of the Paint Horse. With roots deep in foundation Quarter Horse breeding, the early sires of the American Paint Horse have infused in their progeny the Quarter Horse blood, type, and quality that is the basis of this new American breed.

Skippa Streak is the only horse in this section of great sires whose sire and dam are both Paint Horses. What are his credentials for the outstanding position he occupies? First, his sire was fashioned by Quarter Horse blood spiced with Paint Horse coloring in the early breeding tradition. Second, he is an authentic representation of the breed in conformation, blood, and ability. Third, he is a progenitor of very good Paint Horses and gives class and distinction to his get.

Bred by Larry Wiescamp, Skippa Streak carries the blood of two famous Quarter Horses in his veins, Skipper W. and Plaudit, which he received from his sire, Skip Hi. Skippa Streak was foaled in 1964 out of a sorrel tobiano mare, Cheyenne Lil. Nothing was known for certain of Lil's ancestry except that her dam was a Thoroughbred mare on a ranch in Wyoming who in 1959 delivered the filly that became known as Cheyenne Lil. In the registry are a number of good mares whose parentage can never be traced, though they are proved producers of Paint Horses of exceptional Quarter Horse conformation. Cheyenne Lil is one. Her produce show well and perform well and have made her a Leading Dam of Performance Point Earner from 1966 through 1972.

Skippa Streak is a bright-red sorrel tobiano with four white legs, good quarters, and good forearms. His face markings and over-all general body coloring resemble that of his sire. He stands fifteen hands two inches high and weighs 1,250 pounds.

Right from the start, Skippa Streak was as handsome a colt as could be found. Moreover, he was a born athlete. Over the years he has distinguished himself in the all-around Paint Horse field of activity, competing in western pleasure, English pleasure, reining, roping, and trail. Everyone who has seen him has only praise for his disposition, conformation, and ease of handling.

The show record of Skippa Streak is long and commendable. He is an APHA Champion, the 1966 Reserve National Champion Two-Year-Old Stallion, the 1967 Reserve National Champion Three-Year-Old Stallion, the 1968 National Champion Junior Western Pleasure Horse, the 1968 National Champion Youth Western Pleasure Horse, the 1969 Reserve National Champion Aged Stallion, the 1969 National Champion Senior Western Pleasure Horse, and the 1969 Grand Champion Stallion at three of the major winter stock shows, in Fort Worth, San Antonio, and Houston. He has Registers of Merit in western pleasure, reining, English pleasure, and roping. Through 1971 he had earned 100 halter and 176 performance points.

Until 1968, Skippa Streak was owned by Paul Burnett, Wichita, Kansas. In that year he was sold to Bob and Chris Jones, Smithfield, Texas. The Jones family is made up of enthusiastic horsemen and horsewomen. After acquiring their first horse in 1963, the Jones girls, Linda and Lisa, became actively engaged in Four-H club horse judging and competition. The purchase of Skippa Streak in 1968 was their first association with the Paint Horse breed. In 1970, Linda Jones bought her good Paint mare, Mighty Miss. These two were a compatible combination, winning the first APHA Youth Championship and the #1 APHA Youth in the Nation awards in 1970. Her younger sister, Lisa, and her 1967 mare, Hi Spot, followed up the same year by winning the second APHA Youth Championship and the #2 APHA Youth in the Nation award.

When Skippa Streak was purchased by the Jones family, Linda was sixteen years old. A horsewoman at home topside a horse, she trained and showed the calm, easy-going stallion in western pleasure, English pleasure, and trail and at halter. In 1970, Lanham Riley, one of the leading trainers of successful performance horses, rode him in reining and roping events.

Some of the finest broodmares roam over the ninety-eight-acre Jones ranch near Smithfield. Many of the mares are of Wiescamp bloodlines; others are daughters or granddaughters of Tonto Bars Gill, Bert, Mighty Bars, L. H. Chock, Depth Charge, Leo, and Flit Bar. Two top mares are Berty Bug, twice Reserve National Champion at halter; and Levi Miss, the dam of Winning Streak and Skip It. Levi Miss, a Quarter mare, produced Leo's Lucky Levi, at one time the number-one junior western-pleasure horse in the nation and second over all in the AQHA.

The reputation of Skippa Streak as a sire is nation wide. He is a popular sire who consistently bequeaths to his progeny his good action, skill, and disposition. Looking at the records of achievement of his get, one might say that performance runs in the family.

*One of Skippa Streak's finest daughters, Skippetta, A Supreme
Champion. Photograph by Margie Spence.*

A 1967 daughter, Skippetta, is an eye-catching sorrel tobiano who was the 1971 APHA High-Point Halter horse. In
1972, with over 220 halter and performance points, she became
the tenth American Paint Horse Supreme Champion. A remarkable little mare, Skippetta seemed to know how to handle
herself expertly at the performance events, earning Registers
of Merit in western pleasure, reining, roping, barrel racing, and
western riding. She won National Champion Two-Year-Old
Mare at the Kansas City National Show in 1969 and National
Champion Junior Roping Horse at the 1971 show.

The second Skippa Streak filly to pile up halter and performance points on the way to her APHA championship is
graceful, breedy Sugar Streak. When she was only a few months
old, she was named National Champion Weanling Mare in
1970; in 1971 she became Reserve National Champion Youth
Mare; and in 1972 she was Reserve National Champion in
Youth Showmanship. At the close of 1972, with 108 youth
points, 101 performance points, and 93 halter points, she had
more points than any other two-year-old in the history of the
APHA.

Gold Streak is a 1970 son who proved himself a Superior
Western Pleasure Horse and a very good halter horse. Even at
a young age conformation judges were impressed by his appearance. In his weanling year he was the Texas Paint Horse Club
1970 High Point Stallion and was the winner of the Texas and
Oklahoma Yearling Halter futurities in 1971.

Another APHA Champion is Winning Streak, a 1969 tobiano gelding. He was trained and ridden by Lisa Jones in most
of the performance events, displaying once again the versatility
of Skippa Streak's colts. At the 1971 national show Lisa and
Winning Streak won the National Champion Youth Reining.
Other horses featured in every way champion Paint Horses can
be are Skippa Sequita, Skit It, and Skip Oro.

One of Skippa Streak's colts, Skippa Leo, found his way
into Paint Horse racing. He came by his speed naturally from
his dam, Sioux Bingo, who was by Leo Bingo (AQHA 71,355)

by Leo and out of Heart 68 (AQHA 53,512). Leo Bingo is AAA rated and has eleven colts to qualify for their Registers of Merit in AQHA racing. He passed to his get his capacity for speed, his good legs and sound feet, and his fighting heart. Seven of his daughters— and Sioux Bingo is one of them— received their share of these traits and passed them along to become recorded producers of running horses.

Skippa Leo, owned by Edgar E. Robinson, Abilene, Texas, made his start on Paint Horse tracks in 1972 as a three-year-old. His record for the season is one win, one third place, and one unplaced out of three starts. Some of the good horses he outran are Million Heir (winner of the 1971 National Championship Futurity), Jo Stormy Squaw, Misty Moon, Go Lad's Joe, and Slow Danger (winner of the 1970 National Championship Futurity).

From all of the foregoing it is apparent that this line of horses has done its share in spreading the fame of Paint Horses far and wide. For his excellent contributions to the breed, Skippa Streak deserves to be included on any list of great American Paint Horse sires.

31 **HY DIAMOND BOY**

As of this writing, all but one of the Paint Horses discussed in this part are living sires. All of them are horses of true quality, possessing top breeding, good symmetry, muscular power, and remarkable potency. They are some of the most important stallions to influence Paint Horses lineage-wise. Their offspring leave little to be desired and have been endowed by their influential sires with the ability to pass on this greatness to future generations.

Among these stallions the only Paint Horse sire no longer living is Hy Diamond Boy. During his ten years he sired a family of horses that rate with the very best. He is included here because of his influence on the Paint Horse breed, and as his sons and daughters produce outstanding progeny, his value as a sire will become more pronounced.

Hy Diamond Boy was bred by Gyp Young and foaled in 1960 at Poteet, Texas. He was registered in the American Paint Quarter Horse Association by W. L. "Bill" Jones and Wyman Wilkerson of the Western Hills Ranch, Abilene, Texas. When he was seven years old, he was purchased by the late Dr. Mack Daugherty and his daughter, Roann Cartwright (Hy Diamond Boy Enterprise), of Houston, Texas. Bred in the early Paint Horse tradition, Hy Diamond Boy was sired by a Quarter Horse, May's Diamond (AQHA 77,431) and was out of the good Paint mare Parr Lady, who goes back on her top side to some of the finest Quarter Horse and Thoroughbred breeding. May's Diamond was by the Thoroughbred Hy Diamond, and he by the magnificent Hygro. Hy Diamond sired many fast race horses both on the quarter tracks and on the long-distance tracks. Since most of his get were principally sprinters, thirty AA and AAA sons and daughters easily earned the Register of Merit in the AQHA.

The dam of May's Diamond was Flying Bob–My Texas Dandy–bred and preserved the blood of these two outstanding running-horse sires through her fine produce.

There was also running blood on Hy Diamond Boy's dam side. Parr Lady was by Danger Boy II (AQHA 48,052), notable son of Coldstream (TB), who gave to the Southwest many good running and working horses. Danger Boy II also sired Dangerous Girl, the dam of Dual Image (more information on Danger Boy's donation to Paint Horse breeding can be found in Chapter 26).

A sorrel tobiano stallion standing fifteen hands three inches, Hy Diamond Boy was as well made as any Paint Horse or Quarter Horse. He had fine muscle and bone structure and smooth, trim lines. Roann Cartwright said, "Diamond, as we called him, had a wonderful disposition; he was easy to handle and very well mannered. He was a horseman's or horsewoman's horse."

When he was a yearling, Hy Diamond Boy received a bad wire cut on a front foot, which caused him to limp slightly the rest of his life. Despite this disablement, his heart was game, and he did break out to become a good riding horse. Because of the bad scar and limp, however, Diamond could not run or compete in performance events. He was shown occasionally at

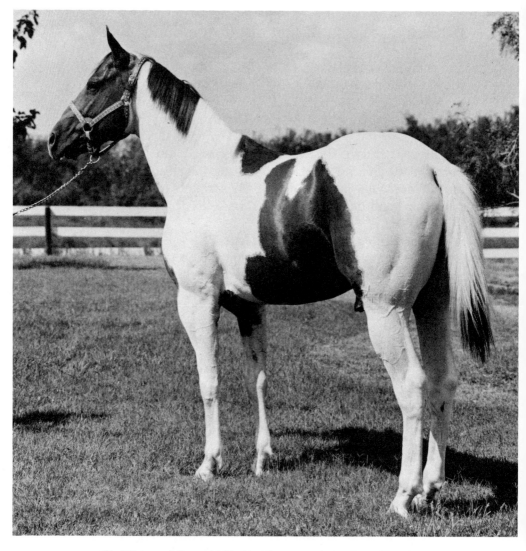

Hy Diamond Boy, 1960–70. Photograph by Don Hutcheson.

halter and even won Reserve Champion Stallion as a ten-year-old at the California Exposition Show in 1969, defeating some of the top halter Paint Horses in the nation.

In early 1969, Hy Diamond Boy was leased by Jo-An Soso, of Live Oak, California, and stood the breeding season at Overo Acres. He sired some good horses during his stay, horses of outstanding athletic ability that have shown well in shows in the western states.

In October, 1970, back home at the ranch just outside Houston, Diamond suffered an attack of colic during the night. He was taken to the clinic at Texas A & M University, College Station, but he died a few days later, on October 28, 1970.

Hy Diamond Boy was responsible for many fine, even-tempered, all-around performance colts, and his daughters are considered valuable additions to any broodmare band. He was one Paint Horse with a very high percentage of colored foals: as Roann Cartwright reported that a good 85 per cent of his get were Paint.

Quality shines in his offspring. On many occasions they earned him the Get of Sire award at such large shows as the Houston Livestock Show in 1967 and 1968 and at all three shows in the 1969 California Paint championship circuit.

Besides possessing the most striking characteristics of shape and disposition that make excellent halter horses, a large number of his get have made good cowhorses. For the varied performance requirements a cowhorse must meet, the quick, maneuverable speed from Hy Diamond Boy's background has proved invaluable.

As a Leading Sire of Register of Merit Qualifiers, Hy Diamond Boy stands high on the list for the period 1966–72, with seven ROM arena colts. Of the seven, three are a whiz at stock work and have Registers of Merit in cutting and roping.

From Diamond's colt crop of 1971, a neat-looking colt, Hy Diamond Reaf, with lengthy muscling, straight legs, and lots of style was selected by Roann Cartwright to become the replacement sire of the Hy Diamond Boy Enterprise. Hy Diamond Reaf, is out of Dixie Albert, the good-producing mother of Rhett Butler, holder of three High Point Trophies from the National Cutting Horse Association.

Hy Diamond Boy's position in the Paint Horse breed as a foundation sire is solid and sure because of sons and daughters like Hy Diamond Bailey, Hy Diamond Billy, Hy Diamond Dandy, Hy Diamond Moore, Hy Diamond Ring, Hy Diamond Girl, Hy Diamond Waggoner, Hy Diamond Robin, Hy Diamond Cash, Hy Diamond Duchess, Hy Diamond Reaf, Hy Diamond Jewel, Hy Diamond King, Dandy Diamond, Diamond Coaster, and Hy Diamond Bar.

Hy Diamond Bailey

One of Hy Diamond Boy's most respected sons is Hy Diamond Bailey. He is a 1964 sorrel tobiano out of Shirley Spark (AQHA 144,644) by Scooter Powers (AQHA 46,911). His second dam is Shirley Jane (AQHA 30,460) by Joe Bailey (AQHA P-4), often referred to as Joe Bailey of Gonzales. An old foundation sire of the AQHA, Joe Bailey of Gonzales became famous for his many good roping and running get like Little Joe, Jr., and Little Joker, the famous O'Conner Ranch stud, Refugio, Texas.

Joe and Ernestine Owings, San Antonio, Texas, purchased Hy Diamond Bailey in May, 1965, from W. L. Jones, Abilene, Texas. At that time he was fourteen months old and had been shown four times at halter, winning three firsts and one second. By the end of 1967 he had an excellent show record. He was an APHA Champion, he had Registers of Merit in western pleasure and reining, and he had been named the 1966 High Point Two-Year-Old Stallion in the South Texas Paint Horse Club and the Reserve High Point Two-Year-Old Stallion in the Gulf Coast and Texas Paint Horse Clubs. In 1967 he was the All-Around Champion in the South Texas Club and Reserve All-Around Champion of the Gulf Coast Club, the 1964 Champion Halter Stallion in both the South Texas and Gulf Coasts Clubs, and High Point Performance Horse in the South Texas Club.

Hy Diamond Bailey is a beautiful, well-proportioned horse, smooth-moving and easy to handle, a trait common to most Hy Diamond Boy colts. He has shown a remarkable ability to

Hy Diamond Bailey. Courtesy American Paint Horse Association.

transmit to his progeny his best qualities and those of his sire. The first pages of his family album are filled with such names as Bow Diamond Bailey, Hy Ginger Bailey, Diamond Bailey, Jr., Paint Rock Candy, Ima Diamond Bailey, and Sparkle Bailey. Through 1974 he had sired fourteen winners and point earners.

Hy Diamond Dandy

W. L. "Bill" Jones, the first president of the old American Paint Quarter Horse Association and one of the most enthusiastic supporters of the Paint Horse, bred Hy Diamond Dandy, among many other top performers. A brown tobiano stallion, Hy Diamond Dandy was foaled in 1965 out of Miss Texas Dandy (APQHA 273) by Old Dandy (AQHA 81,724) by My Texas Dandy (AQHA P-4,900). She represents a skillful blending of

Hy Diamond Dandy.

Quarter Horse and Paint Horse blood, having as her dam a black-and-white mare named Day Break.

Hy Diamond Dandy was a two-year-old when he went to Bonfoey's Fairway Farm, Van Alstyne, Texas. At that time Bonfoey owned several future champion Paint Horses: Hy Diamond Girl, Hy Diamond Ring, and one other fine cutting mare, Uvalde Doll. Hy Diamond Dandy received his early training in roping and reining from L. N. Sikes, a trainer highly respected for his handling of working horses. Sikes has had charge of and has produced many APHA and AQHA champions and developed both Uvalde Doll and Squaw's Stormy Star into national champions.

Purchased by J. W. Tyner, Tyler, Texas, Hy Diamond Dandy won his first performance points in western pleasure in 1970 and received a Register of Merit in this event in 1971. He was a versatile horse; he worked cattle well and yet was a pleasure horse in the truest sense.

Hy Diamond Dandy's career ended in his prime when Tyner lost his stallion on March 10, 1972. His services were beginning to be in demand because the colts he got were attractive in appearance, vigorous, and easily trained, The only sure yardstick to measure a stallion's success as a sire is through his progeny, and his sons and daughters are evidence that Hy Diamond Dandy contributed much to the betterment of Paint Horse stock.

Hy Diamond Girl

Hy Diamond Girl, a National Champion and an APHA Champion, is owned by Roann Cartwright and the late Dr. Mack Daugherty. A sorrel tobiano foaled in 1965, she possessed the intelligence, called "cow sense" in horses, that made her famous for her cutting ability. She is sensible and quiet like her sire, and can be ridden by a woman or child. In fact, under the guidance of Roann she became a top cutting mare and an APHA Champion.

At the 1969 National Show, Hy Diamond Girl was named National Champion Aged Mare and Reserve National Champion Junior Cutting Horse. In 1971 she was the High Point Aged Halter Mare and High Point Cutting Horse in the Gulf Coast Paint Horse Club and received her Register of Merit in cutting from the APHA. She is a fine individual and is a worthy supplement to any broodmare band.

Hy Diamond Ring

Hy Diamond Ring is another of Hy Diamond Boy's daughters to excel at the stock-horse events. A bay tobiano mare, she was bred by C. D. Bruce and was foaled at Santa Anna, Texas, in 1964. A glance at the pedigree of her dam, Chula Judge (AQHA 142,903), will take the reader back to the never-to-be-forgotten King (AQHA). She was sired by the Judge by King. Hy Diamond Ring, therefore, comes by her working ability honestly. She is Register of Merit in calf roping and earned her APHA Champion title in 1969.

Hy Diamond Billy

Foaled in 1964, Hy Diamond Billy, also bred by C. D. Bruce, was the product of mating Hy Diamond Boy to Miss Hill Billy (APQHA 271). A splendid broodmare, Miss Hill Billy was sired by Hill Billy Boy (AQHA P-33,705), of King ancestry, and was out of a mare of Hobo blood.

Hy Diamond Billy was another of those fine cutting horses. The very first time he was shown he won the Junior Cutting at the Houston Livestock Show in 1967 after only six months' training. He was named National Champion Junior Cutting Horse at the National Show in 1968 and received a Register of Merit in cutting during the year. Also competing in NCHA events, he was one of the leading money earners in open competition for Paint Horses.

Hy Diamond Billy has been gelded; but while owned by

Hy Diamond Girl. Photograph by H. D. Dolcater.

Lester Tatum, Brenham, Texas, he sired several good Paint Horses in 1968 and 1969, including Billy Bailey, Billy Big, Billy's Cowgirl, Amber, Hy Diamond Berty, Hy Diamond Roan, and Billy So.

Hy Diamond Cash

The five Hy Diamond Boy offspring looked at thus far are among the ranks of Paint Horses to excel at performance. They have called upon the physical energy and intelligence, but only a limited amount of the speed, of their ancestry. These qualities and their talent have been used to good advantage.

The only colt to draw heavily on his great family background of speed to prove himself on the track was Hy Diamond Cash. He is a sorrel overo out of La Veta, a Paint mare by Show Cash (AQHA 55,452), and she out of Sunbeam Mischief (AQHA 42,301). Show Cash is by Spot Cash, whose sire line goes back to Nick Shoemaker and whose dam line goes back to Plaudit. Some over-all high-quality running horses have come from both these old family lines.

Hy Diamond Cash was foaled in 1965 and during his racing years was owned by Edgar E. Robinson, Abilene, Texas. Making his start in 1968, he participated in stakes and maturity events for three years at Paint Horse tracks. He was described as a very smooth-moving horse who was not excitable under pressure. His record for the three seasons, though not outstanding, was good, good enough to earn him the title of Reserve Champion Running Horse in Oklahoma in 1968 and 1970.

PART VI **THE FUTURE OF THE BREED**

32 THE PAINT HORSE
TODAY AND TOMORROW

The purpose of the American Paint Horse Association, as stated in an earlier chapter, is to promote the breeding and raising of outstanding horses of paint color with the bloodlines, conformation, and distinct quality that will establish the American Paint Horse as a breed throughout the United States. Since the first associations were formed and the standards for the breed were set, some very important changes have been made in the Paint Horse and his environment.

Until the beginning of the past decade most Paint Horses lived in the outdoors, surrounded by the open range. Since 1960, when they were first looked upon as an individual type, the environment, breeding, physical appearance, and ability of these horses have greatly improved. They are now treated to box stalls, brushing and grooming, walkers and exercise pens, and blankets and coolers. They are being trained by professionals and are participating in major horse shows and events across the country. It is apparent from the quality of Paint Horses of today that they have become accustomed to the "soft life" and thrive on these plush surroundings.

313

Since its formation the APHA has grown from 150 members in 1962 to over 4,300 in 1974. One reason for its success and the overwhelming acceptance of the Paint Horse can be summed up in a single word—individuality. Every horse has its individual color arrangement and pattern; no two horses are exactly alike. Each horse is set apart from every other horse—likewise setting its owner apart from the crowd. Each of the present 4,300 members has a different horse (or horses) that does not look exactly like the others of the breed.

Paint Horses have been accepted enthusiastically because they are as good under saddle as horses of the other western breeds. And if another reason is needed, they were an instant success, thanks to the irresistible quality of their colors. The public upon seeing them loved them.

The enthusiasm that has resulted is evident in the increased number of shows, races, sales, events, and affiliated regional clubs that are now functioning in the United States and Canada. By 1975 over 50 APHA regional clubs were listed with the association. These affiliates are not administered by the APHA, but the shows and activities of each group must comply with APHA rules and regulations to be approved by the association. The APHA shows are usually scheduled through local clubs in each state and are conducted according to standards set by the association. The increase in the number of shows is a direct result of the work of the regional clubs.

After organization of the American Paint Stock Horse Association in February, 1962, twelve approved Paint Horse shows were held during that year. The classes were small, but the enthusiasm was tremendous. On September 27, 1962, the Oklahoma State Fair for the first time scheduled a Paint Horse show, and fifteen classes were featured in both halter and performance for juniors and seniors.

Seventeen shows were held in 1963, an increase of about 30 per cent over the previous year. The APSHA finals, later to become known as the National Paint Horse Show, was first held in December, 1963.

The healthy competition of APHA events continued to attract horsemen. Fifty approved shows were held in 1964, followed by sixty shows in 1966. More interest was added to the shows when the association adopted a national point system for awarding registers of merit and APHA and supreme-champion titles.

By 1970 the total number of shows had grown to 174, a 29 per cent increase over 1969, and as many new locations were added to the show and activities schedules, the trend continued upward (see Appendix 9). Paint Horse classes are included as part of the four major winter stock shows held in Denver, Fort Worth, San Antonio, and Houston. At most state fairs throughout the country Paint Horse shows are among the attractions, and thousands of people see these large shows every year.

The climax of the show season is the annual National Paint Horse Show. This show, the largest single show of the year, draws entries from far and wide to compete for the national titles. It began in 1963 as a final contest to determine the 1963 champions. The show was held in December, but through the years the date has gradually been moved forward to a more convenient time when most Paint Horse owners and exhibitors could attend.

National titles are won only at the national show. Under present APHA rules the national show is open to all Paint Horses, whether or not they have been shown during the year. As might be expected, competition is tough, and so only the best horses in the breed are at the national show.

Sometime in the future, when the national show gets too big to handle all the competing horses, the show will be open only to high-point horses from each state. A horse will then have to "earn his way to the nationals." Many changes will have to be made in association rules and regulations before this system can be put into effect. With the continued growth of the APHA and the increasing number of horses at every show, particularly at the national show, this change is a possibility in the foreseeable future.

Lubbock, Texas, was chosen as the site of the APSHA Finals for 1963. On December 8, Paint Horses gathered at the Aufill Sports Arena for the final showdown. The 1963 show was small when compared to the 1974 National Show in Jackson, Mississippi, and only a trophy saddle and nineteen high-point trophies were awarded to the horses that accumulated the most points in halter, performance, and youth activities.

The association's second national show was held on Thanksgiving weekend in 1964, in Hutchinson, Kansas. A total of 134 entries from twelve states vied for 1964 national champion honors in the eighteen classes. The show was arranged in three go-rounds with a different judge for each go-round. Champions were named after completion of the third showing, the national title going to the horse that had accumulated the highest number of points in the three-event judging. Points for each go-round were awarded on a 6-5-4-3-2-1 basis to the first six horses in each class. In 1965, after consolidation of the two Paint Horse associations, the APHA National Championship Show had grown to 144 entries. The show was held in Kansas City, Missouri, on October 21 and 22.

Baton Rouge, Louisiana, was the scene of the fourth annual show, held October 13 through 15, 1966. Owing to the large number of entries, three days were set aside for the judging of the three go-rounds. There were 150 horses making up the 261 entries, representing owners from Alabama, Arkansas, Colorado, Florida, Illinois, Kansas, Louisiana, Mississippi, New York, Oklahoma, Texas, and Wisconsin.

By 1967 a record-smashing 435 entries were in Oklahoma City competing for the twenty-seven national and reserve national titles. The show was held September 25 through 27 in conjunction with the Oklahoma State Fair. Paint horsemen from twenty-two states participated in the show. A new feature was added with the selection of a Miss American Paint Horse Association. The Miss APHA Queen's Contest is governed by twelve basic rules, which include the stipulation that the contestant or her family must be a member of the APHA and that she must be single and between the ages of eighteen and twenty-five. This added attraction has created further enthusiasm and excitement, particularly among the younger Paint Horse owners.

The 1968 national show was once again held in Oklahoma City during the state fair, from September 23 through 25. There were 302 horses making up the 530 entries, from twenty-four states. The number of horses increased by 24 per cent over 1967, and the number of entries increased by 22 per cent over the previous year. A total of twenty-nine Paint Horse classes were judged, including fifteen halter classes and fourteen performance classes. The cutting and roping events featured a jackpot and added money of $2,265.

On August 14 through 16, 1969, the national show was held in Kansas City, Kansas. This location was the farthest north that a national show had been held, and a decline in entries was apparent. At the show there were 172 halter entries, 7 group entries, 106 youth entries, and 169 performance entries, a total of 454 entries.

The eighth annual show was held in Amarillo, Texas, on August 19 through 21, 1970, at the Bill Cody Livestock Arena. A record-breaking 625 entries competed for the national titles in the thirty-seven classes. The show attracted 333 horses from twenty-three states and Canada. A total of $7,793 in awards and cash prizes was won at the show.

After the experience of judging entries from 7:00 A.M. to 4:30 A.M. the following morning, in 1971 the show managers divided the show into a four-day event, though still on the three-go-round basis. The 1971 show, held at the Tulsa, Oklahoma, State Fair Grounds on October 27 through 31, was another record-breaker, with 354 horses entered in the forty-five classes, making a total of 671 entries. Horses came from thirty states and Canada, and national and reserve national championship titles were carried back to eighteen states.

Celebrating ten years, the national show of 1972 was held in Columbus, Ohio, on July 25 through 28. After 650 entries paid their fees, competition was keen as never before. There is

A typical Paint Horse sale.

no doubt that the tenth annual show represented the finest group of quality Paint Horses ever assembled in one arena. The results of selective breeding over the preceding ten years was evidenced by the entrants' nearly faultless conformation, refined appearance, and all-around ability.

The Paint Horse population is steadily increasing. The number of horses registered has increased from year to year, but since a horse census is no longer required, there is no way to determine the actual number of Paint Horses. With registration it is now possible to obtain a fairly accurate estimate, recognizing, of course, that not all Paint Horses are registered in the APHA (see Appendix 10).

Today almost anyone can afford to own a horse. With shows for all ages of riders and all types of riding interests, a huge market has developed for the Paint Horse. Before his "discovery" in 1961 a Paint Horse—even one of the very best— brought only a fraction of the price paid for horses of other breeds. Today the market has shown such an increase that a good Paint Horse that would sell for $400 to $500 in 1962 will bring three to four times that amount.

The first consignment of registered Paint Horses to be sold at public auction was held on March 3, 1963, at Pin Oak Stables in Houston, Texas, in conjunction with the Houston Livestock Show. Forty-three head were sold at an average price of $379.54. The highest-selling individual was a mare, who sold for $1,425 and the second-highest sold for $1,025.

By 1967 prices for the better-than-average Paint Horse had increased nearly 100 per cent. The Broken Arrow, Oklahoma, sale, held on May 27, 1967, averaged $570 a head on thirty-five head of horses sold. The top price paid was $2,500 for a mare, Pachie Moon. A cutting mare, Calamity Sioux, was the second-highest-selling individual, at $2,000.

Another sale held in 1967, the Paint Horse Performance Sale at Sacramento, California, averaged $687 for sixteen head. Speckled Q Ton H, the high-selling horse, was purchased for $3,200.

The Autum Haze Sale, held in Roseville, California, November 29, 1969, established a new high for Paint Horse sales, with an average of $914 for twenty head of registered horses. A bay tobiano mare, Me-A-Butler, topped the sale on a bid of $2,700, and the second-high bid was $2,000 for the stallion Joe Forecast.

With the passing of another three years Paint Horse prices continued upward. On June 17, 1972, twenty-four lots, averaging $1,088, sold at the Tatum Ranch sale in Brenham, Texas. Buyers came from all sections of the United States, indicating the widespread interest that had developed in good Paint Horse stock.

One barometer for judging the success of any breed is the market place. With the market going up, the Paint Horse is also on his way up. In 1974 prices continued their upward trend. At the Golden Opportunity Sale, held in Harvester, Missouri, fifty-three head sold for $59,275, an average of $1,118 a horse. The high-selling horse was a yearling stallion, Snip's Comet, Jr., which sold for $4,000.

Two pretty young ladies riding two Paint Horses: Cathy Jacobs on Snip Bar, Terri Tabor on Rio Retta Bar.

There are thousands of good Paint Horses across the United States, from border to border and from shore to shore. From an indistinct and modest beginning this colorful horse has climbed above neglect, hardship, and obstacles to earn the right to a breed status alongside the other horse breeds of the world. The blending of Arab, Barb, mustang, Quarter Horse, and Thoroughbred blood has helped provide a fine foundation; but it is the record of his own performance and his ability to perpetuate his color and characteristics that have combined successfully with this good blood to produce the Paint Horse of today.

And so this is the beginning, not the end, of the story of the new breed—the American Paint Horse.

APPENDICES

1 BLOODLINES OF SOME OUTSTANDING PAINT HORSES

Ferminio

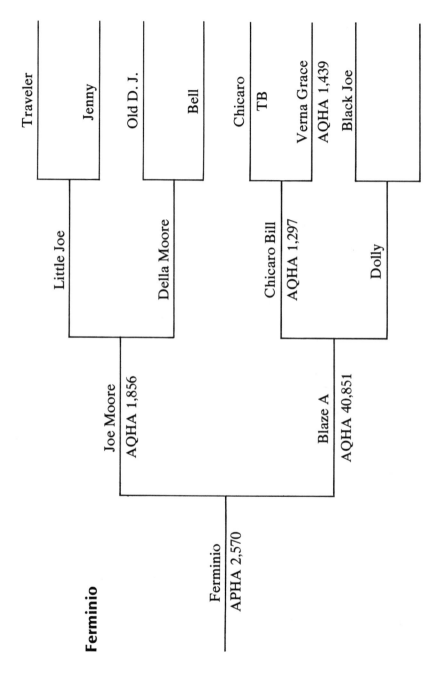

Traveler

Jenny

Little Joe

Old D. J.

Bell

Della Moore

Joe Moore
AQHA 1,856

Chicaro

TB

Chicaro Bill
AQHA 1,297

Verna Grace
AQHA 1,439

Black Joe

Dolly

Blaze A
AQHA 40,851

Ferminio
APHA 2,570

Wildfire

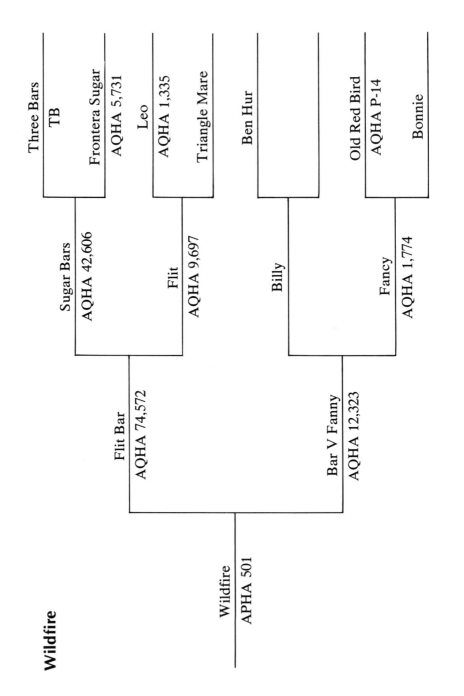

		Three Bars
	Sugar Bars	TB
	AQHA 42,606	Frontera Sugar
Flit Bar		AQHA 5,731
AQHA 74,572		Leo
	Flit	AQHA 1,335
	AQHA 9,697	Triangle Mare
Wildfire
APHA 501
		Ben Hur
	Billy	
Bar V Fanny		Old Red Bird
AQHA 12,323		AQHA P-14
	Fancy	
	AQHA 1,774	Bonnie

Flying Fawago

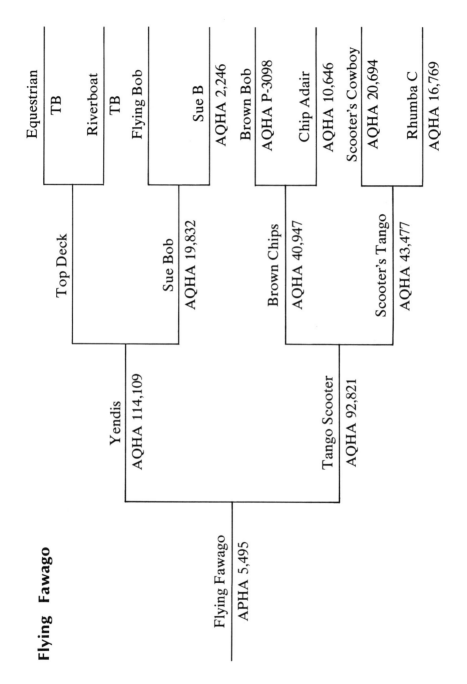

			Equestrian
			TB
			Riverboat
			TB
		Flying Bob	
	Top Deck		
		Sue B	
			AQHA 2,246
Yendis			
AQHA 114,109		Sue Bob	
		AQHA 19,832	
			Brown Bob
			AQHA P-3098
		Brown Chips	
		AQHA 40,947	
			Chip Adair
			AQHA 10,646
Tango Scooter			
AQHA 92,821			Scooter's Cowboy
			AQHA 20,694
		Scooter's Tango	
		AQHA 43,477	
			Rhumba C
			AQHA 16,769

Flying Fawago
APHA 5,495

Dial-A-Go-Go

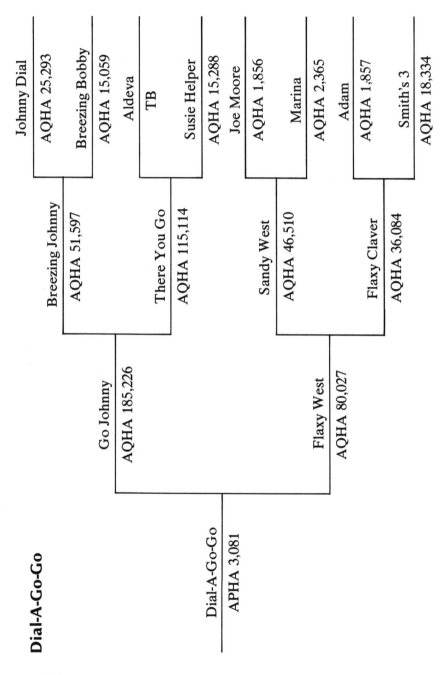

Johnny Dial
AQHA 25,293

Breezing Bobby
AQHA 15,059

Aldeva
TB

Susie Helper
AQHA 15,288

Joe Moore
AQHA 1,856

Marina
AQHA 2,365

Adam
AQHA 1,857

Smith's 3
AQHA 18,334

Breezing Johnny
AQHA 51,597

There You Go
AQHA 115,114

Sandy West
AQHA 46,510

Flaxy Claver
AQHA 36,084

Go Johnny
AQHA 185,226

Flaxy West
AQHA 80,027

Dial-A-Go-Go
APHA 3,081

2 LEADING SIRES OF REGISTER MERIT QUALIFIERS, 1966-74

Sire	No. ROM Qualifiers	ROM's Earned
Q Ton Eagle, s. tob. 60 by Freno (AQHA)	15	30
Leo San Man, d. tob. 63 by Leo San Siemon (AQHA)	13	20
Mister J Bar, s. ov. 61 by Jamina Pondfly 2 (AQHA)	12	26
Yellow Mount, d. ov. 64 by Tetrak Scooter (AQHA)	11	31
Adios Amigos, br. ov. 62 by Ranger's Blue (AQHA)	10	14
Sabru Indio, s. ov. 62 by JoJo	9	18
Balmy L Mac, s. ov. 62 by Balmy L. Dee (AQHA)	9	11
Skip Hi, s. tob. 59 by Skipper's Lad (AQHA)	8	19
Painted Robin, s. ov. 60 by Robin Roy (AQHA)	8	15
Sr Don Juan, s. ov. 60 by Texas Dandy (AQHA)	8	10
Skippa Streak, s. tob. 64 by Skip Hi	7	15
Bay Bandit (AQHA), b. 54 by El Bandido (AQHA)	7	12
Painted Jewel, ch. tob. 64 by Jet Dial (AQHA)	7	11
Hy Diamond Boy, s. tob. 60 by May's Diamond (AQHA)	7	8

Joechief Bar, ch. tob. 64 by Bang Up (TB)	7	8
Painted Lasan, s. ov. 63 by Calhoun's Lasan	7	8

3 LEADING DAMS OF REGISTER OF MERIT QUALIFIERS, 1966-74

Dam	No. ROM Qualifiers	ROM's Earned
Josy Bar, ch. tob. 55 by Skylark Bar (AQHA)	4	9
Poco Snowflake, d. tob. 64 by Kansas Red (AQHA)	4	8
Sky Bar, ch. tob. 61 by Skychief Bar (AQHA)	4	4
Miss Half Bar, b. tob. 63 by Half Bar (AQHA)	3	8
Q Ton Stormee, s. tob. 59 by Sambo W (AQHA)	3	7
Anita Venus (AQHA), s. 59 by Dawson's Wig (AQHA)	3	6
Badgers Lou, b. solid 63 by Pretty Badger	3	5
Maggie Wildfire, blk. tob. 58 by Poco Trace (AQHA)	3	5
Bea's Charmer (AQHA), s. 57 by Tex North (AQHA)	3	5
Q Ton Snapie Zero, s. tob. 64 by Hi Zero (AQHA)	3	3
Crystal Eye, s. ov. 60 by Slow Motion (AQHA)	3	3

4 LEADING SIRES OF HALTER POINT EARNERS, 1966-74[1]

Sire	No. Point Earners	No. Points Won
Q Ton Eagle, s. tob. 60 by Freno (AQHA)	27	462
Mister J Bar, s. ov. 61 by Jamina Pondfly 2 (AQHA)	23	387
Leo San Man, d. tob. 63 by Leo San Siemon (AQHA)	22	563
Yellow Mount, d. ov. 64 by Tetrak Scooter (AQHA)	21	768
Adios Amigos, br. ov. 62 by Ranger's Blue (AQHA)	20	348
Hy Diamond Boy, s. tob. 60 by May's Diamond (AQHA)	18	234
Painted Robin, s. ov. 60 by Robin Roy (AQHA)	16	487
Tinky's Spook, b. tob. 65 by Tinky Joe (AQHA)	16	349
Painted Jewel, ch. tob. 64 by Jet Dial (AQHA)	15	247
Skip's Lad, s. tob. 64 by Skip Hi	15	212
Skip Hi, s. tob. 59 by Skipper's Lad (AQHA)	14	330
Sabru Indio, s. ov. 62 by JoJo	13	232
Joechief Bar, ch. tob. 64 by Bang Up (TB)	13	107

[1]Arranged in order of total points won by their produce.

330

5. LEADING DAMS OF HALTER POINT EARNERS, 1966-74[1]

Dam	No. Point Earners	No. Points Won
Poco Snowflake, d. tob. 64 by Kansas Red (AQHA)	5	251
Josy Bar, ch. tob. 55 by Skylark Bar (AQHA)	4	161
Badgers Lou, b. solid 63 by Pretty Badger	4	155
Skip Lady, s. tob. 63 by Skip Hi	4	142
Q Ton Miss Fanta, s. tob. 62 by McDade Henry (AQHA)	4	101
Q Ton Stormee, s. tob. 59 by Sambo W (AQHA)	4	99
Q Ton Pepsy, s. tob. 57 by Cyclone Red (AQHA)	4	25
Snowball, d. tob. 54 by Buckshot's Pride (AQHA)	3	131
Rosy's Squaw, b. ov. 50 by Little Tom B (AQHA)	3	123
Anita Venus (AQHA), s. 59 by Dawson's Wig (AQHA)	3	117

[1]Arranged in order of total points won by their produce.

6 PAINT HORSES RECEIVING HIGH-POINT TROPHIES FROM THE NATIONAL CUTTING HORSE ASSOCIATION

Year	Horse
1962	Calamity Jane
1963	Calamity Jane
1964	Calamity Jane
1965	Rhett Butler
1966	Rhett Butler
1967	Music Maker
1968	Rhett Butler
1969	Worth the Money
1970	Delta
1971	Edith's Dolly
1972	Delta
1973	Delta
1974	Delta

7 GENERAL SPEED INDEX, AMERICAN PAINT HORSE ASSOCIATION

Speed Index	220 Yards	250 Yards	300 Yards	330 Yards	350 Yards	400 Yards	440 Yards
AAA							
100	:12.00	:13.40	:15.60	:17.00	:17.90	:20.20	:22.10
99	.02	.42	.63	.03	.93	.24	.14
98	.04	.44	.66	.06	.97	.28	.18
97	.06	.46	.69	.09	:18.00	.32	.22
96	.08	.48	.72	.12	.04	.36	.26
95	.10	.50	.75	.15	.07	.40	.30
94	.12	.52	.78	.18	.11	.44	.34
93	.14	.54	.81	.21	.14	.48	.38
92	.16	.56	.84	.24	.18	.52	.42
91	.18	.58	.87	.27	.21	.56	.46
90	.20	.60	.90	.30	.25	.60	.50
AA							
89	.22	.62	.93	.33	.28	.64	.54
88	.24	.64	.96	.36	.32	.68	.58
87	.26	.66	.99	.39	.35	.72	.62

86	.28	.68	:16.02	.42	.39	.76	.66
85	.30	.70	.05	.45	.42	.80	.70
84	.32	.72	.08	.48	.46	.84	.74
83	.34	.74	.11	.51	.49	.88	.78
82	.36	.76	.14	.54	.53	.92	.82
81	.38	.78	.17	.57	.56	.96	.86
80	.40	.80	.20	.60	.60	:21.00	.90

Speed Index	220 Yards	250 Yards	300 Yards	330 Yards	350 Yards	400 Yards	440 Yards
				A			
79	:12.42	:13.82	:16.23	:17.63	:18.63	:21.04	:22.94
78	.44	.84	.26	.66	.67	.08	.98
77	.46	.86	.29	.69	.70	.12	:23.02
76	.48	.88	.32	.72	.74	.16	.06
75	.50	.90	.35	.75	.77	.20	.10
74	.52	.92	.38	.78	.81	.24	.14
73	.54	.94	.41	.81	.84	.28	.18
72	.56	.96	.44	.84	.88	.32	.22
71	.58	.98	.47	.87	.91	.36	.26
70	.60	:14.00	.50	.90	.95	.40	.30
				B			
69	.62	.02	.53	.93	.98	.44	.34
68	.64	.04	.56	.96	:19.02	.48	.38
67	.66	.06	.59	.99	.05	.52	.42
66	.68	.08	.62	:18.02	.09	.56	.46
65	.70	.10	.65	.05	.12	.60	.50
64	.72	.12	.68	.08	.16	.64	.54
63	.74	.14	.71	.11	.19	.68	.58
62	.76	.16	.74	.14	.23	.72	.62
61	.78	.18	.77	.17	.26	.76	.66
60	.80	.20	.80	.20	.30	.80	.70

8. NUMBER OF PAINT HORSE RACES 1966-74

Year	No. Races	Total Purses	Total Startups	Total Purses for National Championship Races
1966	9	$ 1,290.00	12	
1967	8	2,100.00	14	
1968	13	7,949.50	21	
1969	21	14,617.30	41	
1970	24	14,813.14	38	$ 3,859.00
1971	23	23,953.27	32	9,801.02
1972	43	47,129.12	54	19,713.63
1973	37	41,318.89	51	15,403.89
1974	69	83,469.80	94	29,977.00

9 NUMBER OF PAINT HORSE SHOWS, 1962-74

Year	No. of Shows
1962 (APSHA)	12
1963 (APSHA)	17
1964 (APSHA)	50
1965	60
1966	52
1967	74
1968	97
1969	121
1970	174
1971	212
1972	300
1973	357
1974	377

10 NUMBER OF PAINT HORSES REGISTERED IN THE AMERICAN PAINT HORSE ASSOCIATION, 1962-74

Year	No. of Horses
1962 (APSHA)	230
1963 (APSHA)	1,041
1964 (APSHA)	2,310
1965	3,693
1966	5,608
1967	7,747
1968	10,137
1969	13,848
1970	16,000
1971	19,305
1972	22,667
1973	26,998
1974	31,750

11 LEADING MONEY-EARNING RUNNING HORSES, 1966-74

	Money Earned, 1966–74
Shadrach, s. ov. G. 70 by Diamond Charge (AQHA)	$16,207.54
Top Yellow, d. ov. S. 71 by Top Moon (AQHA)	14,593.53
Spoiler, br. tob. S. 68 by Dream Man (AQHA)	13,869.14
Whata Bright Bar, s. ov. M. 71 by Bright Bar (AQHA)	11,707.60
Happy Traveler, s. ov. S. 69 by Ferminio	10,804.51
Danger Spots, s. ov. S. 72 by Slow Danger	10,125.80
Party Gal, s. ov. M. 70 by Lalito Canales (AQHA)	8,373.10
Bang Up 2, b. tob. S. 67 by Bang Up (TB)	8,249.27
Charge Card, s. tob. S. 72 by Hank H Bars (AQHA)	8,092.75
Grey Wonder, g. ov. G. 70 by Wandering Boy (TB)	7,964.48
Paul Bunyon, s. tob. S. 71 by Paul H (TB)	5,793.77

Million Heir, s. tob. S. 69 by Three Jets
   (AQHA)   5,564.38
Mr. Poison Bars, b. tob. S. 72 by Chubby   4,800.89
Super Swift, s. ov. S. 72 by Mighty Deck (AQHA)   4,758.00
Road Master, p. ov. S. 71 by Bar Joe Bailey
   (AQHA)   4,217.95
Miss Decka Reed, s. ov. M. 69 by Decka
   Center (AQHA)   4,074.50
Slow Danger, s. ov. S. 68 by Lalito Canales
   (AQHA)   4,055.61

BIBLIOGRAPHY

American Paint Horse Association. *APHA Information Sheet*. Fort Worth, n.d.

―――. *American Paint Horse Association Stud Book and Registry*. Vols. 2, 3. Fort Worth, 1967, 1970.

―――. *Official Rule Book*. 7th–9th eds. Fort Worth, 1972–74.

―――. *Paints: The Horse with Individuality*. Fort Worth, 1971.

"APSHA and APQHA Consolidate," *Western Horseman*, August, 1965.

American Quarter Horse Association. *Official Stud Book and Registry of the American Quarter Horse Association*. Vols. 1–23. Amarillo, 1941–69.

―――. *Quarter Horse Yearbook 1970*. Vol. 1. Houston, 1971.

American Quarter Racing Association. *American Quarter Racing Association Yearbook and Register of Merit*. Tucson, 1943, 1945, 1946, 1947, 1947 supplement, 1948, 1949.

Beall, Art. "The Cover Picture," *Ranchman*, August, 1962.

Brown, Jim. "Color Inheritance in Horses," *Paint Horse Journal*, March–April, May–June, 1970.

340

Castle, W. E. "The ABC of Color Inheritance in Horses," *Cattleman*, September, 1948.

Crowell, Pers. *Cavalcade of American Horses.* New York, 1951.

Denhardt, Robert Moorman. *The Horse of the Americas.* Norman, 1948.

———. *The King Ranch Quarter Horses: And Something of the Ranch and the Men That Bred Them.* Norman, 1970.

———. *The Quarter Horse.* Vol. III. Amarillo, 1950.

———. *Quarter Horses: A Story of Two Centuries.* Norman, 1967.

———, and Helen Michaelis. *The Quarter Horse.* Vol. II. Eagle Pass, Texas, 1945.

Echohawk, Brummett. "The Spotted Horse Alone," *Western Horseman*, October, 1964.

Fox, Charles Phillip. *A Pictorial History of Performing Horses.* Seattle, 1960.

Graham, R. B. Cunninghame. *The Horses of the Conquest.* Ed. by Robert Moorman Denhardt. Norman, 1949.

Gray, Bob. *Great Horses of the Past.* Houston, 1967.

———. "The Wiescamp Horses . . . and How They Got That Way," in *Western Riders Yearbook for 1967.* Houston, 1967.

Haskell, Melville H. *The Quarter Running Horse.* 5 pamphlets. Tucson, 1945–50.

Huffington, J. M. "Markings and Traits—How Far Do They Go Back?" *Quarter Horse*, October, 1949.

Irving, W. M. "Genetics at Work," *Paint Horse Journal*, January, 1971.

Jones, William E., and Ralph Bogart. *Genetics of the Horse.* East Lansing, Mich., 1971.

"Junior Robertson—First of the Paint Stock Horse Breeders," *Ranchman*, August, 1962.

King, Ferne E. "The Cover Picture," *Ranchman*, December, 1961.

———. "The Rebecca Barrett Tyler Story," *Ranchman*, August, 1961.

Morocco Spotted Horse Co-Operative of America Rule Book. Ridott, Ill., 1971.

Muse, Barbara. *The Grand Twenty.* Trail Creek, Oreg., 1971.

Paint Horse Journal, issues November–December, 1966, through March, 1973.

"Paint Market Shows Growth," *Texas and Southwestern Horseman*, March, 1964.

Pinto Horse Association of America, Inc. *A World of Pinto Horses.* San Diego, 1970.

Pitts, Jim. "Annual Paint Horse Industry Report 1968," *Horseman,* March, 1968.

Reynolds, Frank. "They Called Him Traveler," *Quarter Horse Journal,* May, 1957.

Robertson, Junior, as told to Jane Pattie. "Take Your Rope Horse Slow!" *Horseman,* March, 1967.

Ryden, Hope. *America's Last Wild Horses.* New York, 1970.

Schnaubert, Oscar. "Fast Time," *Texas and Southwestern Horseman,* March, 1964.

Sikes, L. N. "Champions May Come in Small Packages," *Horseman,* March, 1966.

Sires of American Thoroughbreds. Rev. ed. Lexington, Ky., 1968.

"Sixth Annual Paint Horse Industry Report," *Horseman,* March, 1967.

Spence, Sam Ed. "Breeding the Paint Horse," *Texas and Southwestern Horseman,* March, 1965.

— — —. "Can You Tell Tobiano from Overo?" *Texas and Southwestern Horseman,* March, 1967.

— — —. "Cutting Horses Become Flying Horses," *Quarter Horse Journal,* December, 1962.

— — —. "Merger and Growth," *Texas and Southwestern Horseman,* March, 1966.

— — —. "The Paint Horse," *Western Horseman,* October, 1966.

— — —. "Performance as Applied to the American Quarter Horse," *Texas and Southwestern Horseman,* September, 1964.

Teague, C. C. "Origin of the American Paint Stock Horse Association," *Ranchman,* August, 1962.

Temple, Robert S. "Inherited Characteristics in Horses," paper presented at the Louisiana Quarter Horse Association Field Day, Cankton, La., July 9, 1960.

"Third Annual Paint Horse Report," *Texas and Southwestern Horseman,* March, 1964.

Tyler, Rebecca. "Why I Like the Pinto," *Texas and Southwestern Horseman,* February, 1962.

343